This book belongs to:

_____

Inspiration Bible

*The Unseen Force Transforming
Lives Worldwide*

Brought to Life by Emily Gowor

GOWOR
INTERNATIONAL PUBLISHING

Inspiration Bible: The Unseen Force Transforming Lives Worldwide © Emily Gowor 2014

www.inspirationbible.com

First published in Australia 2014 by Gowor International Publishing

www.goworinternationalpublishing.com

ISBN 978-0-9923493-9-4

Disclaimer

Dedicated to all of the people in this world who have wondered whether life is worth living.

A note to parents and guardians,

The stories you will read in this book are undoubtedly inspirational in nature – and many of them will move you deeply.

However, I find that it is within my realm of responsibility as the creator of the project to say that not every story may be appropriate for children and/or teenagers.

I encourage you to use your own conscience and sense of sound judgment in choosing which stories to share with your children and/or dependents – especially if they are under eighteen.

Enjoy the book!

With inspiration,

Emily Gowor
Creator of the *Inspiration Bible* project

When Inspiration Appears

"What lies behind us and what lies before us are tiny matters compared to what lies within us."

Ralph Waldo Emerson

When I first began forming the vision for the *Inspiration Bible*, I had no idea where the journey would take me. I had no idea how many lives would be deeply touched by this book, and even by the process of bringing it to life. I had no idea how inspired people would become at the prospect of doing something so meaningful for humanity. I had no idea that we would find 365 contributors so quickly or that they would be located in fifteen countries around the world. And, I certainly had no idea just how deeply this entire project – the book, the people, the community, and the stories – would impact me as a human being and my experience of life. All I knew in my heart was that I wanted to do something extraordinary in the world. I knew that I wanted to bring my love to planet Earth. It just happened to be a course of destiny to start a global social movement in the process: one that your life is about to be touched by in a meaningful way.

As I write to you, tears are welling up in my eyes. And this is simply because this one book and the entire project behind it have forever convinced me that inspiration *does* exist within every single one of us and within life itself. People walk down the street every single day holding magnificent visions, gut-wrenching and heart-opening life stories, and wisdom inside of them. Brilliance and genius live within us in every moment that we breathe, ready for us to unleash it and inspire people with who we really are. Grand futures exist within our hearts... just waiting for us to receive the inspiration that we need in order to turn them into a reality.

See, the power of an inspired moment is unparalleled. I believe that when we are in a state of inspiration – where we are deeply uplifted and moved – that miracles become possible. I believe that a life built doing what you love is a life of inspiration: one where you wake up in the morning grateful to be alive and thankful for the opportunity to pursue your wildest dreams. And, I believe that when you achieve the heartfelt dream from within your heart, the one that means the *most* to you, that you instantaneously and spontaneously uplift others to do the same.

When I was nineteen years old, I went through a long and challenging eight months of what many would call depression. After completing high school and attending university for six months, I hit rock bottom. I didn't know what to do, with myself or my future. I had just over two dollars in my bank account and no desire for an income or a job; I couldn't see the point. I didn't see a way forwards for me. It was as though the first eighteen years of my life suddenly vanished, and everything I had achieved before that moment – outstanding grades in school included – simply didn't matter anymore. One night, in the middle of 2007, I reached what was to soon become my critical turning point. I arrived home at night, walked in the door and laid down on a mattress on the lounge room floor of the apartment where I was living. I curled up in a foetal position. I didn't sleep, eat or move for twelve hours. I just laid there, feeling completely raw, alone and bare. I remember thinking to myself, "I don't care if my heart doesn't ever beat again."

Everything in my life had lost its effect on me – even many of the people I cared about – except for one thing: my quest for purpose and meaning. I was young, bright, and smart, and yet I felt that I had nothing to live for. How was this even possible? How did I even get there in the first place, where I didn't want to be alive anymore? In hindsight, I can see that I was feeling completely lost, but that deep down inside of me, I knew there had to be a greater reality than the one I was stuck inside. At my core, I knew that life didn't really work that way. The flame inside me hadn't been extinguished yet. I knew that my life was going to require a major transformation, especially if I was going to fulfil my own dreams – and I suspected that it was going to be extremely hard work to build, not rebuild my life, from the ground up. I knew I would have to look within myself deeply for answers, and that confronting the skeletons in my closet wouldn't exactly be easy or pleasant. It was going to be a long journey to choose what to dedicate myself to and stick to it – but it was one that I was willing to take.

From that night on, I made a decision to stay alive. And I set out on a mission: to overcome absolutely anything that stood between me and my having a meaningful and accomplished existence. I wanted to give life my best shot: everything that I had. Not long after that night, I rediscovered my love of writing. In a divine moment when I finally re-touched pen to page, everything became clear. Suddenly, I knew what it was that I wanted to do with my future: I dreamed of writing, speaking and travelling the world inspiring people. I wanted to see the world in all its beauty. I wanted to stand on great stages and speak the words that people needed to hear. I wanted to become an author and publish a long line of books. And I wanted to show people through my determination, spirit and extraordinary accomplishments that it was possible to not to go to sleep at night with their desires hidden away inside their hearts.

That long and painfully lonely night on the floor was the first time that I actually began to love myself for who I really am. I wasn't ready to leave the

Earth yet: I still had the music in me. In fact, I had a whole symphony. I saw my possibilities. I caught a glimmer of hope. I began dreaming again. And I found my inspiration. And ever since 2007, it has pulled me through every single adversity I have faced and challenge I have encountered – from and beyond my rock-bottom moment.

For what is now more than seven years, I have followed this cherished feeling of inspiration down many paths and through the greatest of adventures. It has moved and guided me to achieve many extraordinary things including becoming a multiple published author, business owner, mentor and professional speaker. I have served and inspired thousands of people globally through my pursuits as an entrepreneur – and they continue to unfold and grow exponentially each year. I have been blessed to travel all over the world visiting the most incredible places and winning awards for my writing and achievements while meeting and working with outstanding people.

No matter what I do or which clients, books, businesses and projects I pour myself and my heart into, one thing remains the same: my feeling of inspiration. I have returned 'home' to this in more moments than I can count. When life has been tough and I felt like I had nothing going for me, I have turned inwards and remembered what it is that inspires me. I have reconnected with what I care about and the destiny I feel I was born for. I have done whatever it takes to bring to this essence of inspiration into my daily life. And I have found myself, time and time again. In each moment, I could once again feel that I *did* count, that I *was* significant, and that I had something of awe-inspiring value and heart to offer to the people I'm surrounded by.

Without inspiration, I don't know where I would be. Had I never discovered what my unique inspiration is, I'm not sure that I would be alive today. I'm not sure that I would have stayed... because life wouldn't be worth living without it. I do know without a shadow of a doubt that I would not have been able to achieve what I have so far or had the experiences I have. It goes on from this to say that this very book that you hold in your hands, the *Inspiration Bible*, is a dedication to this unique, powerful and heart-opening energy, an invisible force, which has the capacity to transform a person... and their life. It is now a significant part of my dream and desire to pass on to you the gift that was given to me.

This book is a compilation of stories and contributions from 365 people from all around the world who have stepped forward to share a part of their lives with you. And, they have done it because they care about you. It matters to them that you find your inspiration so you too can overcome your challenges, whatever they might be. They care that you get to know who you really are and love yourself the way you are. They care that you find your power and step into it. They care that you reveal your heartfelt, lifelong dream and devote yourself to it. They also care about the influence that you personally can and will make on this planet by living out an inspirational life. Like me, they know that you are born to be a leader. And, like me, they believe in the unreal capacity that you have to create, manifest, build and sustain a life that you care about so that depression and despair are a thing of the past.

These stories and contributions will uplift you, move you, change you and bring tears to your eyes. They are an incredible testament to the human spirit and what we *really* have within us, as Ralph Waldo Emerson refers to powerfully in the opening quote of the Introduction. You will relate very closely to some of the pieces in this book and feel as though they were written just for you. Others will make your jaw drop. Some will confront you. And many will awaken you. And, in some way – whether big or small – each one will inspire you. You are about to meet humanity through the pages of this book, and in doing so, you will find yourself.

I stand behind this book and the project associated with it, with strength, heart and certainty, because I *know* just how deeply a moment of inspiration can change someone's life... because it changed mine, and this book wouldn't be in your hands without it. This book may very well become your companion on the darkest of days, and in the toughest moments where you feel that life... sucks. It's your pocketbook for finding your heart, overcoming challenges and reminding yourself what you *do* have, instead of focusing on that which you don't. All I ask is that as you read this book, in whatever order you read it, that you have your heart and mind open to possibility – or even a miracle. Don't be afraid to accept help from someone when you are down and out. This book was created for you.

It's time to open up your heart – and get inspired.

With inspiration,

Emily Gowor

26 years old

Author, Speaker & Publisher

Australia

Contributors

1
Our Unfair Advantage

"Why do you say 'Cl-Cl-Cl-Clefairy'?" he said, referring to a Pokémon. It was that moment as a child in grade four that I was first made aware of my speaking stutter. All the way through school, I would dodge every speaking situation. I settled for second best; from giving incorrect answers in class to avoid stuttering, to buying food I didn't want despite being hungry, and clothes I didn't like because they were easier to ask for. I got off at the wrong bus stop because I couldn't say my street, and saw movies alone because I was unable to say the title of the movie my friends were already seeing.

Living in fear everyday got to me. I dropped out of school to pursue my love of hiding behind computers and not speaking to anybody: a.k.a. Information Technology. After three years, I discovered that my plan was flawed. Every employer wanted you to have great communication skills, and I couldn't even say my own name. I felt like I couldn't get employed anywhere. All of this – the past events, pain, frustration and self-sabotage – was a blessing.

It forced me to create my own work and become an entrepreneur. At the age of nineteen, I opened my first business. It was followed by my second business nine months later and a third one not long after. I became obsessed with letting my results speak for me; my actions and my success became my words. If it was not for my stutter, I would have never found this new form of ambitious communication. Our greatest defeat will always be our unfair advantage. Look for yours, and use it to achieve everything you've ever wanted.

Jamie Stenhouse
24 years old
Serial Entrepreneur
Adelaide, Australia

2
Meanings Matter – The Alchemy of Life

*H*ere be words birthed in the fires of the furnace of Life – sounded amidst a seemingly endless war within-without that makes no sense, tearing apart the fabric of lives, ravaging forms, rituals, rites – relationships violently, ferociously, unexpectedly exploded in an outpouring of rage and apparent betrayal.

In the burning heat, *your* eyes appear, *your* face, *your* being, searching for meaning, pleading for sense and purpose amidst the seemingly insane. Maybe your heart, like mine, is aflame. Maybe your soul is crying, reflected in those tears in your eyes. Maybe you're close to the edge because there seems no reason to remain, and death feels the only way to end the pain. I know that space, that searing pain, that surging ache that nothing can contain. You are not alone – not now, not in the past, not in all that lies ahead. I *promise* you, you are never alone, no matter how it may feel right now.

Know this my friend, know this – these are the moments that *really* matter. These are the times when substance, vision, feeling, and *meaning* can truly change. The choice is *yours*. For thus we are fashioned, that meaning is ours to make, ours and ours alone. Feel this. Know this. See this. Right here, right now, *whatever* may be happening.

Nothing matters much until we give it meaning and then, by God, it does! This is the spell of spells, the mantra of mantras, and the remedy to end all remedies: *Meanings Matter*. Therein is the Science of the Divine, of love made manifest – the miracle of your life and mine. Choose the meaning you give things wisely when you are in the fires of pain and suffering, for through your eyes, your mind, *your heart*, Universes are born. Welcome home my friend. Welcome home.

Dr. Kim A. Jobst

56 years old

Physician, Healer & Teacher

London, United Kingdom

3
The Heart and Soul of Education

*W*hat is a *real* education? What do we really want for our children? A *real* education should inspire our children to embrace the miracle of being alive. The Native American Indians believe the moment a baby takes his first breath is when life enters the body. And interestingly, the word inspiration derives from the French, *inspiración* and means 'to inhale or to take a breath.' Of course, we *do* feel most alive when we are inspired. And what is a baby, if not inspiring and truly alive? Like a little angel from heaven, scattering delight and joie de vivre with every giggle; spreading hope for the journey ahead with each wobbly little step.

A real education should preserve this innate joy. Aristotle had it right when he said, "Educating the mind without educating the heart is no education at all."

Ancient spiritual traditions have taught the wisdom of the heart for centuries – qualities of love, gratitude and compassion – and how we can connect with this part of ourselves using simple breathing techniques. And now, neuroscience research proves that this is not some fluffy idea. The heart *is* a bona-fide brain: a complex, adaptive neural network with neurotransmitters that can store memory, has neuroplasticity and is a thinking, learning organism.

In addition to developing the mind, schools must spend time nourishing the hearts and souls of our children, helping kids to remember the magnificence of who they truly are at their deepest core, and how to meaningfully connect with self and others, to express themselves creatively and to live as compassionate beings. We can inspire our children by teaching them how to tap into their inborn heart intelligence. Children *are* the future. And when all schools teach children to consciously connect with the inspiration of heart and soul, humanity will thrive.

Louise Gilbert
43 years old
Transformational Teacher
Melbourne, Australia

4
Be True to Thy Self

*M*y childhood was filled with adult duties. There was no time for the childlike behaviours of playing with dolls or toys. I was born as the eldest of five siblings. My responsibility as their caregiver became evident at age five when my mother chose to leave all of her children in the care of my father who was an abusive alcoholic.

When I was young, I was out with my father one day when a bird pooped on my head. My father, in his infinite wisdom, told me I was the luckiest girl in the world. That has stayed with me throughout my whole life. I worked through the many challenges that came my way, believing I was and still am extremely lucky. I now have four children and four grandchildren. I have travelled down many paths, survived adversity, including sexual and physical abuse, and an unhappy, verbally-abusive marriage of thirty-nine years. I was told that no one would employ me. I went out the very next day and gained employment and have been with the same company for fourteen years.

Six years ago, I liberated myself from my marriage at the age of fifty-five and started a new life – both professionally and personally. I was scared, but I believed I would somehow be okay. I have now done hundreds of hours of self-development and looked into myself deeply. I am devoted to empowering others to be the best they can be, by believing in themselves and pushing through any adversity that they face with a mindset to: *be true to thy self*.

Carmel Cotis
61 years old
Managing Director
Adelaide, Australia

5
Healing the World with Money

J was sure I knew what I was talking about. That's when she slapped me, mid-sentence! "Get out of your head and get into your heart," she insisted. I continued to share what I thought I knew. Again out of nowhere, WHACK! She was right: I'd been in my head, thinking how to 'handle' business, success and life. I had amazing plans, but a complete lack of heart. No knowledge is as powerful as the love that is inside your heart; at least that's what I had learned in just a few slaps to the face.

Following this beautiful wake-up call, I searched for the heart in everything. Through all of my actions, even business. As I was seeking these answers, I stumbled across the Dalai Lama's quote: *"The Western world will be saved by the Western woman."* Which I understood to mean that through conscious capitalism we can each step up and save the world with love.

Most people don't recognize that each and every one of us has the opportunity to heal the world, with the resources we already have. Money is the single greatest hologram of our relationship to our own lives. Many humans blame money and capitalism for the wrong doings on this planet, when actually, it's just a reflection of its handlers.

What if money could be made by expressing love for others? This exists already: social entrepreneurship is the answer to increasing the flow of love on the planet, ending wars and even poverty itself. I am saddened to think that any of us could believe money is evil. That is childish blame. Murderers murder people, not weapons. By stopping the excuses and bringing heart into business, we will mature as a species and heal the separation between love and money.

Rossco Paddison
30 years old
Heart Centred Money Maker
Gold Coast, Australia

6
My Little Legend

I have just watched my youngest of four children play his first game of football. The smile on his face was contagious. The pride he had in himself was clear. He barely got to touch the ball, but when he got put up as ruck for the ball throw the whole team started yelling, "Go Bailey!" As the ball went up every other child stood back, even the players from the other team. The ball came down and Bailey caught it; every child on the field cheered. He turned, ran a few steps, kicked the ball and the game continued. Seeing all of the players on the field, ages ranging from six to ten, stop and cheer for my son was amazing. The fact that even the other team was rooting for him was inspirational.

You see, Bailey was born over ten weeks premature. He spent nine weeks in the Neonatal Intensive Care Unit. The first few days were touch and go. We didn't know whether he would even survive, let alone grow up into the boy he is today. Due to his premature birth, Bailey has Spastic Diplegic Cerebral Palsy. We didn't know whether he would ever walk independently, let alone run out and play a game of football.

Bailey is seven years old right now and truly believes that he can do whatever he puts his mind to. Not only has he conquered so many milestones, but he has also stood on stage in front of nearly 200 people and been interviewed about his disability. Bailey is an inspiration to everyone around him. He has a heart of gold and is the most determined and strong-willed person I have had the pleasure of meeting. My husband, his two brothers, his sister and I couldn't be prouder to have him in our family.

Jenni Reiffel
32 years old
Company Founder, Investor & Author
Adelaide, Australia

7
Painting the Future

I walked down the aisle, a radiant bride. There was no fairy-tale ending for me though; it quickly turned into a nightmare of abuse. I believed that I had no choice in the matter and that marriage was for life. During this time, I started painting, and the time I spent in art class each week became my refuge: a place of peace and nurturing.

Like many people before me, I thought having children would somehow magically change things. It didn't. The situation only became more abusive. I believe that during time I spent painting in the night hours, whilst the others slept, a connection to source was developed. Comfort and stress release was the result. After many years of suffering, depression, and struggling to function for my girls, I suddenly knew: I had to *be* the change so that my daughters and I could live in safety and harmony. Life soon became easier with much laughter and joy. My paints soon lay neglected.

Then like a bolt of lightning, my little brother was diagnosed with cancer. I chose to become his carer; an experience that was an emotional roller coaster ride for two years. A strong bond developed during the struggle with life and death. We held hands as his life passed away at fifty one-years-young. He died with the masterpiece still in him.

This time of deep loss was a huge awakening for me! I realised I was living life aimlessly and my masterpiece was also still within me. I made a commitment then to embrace art and creativity, no matter what. This decision empowered me to use art to process and release my grief, and all that comes with it. Within the creative space, I have opened up my heart and found my inner wisdom. Now, I live my masterpiece – each and every day.

Rhonda Brown

63 years old

The Creativity Queen

Wishart, Australia

8
Pick Yourself Up, Dust Yourself Off and Keep Going

J'd hit rock-bottom several times. I even considered opting out to ease the pain, but a voice inside wouldn't let me quit. We all suffer heartbreak at least once. Some never risk it again, lest they re-open the wound. I felt alone before my marriage ended, but stayed longer than was healthy for the love of our children. Married too young, financially pressured and focused on parenting, we had drifted apart. I married again, this romance felt right: the girl to share the rocking chairs. We built businesses together, bought properties, and created a mini-empire, laying the foundations for our dreams. Yet that journey changed us: we were lashed by a storm of struggle.

She yearned for a simple life and the freedom to travel. I revelled in my entrepreneurship, battling to create the vision I thought she wanted. We both became burnt-out workaholics. When she ran away, part of me left, too. Questioning my life's purpose, I found that my saviour was my need to be a brave and present father.

Rising up from despair, I re-committed to my spirit, rebuilt my business and rebuilt myself. I connected with the wonders of nature, enjoying the freedom of a road trip. I swam with mantas, dolphins and a whale shark; I bathed under waterfalls and inhaled the serenity of spectacular landscapes. No longer seeking another to complete my soul, I found one to enhance it. Tested again, nearly losing everything in the global meltdown, I re-discovered my own 'best friend' within – the one constant and inspirational voice, my companion, my messenger, the survivor – my own authentic self. Listen to your soul – it knows your true values, the answers you seek and answers to questions you haven't yet asked. Trust your instincts. Listen, love, breathe and live, my friend.

Tony Inman

53 years old

Business / Lifestyle Strategist & Author

Perth, Australia

9
11 Quotes from My Heart

"Why be ordinary when you can be extraordinary?"

"Be *grateful* for what has been, and be *inspired* by what could be."

"Purpose is the tune in your heart. Living your purpose is to sing it."

"Life is not risk-free. It was not meant to be. Life calls on us to extend ourselves, to evolve, and to be the absolute greatest we can be. This does not take place in our comfort zone."

"Struggle and challenge are two completely different things. Struggle is what you feel when you try to put a square peg into a round hole. Challenge is when you rise to the occasion and step out of the comfort zone to achieve something meaningful."

"Each soul seeks uniqueness, so that it can express, to itself and others, its true beauty and purpose in life."

"To be ordinary or extraordinary is not a birthright. Neither is it a result of chance. It is a result of choice, and we make that choice when we allow *passion* into our life and work. Passion is a game-changer, the *one thing* that changes *everything*, because it uses the strongest force of all, which is *love itself.*"

"Change is always only one new choice away."

"A man makes his wisest choices when he knows what he is here to do in life."

"It is in the heart we experience life itself, whereas our mind chooses the direction."

"I believe one of the most pressing issues is to learn from the *feminine*. Collaboration instead of competition; compassion instead of judgement. Heart *and* mind instead of only mind. We cannot change what has happened, but we can courageously map a new way forward by drawing equally on all gifts, abilities and insights, that come from simply being born a human."

Jesper Lowgren
49 years old
Transformation Thought-Leader
Sydney, Australia

10
Our Angel

*M*y life before our angel was beautiful. But I was too busy with plans, career goals, and an active toddler to notice. Looking back, I can see how blissfully unaware I was of how dramatically life was about to change. She was eight days old when the first seizure occurred. Then there was another, and another. Panic buttons at triage caused fourteen doctors to appear out of nowhere. MRIs. Intensive Care Unit. Tests. Countless needles and drug trials. Hundreds of seizures, one-after-another. Then, amidst our terror and clambering for hope, the big blow. It's impossible to describe the shock of hearing your baby will forever be 'vegetative.'

Depression followed. There were considerations of whether I could allow her to live like this, my own suicidal contemplation, and guilt over what it would mean to leave my three-year-old.

Three years on, she has changed us in ways we didn't know were possible. She has brought love to our lives unlike anything we have experienced before. She lights up the world with her smile and every small measure of progress brings us unspeakable joy. Despite those dark days, the terror and unimaginable impact of shattered dreams, with honest reflection, we wouldn't change her.

Her journey has broken us into the tiniest of fragments and invited us to create ourselves anew. In our rebuilding, we have had the rare opportunity to choose which parts we wanted to keep—and which we no longer wanted. We've discovered a raw vulnerability, and are now alive in ways we never knew to access before. While the path may not always go as you expect, I hope you muster the courage to trust life and have the patience to allow it to unfold and reveal its soulful, divine perfection. Because, if you let it, it always will.

Jasmine Platt

34 years old

Spiritual Development Coach

Auckland, New Zealand

11
Only Now

Quantum time expands –

Before, After – Only Now.

Sighing of the Wind.

Charles Rawlings
55 years old
Lawyer, Scientist & Author
Winston-Salem, United States of America

12
We Are All Like Mum's Rose Petals

*W*hen my daughter was five years old, she was being bullied at school for being a mixed child. She has African and European blood. Eventually, she did not want to go back to school. One day when I picked her up, she was in tears. I spoke to her teacher and then had a nice, quiet, calm word with the bully who was only a year older than Michelle. When we got home, I knew my daughter would be scarred for life if I did not handle this situation properly.

As we unpacked the school bag, I asked Michelle to come to the kitchen to help me prepare dinner. As we were about to set the table, I noticed my collection of rose petals was nicely placed on the table as decoration. I said to Michelle, "Honey, what do you see in that African basket?" She answered, "Dried up rose petals." I asked her what else she could see and she said, "They look a bit dusty, but they seem to have different colours; some look really dark red, those ones look a bit yellow, and the those other ones look like they have once been white."

I said, "Exactly, that is how we all are as people; we come in different colours, but we are all the same. Just like these rose petals." She looked at me and smiled. I asked her if she understood what I was saying. She laughed and said, "Yes mum, we are all the same and we are all beautiful, just like your dried roses." Bullying kids for being different in culture or ability happens a lot in schools. But, I know my daughter is empowered, and she knows that we are all the same despite our external differences.

Nkandu Beltz
31 years old
Author & Speaker
Horsham, Australia

13
The Pull From Within

*J*often ask myself, "How can I get inspired again?" It's as if I had 'it' and lost it somehow. Let's be honest: we all lose our inspiration every now and then. I'm sure it's something you've experienced too. I'm not ashamed to admit that I'm a workaholic, and so I'll use this example from my working life to explain how I find inspiration with the hopes that you too can find inspiration when you need it.

Quite often, when I feel as if I'm struggling, I imagine a successful future version of myself who has achieved what I am aiming for. I ask him, "Why the heck am I working so hard?" The vision of my future, successful self, standing there, having achieved the outcome I desire is enough to convince me why I am here on this planet and BOOM! I find my inspiration again!

Now, the real secret is to grasp this inspiration and take action immediately. By taking action and creating momentum, you become the doorway to allow the magic of your inspiration to appear. I believe that being motivated is the 'push' and being inspired is the 'pull.' The key difference here being that motivation comes from external forces, pushing you to get results, whereas inspiration comes from deep within: your core. When you react from within, you're on fire and become alive again. I'll leave you with a few questions to connect to your core. Ask yourself:

- What keeps you awake at night, even when you're tired?

- If you take your last breath tomorrow, what do you want to accomplish before you die?

If that doesn't light you up, you're still not there. Keep going. You will achieve the inspiration you desire – and it will help you achieve amazing results.

Poy TB

31 years old

Coach & Entrepreneur

Sydney, Australia

14
Life Mastery

J used to work in the city and, during lunch, I would go to a small park. Every Tuesday, there was a Buddhist monk named Joe. He sat there with his A-frame and answered questions people had while passing by. One of the things I am interested in is religion. So, the monk and I started chatting regularly. We talked about many things including religion, life, food, being a vegetarian, money, and so on. He owned, except his clothes and mobile phone, absolutely nothing. His understanding was that money is something to avoid, thus he did not want to have any possessions. I confronted him on this, and soon realised that his idea was that money is 'bad.'

To me, money is neutral. It can be used for things like building schools, growing charities, providing jobs to people, or helping to find a cure for cancer. Money can also be used in other ways: for corruption, funding research to develop weapons, and so on. Money has no emotion. It is simply here to serve us. We are the ones who give it purpose. We are here to master our lives, and money is one of the components of doing this. If you work for it, for the rest of your life, you become its slave. If you make money work for you, you are its master, and you can focus on what you really love doing. Money, then, is a by-product of the success you deserve.

A monk can have no possessions and still be a slave to money, because he relies on and, in a way, is a burden to others. If, however, you empower yourself, save and invest, you can do more of what you love, get paid for it and in turn provide value to thousands of other people. That is life mastery.

Juraj Benak
32 years old
Entrepreneur
Brisbane, Australia

15
Strangers

Two strangers walk by

Just a nudge of two shoulders

Passing through the crowd

Two strangers stand closer

A line in a coffee shop

Simply unaware

Two strangers collide

An apology exchanged

Two strangers no more

Two unlikely friends

Lounging in a warm café

Sharing their stories

Two warm mugs in hands

Both hearts now even warmer

A spark ignited

Two minds uniting

Inspiring one another

Each showing the other

That they can change the world

Rachel Watt

15 years old

Student

Melbourne, Australia

16
Comprehending Sadness

Comprehending sadness has been, by far, the most inspiring journey of my life. That might sound strange, but I assure you of its truth. See, for me, sadness comes in many forms. Sometimes it's not living up to my own self-concept. Sometimes it's losing a loved one or having a precious item damaged or destroyed. Sometimes it's the missed possibility of love or the cost of going after it. Then there's the sadness of being unfulfilled by the stresses of living a life I didn't love, all the while seemingly incapable of admitting to myself my vision of the life I'd love.

I was taught that our 'fantasies' create our 'nightmares.' I know that's true. But for me, there was something greater in sadness that I had to uncover. I figured if it exists anyway, regardless of how we make it, it must have a reason, as worthy of a life created by the Universe itself and experienced by a gathering of stardust. "My God," I asked, "How is my sadness part of my journey?"

I remember staring at a mirror after having yet another 'fantasy' broken by the loving values of the other person. I stared at my own reflection, asking whatever higher power there is, why I was given the assignment of experiencing so much emotion. That's the first time I can recall, that I heard the sound of my soul.

"Your sadness is the source of your strength."

Such a simple idea, but so easily missed by people, including myself. But its actuality is beyond fallacy. Those moments of sadness. We are so blessed to have them, for it is within them that we feel it, and listen, and can see our true nature, our true self that is inspired beyond measure.

Stephan Gardner
30 years old
Visionary Life Coach
Toronto, Canada

17
The Gratitude List

*E*very night I write a gratitude list. These are my top ten choices for the life I've lived so far. These are the things I am grateful for:

1. Random acts of crying: you appear at wholly inappropriate moments, yet I will always cherish you for the emotions you allow me to experience.
2. Money: you may not always be the quantity I wish for, yet you certainly know how to keep me in the quality lifestyle of global travel and knee-high boots to which I have grown accustomed.
3. Change: you consistently poke, prod, challenge and anger me, yet I always come back for more.
4. My feet: you move me (pun intended) and have allowed me to walk in some of the most serene and scenic places on the planet (and just quietly, I think you are two of my more attractive assets).
5. Relationship break-ups: you were always the toughest of decisions, yet I never regretted you.
6. The boy in grade three who took to calling me "Dead Bra" (a pretty clever take on "Deborah" for an eight-year-old, if I may say so): you gave me a thicker skin and the inspiration to change my identity to the infinitely more fitting one of "Debbie," for the next twenty-three years.
7. My crazy hair: you continue to teach me acceptance and appreciation for that which I will never hope to control.
8. My work: you have not often been what I expect, but wow, you have been fun.
9. Dry socks: after ten days on the Kokoda track, you will always be magnificent in my eyes
10. My self: you inspire me daily.

(Plus, the usual suspects: my partner, family, friends, hammocks, sex, avocadoes, the word "nifty," and my teddy bear, Herbert. You guys go without saying.)

Deb Campbell

34 years old

Event Manager

Melbourne, Australia

18
The Present

One of my favourite quotes is from Deepak Chopra:

"This moment is as it should be because it took the entire Universe to make this moment. When you struggle against this moment you struggle against the entire Universe."

The present moment is always 'perfect' because it took the entire Universe to make it. I know and trust that the Universe has a greater wisdom, a supreme intelligence and a magnificent divine order that we may not see at the moment. Our entire lives are a sequence of present moments, maybe billions, trillions, or quadrillions... So, if it took the entire Universe to make each present moment, how can there be mistakes or errors? Every present moment holds a precious gift.

This precious gift might be wrapped inside an ugly wrapping paper in the form of a disease, an accident, someone we dislike, someone that mistreats us, loss of a job or money, loss of loved ones through death or divorce... you name it. Sometimes it takes us minutes, hours or days to unwrap that ugly package. However, most of the time it takes us months or years to find the precious gift inside. Unfortunately, some people never unwrap the package and therefore miss out on the gift.

The ugliest wrapped gift I received was at age thirty-five. My husband had an affair and walked out on me. It was the most painful moment in my life, yet it was also the most precious gift. I set out on a journey to be my authentic self, do what I love, share my unique gift, and inspire others live an empowered meaningful life. So, next time you are faced with ugly gift-wrap, be curious. Ask: "I wonder what gift is in this package for me? What unique and special gift is this experience is giving me?"

Dr. Marcia Becherel

53 years old

Human Potential Coach & Speaker

Brisbane, Australia

19
Journeying from the Many to the One

J've been a scientist pretty much all my life, studying life and its intricacies from the inside out. Becoming highly specialised in my field over the years, I gradually became more humble before the intelligence that governs life. As I delved deeper into the multitude of tiny molecules that make life possible, dissecting the enzymatic pathways regulating our genetics, the more I felt compelled to step back and explore the infinite macro.

From the apparent 'many-ness' complexity of creation came the void to explore the 'one-ness'; the simplicity underlying evolution. The more specialised I became, the less I really understood life. Studying the mechanics of life did not suffice! I was drawn towards the hidden Laws of Nature and human experience, realising that matter without spirit is motionless and spirit without matter is expressionless.

Scientists are often regarded as open-minded and willing to embrace change. From my insider perspective, the rules of the game keep you bound in the materialistic model of life. The classical scientific reductionist approach teaches us the illusion of understanding life. Life is more than the sum of its parts. Breaking free from this conditioning is not an easy task. However, once you give yourself permission to break free from the reductionist shackles, you open up Pandora's Box.

After more than fifteen years of dedicated and focused research in life sciences, I realised the study of life cannot be meaningful without embracing the infinite micro (body) and macro (mind and spirit) domains of existence. Progressively, I awakened the purposeful leader within, clarified my mission and embraced my uniqueness. Today, I witness the One and the Many around me on a daily basis. This helps me to appreciate life's hidden order, for life is but an endless series of journeys between the One and the Many.

Dr. Olivier J. Becherel

42 years old

Researcher, Educator & Coach

Brisbane, Australia

20
Your Guardian Angel

*A*s I look at you with love, I see absolute love and joy. From the moment we connected, I knew there was so much more to you. I saw the sparkle in your eye, as you came into this world and it gave me so much joy to see you, with your tiny little hands and tiny little toes. You were a miracle, an absolute beauty who chose to come into this world and make life so much brighter for those around you. You are a ray of sunshine, a breath of fresh air. You light up the world wherever you go. Even on your gloomy days, that spark still exists inside you.

I am here to remind you that this spark can never be put out. You are the sun; you are the shine. You are here to do magnificent things. As I take your hand, I ask you to believe in yourself, to know that all will work out for the best. What fills you up and gives you joy and pleasure? Do not let others influence you and talk you out of what you already know is right for you; for you get to choose. You get to be in charge of you. I tell you this because I love you. I want to see you be the best that you can be, not for others, but for yourself. You are worthy and deserving of your true heart's desires.

Are you ready to accept what is possible for you? Are you ready to believe and trust in yourself, no matter what others tell you? Are you ready to soar high and not look back at the past? Are you ready to take a chance on yourself? I will be with you every step of the way. You are never alone. Talk to me. I will listen.

Your Guardian Angel.

Erica Morris

41 years old

Intuitive Healer & Spiritual Teacher

Berwick, Australia

21
Grateful to Survive

*J*t was a clear sunny day. Music was playing on the radio. I sat patiently at the traffic lights thinking about the magical European holiday I was going on the following day. The lights took forever to go green. Finally, as they flicked over, I put my foot on the accelerator. For the next few seconds, the world still seemed, well, normal. The sun still shone, the music still played, and my thoughts were still on my holiday. Then, out of the corner of my eye I saw it. Large, fast, and terrifyingly close.

As I turned my head, I saw a three-tonne tow-truck just metres away. I tried to swerve. But, there just wasn't enough time for me to get out of the way as it sped through the red light. I remember seeing a flash, hearing a loud bang, and air bags going off throughout the car. I remember thinking, *I can still see the sun, I must be alive.*

Miraculously, I wasn't killed. The car was a complete write-off, but I was okay. In the following months my body suffered terribly. My back, neck and shoulder were traumatised from the impact of being hit at 70 mph. I spent hours in chiropractic, massage, undergoing x-rays and scans. I felt frustrated, angry and upset. I started to think how I could be grateful for the crash.

I remember the paramedics telling me how lucky I was to be alive, saying if the car had been smaller or older, I'd be dead. I became grateful for being the first person at the lights. By being there, I had saved another person's life. It was then that my traumatised body started to heal. The pain started to subside and so did the frustration, anger and upset. It's amazing what can happen when we change our thinking.

Caroline Shaw

45 years old

Marketing & Business Consultant

Perth, Australia

22
Mentors Are Believers

*T*hroughout life, regardless of age, financial situation, knowledge or certainty, we all have an innate dream, a longing to do something amazing and life changing. Everyone has this within themselves, but sometimes we just need the right guidance and mentorship.

I discovered my dream and burning desire at fourteen, when I first started playing the meticulous and miraculous game of golf. I was introduced by my father and relatives, who had minimal skills and talents, but taught me important lessons along the way. After trying many private lessons from different teachers and coaches, I felt like I wasn't connecting with these people. This was my dream! I didn't want to just get advice or guidance from anyone; I wanted someone who spoke with inspiration, dedication and patience. As the saying goes, "When the student is ready, the teacher appears." I was ready!

I met my mentor, Jeff Wagner, in 2003 at St. Michaels Golf Club and remain friends with him to this day. Jeff taught me many things about golf – from technical skills and game play to practice routines – but what most resonated with me, what filled my void, was his remarkable ability to communicate his life experience in a simple, yet effective, form to assist my golfing career.

"Golf isn't just a game, it's a way of life." "This isn't a one or two-year plan, this is a twenty to twenty-five-year plan, so practice and work towards that." Jeff would say things like this, and I would completely agree, like he was speaking to a different me – the 'me' that had the dream! Jeff's mentorship was incredibly helpful, yet challenging. My advice is to find a mentor who believes in and connects with you; someone who sees the dream within you. Then watch your dream ignite and propel you forwards!

Luke Papallo
28 years old
Counsellor
Sydney, Australia

23
Change Is Not Optional
– It's a Fact of Life

*I*n the last 200 years of human history we have gone from steam, to electricity, to the Internet. To think, this only represents a fraction of the time we've spent on this planet. Back when my father was in business, you could survive two decades without changing your business model. As soon as we ticked over into the new millennium, that time was halved to a decade, as we witnessed the proliferation of the Internet. By 2010, we witnessed the smartphone revolution, and the time was halved again. As 2015 approaches, we will enter yet another wave of disruptive innovation, and we will be compelled to adapt, yet again.

To that end, I would hazard a guess that fifty percent of the jobs and industries that exist now, won't exist in twenty years' time. So, what can you do when confronted by a world of neverending change? You could live your life in fear that your industry or job will be made redundant by technology. Or, you can embrace it! Because, with these threats come massive opportunities for growth and innovation. The Internet saw an entire industry pop up out of thin air. While some resisted the change, others saw it as an opportunity. The most inspiring stories I have read have been the stories of young entrepreneurs building something from nothing in their parents' garage. Disruption creates opportunities. It's your job to make the most of them and ride the wave of innovation.

Mark my words: the world will belong to those who can embrace change. To that end, adaptability will be one of the most important skills that any human can possess in the future. My question for you today is, "Are you prepared?" Don't wait for change; create it.

Chris Hooper

27 years old

Entrepreneur & Accountant

Adelaide, Australia

24
The Mystery Girl

*K*nown as 'The Mystery Girl' in 1978, by a medical team, at eight years of age, I miraculously survived a stroke. I had extremely unusual, serious findings in my diagnosis – losing my ability to walk and talk. Doctors reported to my parents that I would never walk again. I am lucky to be alive.

Facing a long period of rehabilitation to walk again and use my arm, I learned that there's no such thing as 'can't.' A few years ago, I was asked a question that puzzled me at first: "Donna, what can't you do since having the stroke?" This confused me, as I have always tried to focus on what I *can* do, rather than what I *can't*. My response was: "I have never felt confident to run since 1978!"

My first tentative running steps, in November 2012, began with only thirty steps before having to stop and think *I definitely need help!* Coached by two running experts, I started with a fun run goal of 5.3km in January 2013, and was determined to run the 42.2km in October 2013. Yes, there were times of frustration, but my coaches kept saying, "Baby steps, Donna, baby steps." So true! I did that when I faced rehab to walk again with 'baby steps,' and now I was doing it all over again to face my challenge of running.

I ran my first full marathon in October 2013. I took on this challenge to raise funds for the hospital that saved my life and to encourage others. If reaching a goal seems tough, remember your reasons 'why' you want to reach it, and that 'there's no such thing as 'can't.' I feel privileged to use my unique story to encourage and inspire others; for I believe this is my mission.

Donna Campisi
43 years old
Speaker, Writer & Humanitarian
Melbourne, Australia

25
Never Give Up

*T*he story I want to share with you as you read this book is one that I experienced in my own life. As the heading suggests, I want you to never give up on your dreams in life no matter how small or insignificant they seem or how others make you feel about them. Listen to the inner voice guiding you to go for what you want. That voice already knows what you really want to do in life. Very few people take notice of what their intuition is trying to tell them. Those that do are amongst the greatest entrepreneurs and business leaders in the world and have had the biggest impact in their respective industries.

I went through the early stages of my life ignoring my intuition. It wasn't until I attended *The Breakthrough Experience*® with Dr. John Demartini in 2010 that I started to really listen. I gained a different perspective on life, and the greatest message that I was able to take away from that weekend was: "Go for your goals, regardless of what people say."

Since that weekend, I have been working on my dream of owning a global business. Despite what you may hear from leaders, business success doesn't just happen overnight. It can take months, or even years, of hard work and endless effort behind the scenes before it goes anywhere. But it is worth it. Just know that you have a special gift to share with the world, and don't let anyone stop you from being who you most want to be.

"Stay hungry, stay foolish."

Steve Jobs

Ala Almaet

28 years old

IT Specialist & Entrepreneur

Sydney, Australia

26
Self-Love Is All There Is

*A*s I woke up from another overdose, bewildered by my drive to self-destruct whilst living a life many would dream of, I experienced a life-changing realization: I had lost myself! I was living a glamorous life of luxury, making money, playing with all the toys and having all the friends my heart desired, but I was in inner hell.

I reflected back to my first twenty years of life: I was incarcerated, beaten, shot, stabbed, raped and gang raped until I escaped in my early twenties. I realized that amidst all that outer hell, imprisoned and isolated from the world, I was in inner *bliss*. Since escaping, I had built a great life of fun and laughter, but I was in inner *hell*.

After my escape, I sought love, acceptance, and self-worth outside myself and forgot the ritual that kept me connected to my authentic self during my years of incarceration. Through this ritual, I built a strong sense of self-love, belief and worth. I knew I would live a powerful life, and that gave me phenomenal courage to survive the torture. But, when I escaped, I forgot about my inner connectedness. It ebbed away until I was emotionally destitute — missing my inner authentic connection — leaving emptiness that nothing external could fill.

The life-changing realization I had after that last overdose took me on a journey back to myself. I built a life of inner and outer heaven with joy, love and compassion based on building self-love. Working with people globally, I recognize that same emotional destitution in so many. Take the shortest, most transformational journey of your life — from your head back to your heart! The single most important thing you can do in your life is to truly unconditionally love yourself for exactly who you are, as you are. You are *perfect*; and you deserve your love.

Judy van Niekerk
46 years old
Author, Healer & Trainer
London, United Kingdom

27
On Resilience

*T*he great tales of resilience are closely intertwined with the great tales of success. I am fortunate to have personally heard many of these tales. I recall the victim of high school bullying who was unanimously elected as a captain of that school two years later. I recall the student who failed four subjects in his first year of university and went on to graduate with honours. I recall the entrepreneur who was told he had the worst business idea ever and went on to co-found a new company that beat Harvard, Yale, Stanford and MIT into the finals of an international business competition.

These are extraordinary tales, all of them, and all with a common thread: the archetype of the individual who journeys from setback to success. It's the classic success story. What is often left unsaid, though, is that which lies beyond these turnarounds and these comebacks. It is the transformation of the character in these tales.

What becomes of our resilient protagonist in these tales? More to the point, who does he become? The great Danish philosopher Soren Kiekegaard once noted: "Life can only be understood backwards; but it must be lived forwards." Perhaps our challenges can only be understood backwards. In hindsight, as we reflect on the obstacles we have encountered, we suddenly realise why we had to endure them. Resilience, essentially, is to continue living forwards, even if you may only understand backwards.

Can you continue to live forwards, despite understanding not being achievable at present? Can you continue through challenges with resilience, with faith that you are being moulded into someone new? I believe that it can be done. The other main, common thread in those original tales I told is that I am the protagonist in all of them.

Ben Luks
26 years old
Online Marketer
Adelaide, Australia

28
It's CAN-cer

Sitting in bed with views of sun-soaked Melbourne city from the tenth floor, I turned to look at the doctor sitting on the end of my bed. I'd been in hospital since just after Christmas when a tumour was found. I was about to find out how serious it was. The oncologist carefully spoke: "Cameron, you have a grade four brain tumour, the rarest, aggressive and most hard-to-treat tumour."

Slowly it sunk in: I have brain cancer. The average lifespan is five to six months; over eighty percent die in two years and over ninety-five percent die within five years. There is a zero percent survival rate. What would *you* do? I examined my life and what I wanted it to represent. I thought about the impact my life would have on those around me. What will they say when I die? Will they be happier that I had lived and died than never really lived?

I have learned that life isn't how *long* you live but how *much* you live. How much you *give*, not how much you *take*. It is not measured in money or time, but in experiences and impact. We all impact our world. I have seen the impact that the first smile, from a child who has never moved on their own before, can have on a room. Joy and memories are important. Children facing obstacles many of us couldn't fathom have positively changed the world of those around them. So what are we going to do? What is your impact?

I choose to risk truly living; to risk failure in the hope of bettering the world. I am doing the things I dream of and things that reasonable people believe impossible. I am not going to let a shortened life get in the way of living my life fully. How are you living yours? What do you want your life to represent?

Cameron Gill
36 years old
Superhero Creator & Entrepreneur
Melbourne, Australia

29
Noodles

*J*n the winter of 1997, I was in Hokkaido, Japan on an exchange program. I was with my parents in a noodle bar, in thick, heavy coats; the snow drizzling down outside. My proud father, with boast in his voice for his son, started to wax lyrical about the things he knew about Japan. As our hot ramen noodle soup came to our table and Mum scooped a generous portion of hers into my bowl, Dad proceeded to tell a story that fit the occasion. It was his take on a short novella by Ryohei Kuri entitled *Ippai no Kakesoba* (in English 'plenty of noodles'). To this day, its impression has stayed with me.

A recent widow walks into a noodle bar with her two boys on New Year's Eve to reflect on the year ahead and honour their deceased father who had promised to take them before his passing. The family was left with financial hardship and could only afford one serve of noodles. The owner of the noodle bar listened to the conversation as the mum taught the boys resilience and gratitude.

"One serve is plenty, we don't need more than that," she said. Moved by what he heard, but out of respect for their sense of pride, the owner hid an extra portion of noodles into their one serve without them knowing. Year after year they returned, and year after year they ordered one serve. Every year the owner gave them an extra portion. The boys, now adults, become distinguished professionals and their financial woes were long gone, but when they return to the noodle bar they still only order one serve in memory of their roots.

From that story, came many poignant lessons: the need to appreciate life and its journey – my own and that of others – and to celebrate it in humble ways.

Seung-woun Yi

37 years old

Teaching Mathematician & Entrepreneur

Gosford, Australia

30
The Voice Journey

The words are sometimes hiding
Behind the thick brick walls
With only glimpses of shining gold
Peeping through the holes
They must be golden wisdom
That want to see the day
They must have lots of power
To reach that light today
To wonder in despair
To overcome life's slope
To be the voice of woman
That fills the world with hope
To reach the silver lining
Behind the heavy bricks
Reach for bright blue skies above
And feel the voice release
Release your inner power
Feel liberated through
Be like angel's feather
And spread the message true.

Ella Kushnir
50 years old
Communication Expert & Author
Sydney, Australia

31
The Only Black Belt

So, what are the 'must-haves' for becoming a karate black belt? Typically, you might say hard work, talent, focus on the end goal…and so on. Well, all of these are true, but perhaps most important of all are determination and focus.

I originally started training in martial arts with a group of friends. We started at the same time and had all decided to join the local karate club after being inspired by Bruce Lee movies and various other action films. We all thought it would be fun to be able to have that same amazing level of fighting ability, finesse and fitness. As a natural part of the process, we had to undertake gradings every three to six months, where we would be examined on how well we had learned patterns of movement, techniques and general ability.

There are ten stages from novice (or white belt), to black belt, with each step becoming progressively more difficult and challenging. Surprisingly, as I advanced to each stage, at least one friend or two would drop out, believing it was too hard, or that too much effort would be involved, or they simply lost the motivation, allowing 'life' to get in the way. By the time I was one step away from achieving my black belt grading, I was the only one left!

The day of the black belt grading drew near; it was worse than preparing for exams, as the consequences of not being prepared were worse than just getting an 'F' grade…the consequences were most likely a good beating too! The focus, meticulous training and determination paid off, and I eventually came through with flying colours — exhilaration and huge relief followed. The amazing thing however…was that this was only the beginning of my journey!

Geoff Alexander

44 years old

Digital Marketer

London, United Kingdom

32
Your Body Speaks

*Y*ou shine when you are living and speaking your truth. Your life is your creation. There are no limits to what you can achieve when you connect to your true self.

Your body has an in-built mechanism to let you know when you are off purpose. Symptoms are your body's feedback to get your attention and get you back on track. You may have loss of energy and vitality, weight gain, digestive problems, as well as chronic pain and stiffness. The key is to listen to your body speak and ask yourself some questions: "Am I expressing my truth?" "Am I living according to someone else's values?" "Is there emotional stress I am not letting go of?" "Are my buttons being pushed?" and "Is the life I am living a true reflection of who I am?"

Observe how you physically feel when you are being true to you. You are more vibrant and energetic. You are like a magnet. People are attracted to you. You are able to manifest what you desire. You live with presence, confidence and certainty. You make healthier choices. You look and feel more youthful, more alive and certain.

Remember: you are in charge. You are an inspired messenger, here to share your own unique talents and gifts to the world. It's in that space of being your authentic self that you find your calling, your purpose. The fact is, your life is about *you!* When you make your life about everyone else's wants and needs while ignoring you own, you shrink yourself, you play small, denying the world of your true magnificent expression that is *you*. Listen to that inner voice. Listen to your body's feedback to help get you back on track. Give yourself permission to express your true self. Leave your mark. Be you!

Dr. Dave Tuck
45 years old
Wellness Coach & Chiropractor
Dallas, United States of America

33
Awaken Your Divine Self

'*I*nside' is just *you!* A divine self with a mission and purpose. There's clarity and certainty. And then *life* happens! How difficult it is, to stay attached to that inner world, after all the childhood and social conditioning! Authority figures tell you how to be; media and peer groups sway you; some experiences clip you. Your edges blur. Why you are here, and how best to truly express yourself, are eclipsed by the innate desire to belong and fit in. Hoping to please and doing what's right, you feel increasingly powerless and insignificant, falling between the cracks of other people's desires and expectations.

It's possible to reach adulthood and feel you have lost touch with your divine self altogether. Yet, there will come a pivotal point, a moment, when that unique voice within will look at the life you have made and will urge you to ask: "Does it have to be *this* way?"

The response is *no!* Permit yourself to ask two key questions: "Who am I?" and "Why am I here?" Your personal journey back to *you* requires you to expand your self-knowledge, self-worth and self-love. Reflect on your life; dig a little; the answers are like gems waiting to be plucked from the rock-face. In your past, every person you've ever met, every event or experience that happened to you has honed your character, qualities, skills and attributes. Your specific challenges have defined your focus and destiny. In the now, rediscover what and who gives you delight, and where you feel at home.

Listen to your intuition: make definitive shifts that 'feel right' and do only that which makes you feel alive! Trust your divine, authentic self. Own your identity! You are *unique* and *amazing!* Show *that* to the world!

Tania Tuck

47 years old

Emotional Wellness Specialist

Dallas, United States of America

34
Her Heart

*O*n a cold morning in May, a five-year-old girl was admitted to hospital. Through no fault of her own – not bad eating habits, smoking habits, nor poor decision making – this innocent child was born with a hole in her heart that would likely end her life, without intervention.

Bravely, the young girl faced her fear. And the doctor took a knife, cut into her young body and, with her tiny heart beating in his hand, sewed up a hole like a person might sew up a torn shirt. The operation was successful, a miracle of the modern world. The brave young girl went on to become my closest friend and the inspiration of my life: my sister.

She did nothing to create the hole in her heart, yet before she had been in the world for six years, she had faced her own death – and beaten it. In all my travels, I have yet to find a heart that functions so well as my sister's. She tirelessly loves life and all those who are dear in it. She is the face of strength for so many other 'heartkids' and families bravely facing their own similar situations. Many have gone on to inspire others; many have lost the fight along the way.

I live in daily gratitude for what I have. Many will say that it's been the secret of a fortunate life. My sister taught me that sometimes there's a hole in your heart and it can challenge your whole world –but *you get to choose* how you face it. Sometimes it takes a hole to be fixed for us to appreciate the gift that we get to live every day. Most of all, my sister taught me that when you give yourself permission to be inspirational, you give others permission to do the same.

David Cervelli

31 years old

Business Performance Consultant

New York City, United States of America

35
The Legacy of Insight

When I was young, I had an athletics coach named Keith. Early in his life, Keith witnessed the Hiroshima bomb go off. As a side effect, he lost his eyesight completely and became blind. I used to walk up to his house, in our little town where he lived, to pick him up. He would walk down with me, holding on to my arm as I guided him the whole way. We'd walk across the paddocks with cows in them, and I'd lift up the barbed wire fence for him to climb through.

We would arrive at the sports oval where he volunteered to train fifteen to twenty kids. Although he couldn't physically see us, he was developing some of the best athletes. He would use his other senses to coach us. We would run around the oval doing laps, and when we finished, he'd place his hand below our hearts to feel our heart rates. He would use the power of insight to train us. We played tricks on him to see if we could catch him out; but somehow, he always knew.

His influence led me in an amazing direction in life, as I became a champion athlete in Australia. I learned to visualize and work with my other senses whenever I felt weak during performance. Keith placed a huge level of trust in me to guide him; and in doing so, he taught me to trust and guide myself. When I can't see the answer, I know there is something else, a bigger order, going on behind the scenes that can't always be perceived with the eyes. My legacy to you is to say this: trust what you've already got, because that is what makes you who you are. Utilize your strengths and talents. See the inner leader. Close your eyes and trust yourself.

Sam Norton

34 years old

Leadership & Executive Business Consultant

Sydney, Australia

36
The Death and Life of My Soul

*L*ast night, standing at the edge of the cliff, I dared to look down and see the breathtaking beauty of the scene in front of me. I saw a sheer drop with the rainforest below me, birds circling, and I remember feeling life pulsing all around me – the plants, the trees, the animals, and the forest. Before I could even hear the voice saying, "Are you ready to jump?" I already knew I was.

Everything in my life had led me to this moment. Knowing that I was jumping to my death felt beautiful, for I knew it was the only way to feel alive. As I took a step forward, my breath quickened and my body shuddered. As I leapt off the cliff with a graceful sweep, golden wings, three times the length of my body, stretched out with a strength and agility that suggested they had been ready for this moment for an eternity.

I flew and circled down the cliff, and realized I could fly through and into the opposing cliff edge. I was flying as if the molecules of the land were nothing but my thoughts. I flew into the city and through the buildings—one-by-one I conquered them; each one cementing this realization in every part of my being.

This was all a dream; a visualization that I had. Life is the reflection of my heart. I can be anywhere, do anything, and be anything as I am everyone. I realize every person, every act, every dream, every manifestation is made as perfect, because it's made by God and made by a part of me. That moment of true oneness felt like it was different – it felt it was going to stick. The realization penetrated every cell in my body and I knew this was it; life would never be the same.

Paras Yazdani
35 years old
Photographer
Melbourne, Australia

37
Simon's Story

*A*t age sixteen, I left school for a career in retail. By eighteen, I was the youngest manager in my home state for an international retail chain. At twenty-three, still climbing the management ladder, I was poached by another retail chain. By twenty-four, I was married, and at twenty-six, the first of two children was born. I supported a mortgage and a family. At twenty-nine, I became a dad again, bought a bigger house, had a better job, and earned more money. At thirty-three, I built my first business, which ran for eight years. I achieved all this by dedication, application, and doing the hard yards. It was a rich life but not, however, a happy life.

Through divorce, I'd lost my wife, kids, and my big house. Soon after, I lost myself. I'd crashed. By thirty-five, I was an alcoholic and had been diagnosed as manic-depressive. At thirty-eight, I attempted suicide by driving my van into a telephone pole. I spent twelve weeks in hospital, six months in a wheelchair, and it was a year before I could walk unaided again. I rebuilt my entire life from the ground up.

That old life, and the tragedies in it, were my choices. In that life, I had countless opportunities to choose another path. I didn't take them. I don't believe in right or wrong choices, only good or bad. Both lead to the same destination, but the bad ones have a more interesting journey. My new life and my new choices have seen me become a man driven to help make a difference in the lives of others. I'm finally happy. Your power in life resides in your choices. Take the time to choose 'good.' Be tough, get strong, work hard and be the success you know you can be. You can choose to be happy. Do so.

Simon Clark

46 years old

Change Agent

Melbourne, Australia

38
The Simplicity of Life

When was the last time you stopped to think about what is truly important in your life? Maybe the answer is never. You're too busy living your life, after all. Going to work, looking after your children, visiting friends, planning holidays; there's so much to do. But how much of what you do, is done simply because it is what you do?

At our very core, we are all simply seeking happiness. We do it in many different ways, but that is what we are looking for. The key is simplicity. How many things in your life are actually contributing to your happiness? How many of them are really just junk, cluttering up your time and space?

Stop and listen. Allow yourself to be guided by your inner voice. The most effective way I know of doing this is through meditation. If you're not a regular meditator, start now. Just fifteen minutes a day will make an enormous difference to your life. It instils a calmness in you that tempers life's ups and downs and improves your resilience. It amplifies your inner feeling of knowing what steps to take whenever you're unsure on the surface.

Don't wait until a tragedy forces you to take stock of your life. Take the time to reflect on what you do have in your life and what is no longer serving you. Get back to basics. Grow some of your own food. Switch off the television for a month. You might find you have no inclination to turn it back on. Read books instead. Paint. Listen to beautiful music. Learn an instrument. Spend time in nature. Say, "I love you" to at least two people every day – and make sure that one of them is you.

Dr. Haley Jones
45 years old
Author & Speaker
Canberra, Australia

39
Universal Love

J was angry. I had asked my daughter Jade, age nine, to do something and she had not bothered. I scowled at her and said, "Jade, I am so cross with you." She looked at me calmly and replied with a smile, "But I know that even when you are cross with me you still love me, Mummy." I was taken aback. "Yes. That's true. But how do you know?" Without hesitation she replied, "I just know. You show me in lots of ways that you love me." She proceeded to list some of the ways: listening to her, smiling at her, spending time with her and hugging her. I was astounded! Children are very observant. To me, these were little things that took no effort to do, but to Jade they were clear signs of my love for her.

In the same way, the Universe shows us in a myriad ways how much we are loved. But we do not recognise these signs of Universal love, because they seem small and insignificant to our adult minds: people smiling at us in the street; a stranger offering help with something; a friend wanting to spend time with us; a colleague buying us a coffee. But what would our daily lives be like if these 'small' things did not happen? For me, it would have far less colour and be far less pleasant.

So grab a piece of paper and a pen and make a list of all the pleasant 'little' things that have happened to you in the last seven days. How do they make you feel? We are loved every moment of every day. We just need to be more observant. We need to open our eyes, ears and hearts to see the evidence of this love. Are you ready?

Christie Pinto

47 years old

Author, Coach & Healer

Sydney, Australia

40
Kindness

*S*he astounds me even now.

As I stand there, fifteen years old and homeless, looking into her eyes with the naivety of a teenager. She returns my gaze, waiting on the threshold of her home, considering me. I offer her all the money I have. One week? That's all this money buys: A room. She sees me; she sees more than me; she sees inside of me. I'm hopeful. Can she see I'm alone? Yes, she sees it. It's right there, like a cloak. How else does a child stand on the doorstep of a stranger, wanting accommodation from an advertisement in the paper? "You can stay," she says. I breathe a little deeper. She smiles. My chest begins to expand.

She reaches out to touch my arm. I am automatically drawn to her touch. It's warm and inviting. Moving over the metal frame of the door, she invites me in. I trust her. She expands her kindness into the tangible, extending the value of what the money buys. Doubles my single room rent to two weeks, including food. I'm surprised. Happy. I want to repay her gesture. I clean the house. My room is tiny. Her heart is big. She is small and big at the same time.

I am tiny. She changes my path. I have security and possibility. She has assurance that she's a good person. I still don't know her name. It's been twenty years since I met her. She showed me pure goodness. I'll never forget what I saw, felt. I've passed it on to others. Does she even know she made that much of a difference? I hope so. The kindness of strangers, even the smallest impact, has a positive effect on all involved. It may even change a life.

I am grateful. I am flourishing.

Suzanne Waldron
35 years old
Human Behavioural Specialist
Perth, Australia

41
The Bonsai Effect

Compassion has caused me to see that the ancient art of Bonsai has not only been applied to trees, but is prevalent in human life through social, cultural and religious conditioning. Social behaviours of our lineage and traditions have wrapped an invisible copper wire around our beings and we have been emotionally, mentally and spiritually clipped and pruned like a Bonsai. Our natural state has been distorted far from our true spiritual, authentic design.

I have seen it take some people up to twenty years and more to escape this invisible debilitating copper wire. It takes time for the natural growth to come back and for the photosynthesis of love, light and energy to restore these people to their God-given eternity and destiny.

The art of freeing someone's mind is much more intricate and delicate than the art of Bonsai; however, look closely and there is a similarity. We should do everything within our power to let the light, love and energy restore. Where possible, with the right soil, nutrients, light and rain, and the right physical, emotional, mental, spiritual and financial environments, unprecedented transformation takes place.

Most people have been restricted in their self-expression; they have been limited in their own ability to share, experience, give and receive true love. We arrive in this world oblivious to what is really going on, and in many cases, by the time we wake up it is too late: our life has nearly passed us by. Many have found that the art of de-bonsai-ing one's life is the most rewarding self-expression of their existence. Seeing someone straighten-up after being knurled and twisted, suffocated and cut off, is invigorating and enriching. It gives me goosebumps when I see people find their authenticity and freedom – and come alive.

Frederick Krasey
61 years old
Business-Life Trainer
Melbourne, Australia

42
The Meaning of Pain

From the tender age of five, I learned the meaning of pain. Today, I call this 'a blessing,' yet back then I called it what it was: pain. When my older sister decided to run away from the family, she challenged all values, pushed all boundaries, and struck the bow of pain straight into my parents' hearts. I witnessed and felt the brokenness of my parents. It changed the family dynamic, creating deep ridges within the heart and leaving memories that followed me well into my adulthood.

Although so biologically young, I remember my decision clearly: "I'll never do what my sister has done." I had carved into my subconscious a new path, a new way of thinking. I decided not to stretch any boundaries. The responsibility that came with this decision, followed, influenced, and, at times, tormented me until I reached my late twenties.

Looking back, I shivered at the realization that my life, up until that point, was turning into what I had vowed it wouldn't become. To stop the process from repeating itself, I had to pause, think and allow the past pain to surface so that I could feel it and heal it. I call this 'my season of brokenness.' I was not done until I embraced it all. I was not done until I realized that any obstacle that comes into my life serves me, helping me to overcome pain and be victorious.

I embraced what I call the 'Principles of Strategic Gratitude' and came to the full realization that anything positive has a negative attached to it and vice versa. My heart lightened, and its arms of gratitude have extended to accept and embrace every positive and negative situation that was, that is and that will be. In like manner, I have become equally a master of success and a master of failure.

Claudia Carmen Anton

44 years old

Naturopath & Igniter of Feminine Fire

Melbourne, Australia

43
A Transformed Relationship

*M*y partner and I called the 'in love' state we were experiencing when we first moved in together 'Blissylvania,' but something had gone wrong over the years, and we'd arrived at the point where we were both frustrated, resentful and cool towards each other. In fact, there were times when I didn't even like him, and I'd begun threatening to leave.

As we had three young children, I figured we should make one last attempt at repairing our relationship, so I contacted a counsellor. We spent our first session sitting at either end of his couch but as the months passed we grew closer, and I began to truly value myself for the first time. So, when we seemed to hit the wall again, I decided that while I loved him, I wasn't prepared to live with his depression. I would rather grow than stay in a stuck relationship.

I must have been coming from a very clear and congruent place when I made this decision because my partner stepped up in his commitment to me and our family in such a significant way that others commented. He dropped his depression so abruptly and completely that I was staggered by the realisation that *he had literally been playing a role to support my growth*. While I didn't value myself, he didn't either – a brilliant way to push my buttons and rouse me to seek change. As soon as I did, he did. He might have been playing that role unconsciously, but it sure worked.

I'm very grateful to the skilful counsellor who worked with us during that year, to my partner for irritating the hell out of me, and to myself for having the courage to grow. That was ten years ago and today we're closer than ever.

Liliane Grace
50 years old
Writer, Speaker & Educator
Ringwood, Australia

44
Living Your Life in Flow

I have always had a lot of faith. Like many of you, I have attended numerous personal development programs and spent years soul searching to the point where it seemed there were no more layers to peel. However, subconscious self-sabotage would still rear its lovely face and old patterns would re-emerge. One day it clicked: I had spent so much time and money attending courses and shifting belief patterns, yet the one thing I hadn't changed after many years was how my physical environment was laid out or the colours I surrounded myself with.

You see, we are a product of the space we live in: how we place our furniture, the colours and images we see. They contribute to how we feel and what we attract into our lives. Everything around us emits a vibration and makes us feel as though life is easy or as though we are swimming upstream.

I started experimenting with colours, numbers and furniture placement in my home and business—everything from the colour of my underwear to candles and table cloths. I noticed my impression of myself and how I felt changed. I started to love myself the way I am and for who I am: a unique being that receives and sends energy and lives life with flow. My health, relationships, career, travel and creativity all opened up.

To help you start the journey of living your life in flow, I leave you with this tip: Light an orange candle: the colour of change. As you do, set an intention for the changes you wish to make. Now, clean your kitchen with orange spray. The kitchen is the place where you nurture yourself. Cook a nourishing meal for yourself using each of the hotplates to represent the different areas of your life. Enjoy love and bliss.

Rieta Mistry
47 years old
Energy Flow Creator
Brisbane, Australia

45
From Heart to Hands

"Lines of spirits joining,
fingers to my chest.
To write at will what I feel to say...
the very golden best.
Tears that stream,
from face to floor,
trace memories of my past.
Of times I struggled dearly,
in high school English Class.
Logic would have me abandon,
my love for the written word.
But my soul would keep on knocking,
till its truth was finally heard.
Years have passed
along this path,
as an artist I played my part.
Trust the hands to do the work,
in honour of thy heart."

Jon Low
28 years old
Writer & Speaker
Sydney, Australia

46
The Nature of Life Living Us

J broke bread with a dear soul mate one night. We'd had a period of silence from one another for a few months to help us move through a change in our relationship. One thing I discovered through him four years ago was this: "When you're free to stay, you're free to go. And when you're free to go, you're free to stay."

We dove into 'the illusion' of letting go. Do we really let *go?* My experience is that letting go is a falling into oneself, through a deep acceptance of what is: letting it *be*. It has nothing to do with the person or situation. It has everything to do with our own sense of 'whole-iness.'

Just like an autumn leaf that has changed its colours and fallen away from the tree, ever so gently floating to the ground, there is no fear of separation, no suffering by the tree, the branch or the leaf.

The leaf doesn't say, "Oh no, I'm falling, the branch let me go," nor does the branch say, "The leaf left me, I'm all alone now." Nor does the tree doubt its purpose. They all merge into an understanding of their new expression and experience of life. That is freedom. That is love. That is necessary.

We fear what we don't yet understand. There's beautiful wholeness when we allow room for what is necessary for our own evolution and extend the loving freedom to others. How can you extend loving freedom to yourself right now knowing there is nothing you need to DO to be loved, no part of you that is not welcomed? Every feeling is worthy of you. To feel life's contrast is *love* working through you, as you. Let it *be*... love.

Priscilla Bokhara
45 years old
Author, Speaker, Mentor
Stirling, Australia

47
Free

Surrounded by the thousand candle lights

Our hearts are set on fire

Shyness gone

Gifted with a new strength of awareness

We give courage to love and different shades of understanding

...Free like the waves of the oceans

Does love conquer at first sight...?

We were overcome with curiosity of our bodies

...Until we reached purity of light...

Never were two sparks made for each other

We are free...

Kameron Sergei-Kleut

41 years old

Actor, Consultant & Advisor

Sydney, Australia

48
Ade's Story

I discovered through painful and very testing personal experiences that, regardless of our situation, it is how we choose to respond that says everything about us – whether we like it or not!

On the evening of July 20, 2011, I suffered a serious stroke that required urgent lifesaving brain surgery under an induced coma – which I was not expected to survive! I spent seven months in hospital learning to breathe independently, sit upright, and now I am in the process of learning to walk again.

As I lay in bed with rails around the edge, I felt like a caged hen fantasizing about becoming free-range. At one stage, I was not able to work out how to press the nurse button to call for help. It was at this time that I realized that the battle is truly won and lost in the mind. I knew that if I were to keep a positive mindset and heal my body, I would have to develop ways to stay sane and happy. I developed my own personal toolkit.

First, there was the tool of appreciation. I remembered the famous Jewish proverb: "I felt sorry for myself because I had no shoes... until I met a man who had no feet!" Every morning and every night, I would bookend my day by asking, "What are five things that I can be truly grateful for?" Even in tough times, there is always something.

My second tool was to always look on the bright side of life. I continually asked myself, "What is good about this; is there a funny side to this situation?" These two questions, among many others, literally changed my life. How we see the world reveals who we are, rather than revealing the world itself!

Mr. Ade Djajamihardja

45 years old

Producer, Author & Speaker

Melbourne, Australia

49
A Message to My Granddaughters

*M*y Darling,

You are beautiful; you are loved; you are special. I watch over you, sometimes near, sometimes from afar, but the invisible threads binding our souls are always there. Our special bond helps me guide you and share love, light and laughter. You are open, curious and delight in everything you approach. I encourage you to love yourself, as you become an amazing, confident, sensual woman.

Look within; appreciate your inner beauty and strength, because life comes littered with glad and sad moments from miniscule to monumental. Now don't have a 'tanti.' Brace yourself; there will be highs and lows, great and shocking times. Doors will open, close gently or slam shut. Each decade that passes will challenge and celebrate your confidence.

A curly point – 'beauty' opens doors, but what happens when you open your mouth? Have you learned to speak with kindness, joy and love? Have you learned the lessons of openness, honesty and trust? Have you learned the utter joy of laughter? These lessons will help carry you over the rocky times.

As you mature, you will understand sensuality apart from sexiness. Sensuality is an attitude of the heart, the way you move, talk, act. It is the lure of promises not yet delivered, reflecting your personality. Sexiness, my dear, you already understand! Your innate wisdom shines through and teaches me so much! Your intensity, vibrancy and energy continually delight and amaze me. Already your inner confidence and sensuality radiate love and kindness. Continue to feed it with positivity; if you stumble, pick yourself up, dust yourself off and try again. Never underestimate the potent qualities of confidence and sensuality.

From my heart to your heart, darling you are beautiful, loved and special. You can do it! I am here for you, always.

Di Riddell

65 years old

Confidence Coach

Nambour, Australia

50
My Tragic Opportunity

*S*tatistically speaking, I should be dead. My injuries were extreme; the witness to my car accident was surprised he found a pulse. Following the induced coma, the recovery outlook was not exactly encouraging: brain damaged, blind in my right eye, with three quarters of my face deformed. Suffering with anxiety and Post Traumatic Stress Disorder, I would require anti-depressants.

Although the damage isn't obvious to others and it's a miracle I'm not brain damaged or blind, the story does not end there. 'Survival and recovery' feel endless, as I live with permanent consequences from my injuries. Sometimes I can't stand my reflection. I don't recognize the person looking back at me, as *me*, but more like a deconstructed, damaged image of me. I am tormented by this image I can't escape, recounting indescribable physical and emotional pain, panic and vulnerability. Then I remind myself that this could have been so much worse and I am grateful.

I learned that survival is not about getting back what I had or wanted. It's an opportunity to create a new future with new goals. Whilst my reflection is a painful trigger point, it's also a reminder that in my darkest hour I discovered I am brave. I learned what is truly important in life, for me. I found courage to unashamedly be me. I now have a greater purpose – to help others deal with trauma.

I rejected the use of antidepressants by never accepting a situation as only negative and blatantly refusing to believe I am a victim. What's kept me going is the dedicated search for what I call the Tragic Opportunity. That is, looking for positives and lessons in an otherwise negative situation by asking, "What's the lesson, and how can that help me be better?"

Deborah Stathis
34 years old
Post-trauma Coach
Melbourne, Australia

51
Finding Your Own Strength

I left my own country, Japan, at the age of twenty-three and came to Australia. I was absolutely lost in life. Many issues that were happening at home meant I couldn't go back. Living in a foreign country with no confidence in my English or life skills was tough. The only thing that helped me was my relationship with my ex; when it ended with him having an affair, I completely broke down. Receiving an unexpected call from a stranger, telling me that she was pregnant, was devastating.

The events during my first five years in Australia smashed my belief system. I asked myself, what have I done so wrong to put myself in this situation? I didn't know what was true, what was right, or who to trust anymore. Something had to change. My next step made no sense to the people around me, nor to me, but I moved to Melbourne. I had never been there, didn't know anyone there, and had no job or house; yet something was telling me to go. Whatever I'd been taught in my life wasn't working; I had to take a new approach to move forward. My last option was to follow my intuition.

I started doing things that I enjoyed, instead of what others thought I should do. I learned to improve, trust and love myself. My life completely shifted. Facing my fear of the unknown paid off more than I ever expected. I believe we all have the strength to get through our challenges. Although those testing times can be very painful, they push us beyond our limits and provide an opportunity to discover what we're truly capable of.

Maki Kanazawa

38 years old

Facilitator & Healer

Melbourne, Australia

52
Follow the Inner Voice

J was fifteen, in high school and dreaming of going to university. Then someone told me I was indigenous and therefore not smart enough. Apparently indigenous people did not go to university. They didn't know I was in the top two percent of my class. How could I not be smart enough? But I was young and didn't know any better. So, I listened to what they said and slowly lost sight of my dream.

I lost focus; my grades dropped, and I barely made it through high school. I left school and waited tables. I had no purpose, no power, and no direction. I was depressed and started to drink and take drugs. I hated my life, and I felt like a failure.

At age twenty-three, I woke up with yet another hangover. I felt miserable. I was sick of going nowhere and doing nothing of value. Surely there was more in the world for me. Surely I could do the things I had dreamed of, even if I was indigenous.

Something had to change. It was in that moment I made a decision to stop listening to others and start listening to myself. It was time to go after my dreams. I stopped drinking and taking drugs, and I enrolled myself into a degree at university. I got focused; I had direction; and I had purpose. And four years later, I had my degree. Ever since, I have been on a mission to make all my dreams come true – no matter what anyone says. In the end, it doesn't matter who are you are, where you come from, or what others think of you. We are all worthy of making our dreams come true. If I can make a change in my life, then so can you!

Bridgette Williams
32 years old
Academic Skills Advisor
Brisbane, Australia

53
Find Your Why – Love Your Purpose

*M*y journey began early on the day I was born, when my father decided to leave me with my mother and two young siblings, without money or support – a seemingly selfish and callous decision. That single event set a course for my life and what I have become today. What neither my father nor I realized at the time was that he set me free to be whatever I wanted in this world.

I didn't have an example for what I 'should' be in many aspects of life. I had to work it out by myself, research, choose and create, rather than replicate. I had to seek out information, assess the best decisions and trust my instincts. Everything I have and believe in has been my choice. This background explains my commitment to self-improvement. I have worked hard at gathering knowledge through formal education, searched out best-practice alternative thinking, and challenged myself to be the man I wanted to be.

I never really thought much about my mission in life until my eldest son, Hudson, seven-years-old at the time, asked me what I had dreamt of doing when I was a kid his age. I thought for a while and realised that all I really wanted to do was work in business. I saw the love my grandparents had for their own business crafted around their values and family; something that I wanted to take on as I built my own profession. I shared this with Hudson. His response was touching: "Well Dad, you get to live your dream then." And I guess he is right.

Andrew Ford

43 years old

Personal Brand Creator

Melbourne, Australia

54
Finding My Own Truth

*U*pon hearing Marianne Williamson's poem, *Our Deepest Fear*, I sensed a stirring deep in my soul. But at the same time, a sense of fear, unworthiness and disbelief as she addresses each one of us to rise up and know that we are wonderfully made – no matter what is happening in our lives at any given moment.

Life has been an exciting rollercoaster ride between moments of uncertainty and what I now know as 'the truth.' I have lost my footing, where my limitations have taken over and held me back from doing what is my Godly DNA to achieve. And, I have become the ultimate observer, creating unlimited possibilities, crashing through comfort zones and loving the excitement of taking action steps. As I now connect, learn and grow on this incredible journey, the beautiful truth keeps shining through: we are all part of this fascinating matrix, inextricably intertwined with those who have something to teach us and vice versa.

Whenever I find myself struggling and searching for a solution, God puts me in front of someone or something that guides me towards an answer. Other times there is a realization that my challenge is very self-centred and I need to give it up, let go, take my eyes off myself and adhere to the ultimate truth of being the overcomer that I was born to be.

I am now inspired daily by this truth and my purpose to show others that they are, indeed, children of God who no longer need to play small, and that they are a mine of infinite potential with the ability to create anything they choose. Are you, too, ready to play full out on the big screen of life and be the overcomer?

Jan McIntyre
61 years old
Social Marketer & Educator
Brisbane, Australia

55
Driven By My Brother

When I was seventeen-years-old, I finished school and moved from Melbourne to Brisbane to be closer to my brother and Dad on the Gold Coast. As younger brothers do, I had always idolized my brother, and now wanted to hang out with him as an adult, not just a younger sibling.

One of the first nights in Queensland, I was sitting in my older brother's apartment on the Gold Coast. I knew that he had a lot of difficulty while we were growing up. He suffered with our parents' divorce and often found himself in the wrong crowds at the wrong time. I knew that he had suffered depression and it had lead him to some heavy drugs, but that night he told me that he had tried to commit suicide. I didn't know.

I also didn't know that one of the only reasons he was still here that day was because of me. In that dark moment, before making what would have been a horrible mistake, there was something that stopped him. He told me that it was me. It was because he had a younger brother that idolized him, and because of the example that he would be setting for me, that he chose to stay.

That day, I committed to him that I would join him on his personal development quest, and we signed up to be front row at the Robert Kiyosaki personal development seminar. His was then the first book I had ever read by choice: *Rich Dad, Poor Dad*. From then on, I decided that I was going to live a life where I would be an example to others. Anytime I'm having a bad day, I think back to that moment and I remember that it's never that bad. There's always a way out.

Daniel Kalnins

28 years old

Co-Founder of BreakThrough Apps

Melbourne, Australia

56
34 Kilograms

Weight loss and getting fit is more about the journey and the person you become than your dress or pant size. Losing a third of my body weight at twenty-six was only the start to the new life I have created.

Since I was a young child, I had always been chubby, but over the years I got fatter and my confidence and esteem took a huge hit. I was verbally bullied on a regular basis. Even my own friends wouldn't pick me when it came to school team sports. By the time I was in my twenties, my weight had reached 96 kilograms, which was a lot considering I am short. I was inactive, shy and lacked confidence. I spent most of my free time in front of the computer or TV.

A conversation on my twenty-fifth birthday catalysed my weight loss journey. The next day I signed up to the local gym and within a week I had started. Going from someone who ate poorly and didn't exercise to someone who exercised twice a day, seven days a week, with a clean and healthy diet was easy for me.

It took me under a year to lose 34 kilograms, which I have maintained for over six years now. Since losing my weight, I have done things I would never have thought I could do, and all because of new-found confidence. I now want to explore and experience everything life has to offer. This is totally the opposite of the overweight person I was. I have been skydiving, abseiling, and rap jumping, and I've gotten involved in martial arts, acrobatics and dancing, with more to come.

I didn't just shed my fat: I also shed the old 'me' and stepped in a new, confident and healthy person.

Jason Best
34 years old
IT Solutions Consultant/Developer
Brisbane, Australia

57
You Are a Miracle!

*E*very being is a miracle. We must teach each other that *we are all the same* regardless of any arbitrary label we use to separate ourselves from one another and our own divinity. I believe it is our responsibility to awaken to our experiences and observe what our actions and non-actions do to us; as individuals and collectively. Do you feel that there must be a better way to live? Do you sense the urgency to re-organize, re-prioritize and seek things truly worth valuing? We must move away from fear and living from our ego toward love and living from our soul. Our egos exchange fear and nurture separation, while our souls exchange compassion, forgiveness and love.

This is why we are here: to learn how to live from our soul and not our ego. After thousands of years we still value objects, convenience, blame and excuses. The time to end judgment and excuses is now, but it must begin with *you*. It must begin with you and your choice not to judge anything or anyone, including yourself. When we judge others we truly dim the light of our own soul. It is so basic, so clear, yet we still stray.

We must have faith. We must trust in our divine path of instinct and no longer ignore our duty to always do what is right in every moment that there is a choice. Practice love, acceptance, and forgiveness; do not pass judgment, do not assume, do not jump to conclusions. Begin to awaken so that horrific tragedies both man made, and 'made' by nature, do not happen in vain. May your higher power bless you. May you find your faith. May we lift one another through compassion and by living from our souls.

Pamela Horton

44 years old

Soul Advocate

Sarasota, Florida

58
A Single Mother

J was just twenty-nine when, in 1992, I discovered I was pregnant. I was not married or in a 'stable' relationship; my one true direction was my job in nursing management. The surprise pregnancy unleashed a flood of emotions, rising and falling with the wild current of my hormones.

I did the only thing I could do: I called home. Soon enough, I was once again living with my parents, leaving my career, friends, and all sense of my life and purpose as I knew it behind. I became a statistic. I was a stereotype. Reliant on family, community, and government assistance, I was a dependent with a dependent. Like many in my position, I struggled with a sense of not being good enough to provide for my own child. Living with my parents, I took a calculator to the supermarket so I wouldn't come up short.

My days and nights merged into one, alone with a sleepless infant. My internal war droned through it all until, maternity leave over, I returned to my nursing career. My parents moved to help me with childcare. Years have now passed, and with it the realization that I had stability and control during that time. I made the choices regarding my son's care and education and provided a loving environment. I chose his name, his clothes, his hairstyle, where we lived and how we lived. I went from dependency and reliance to independence and self-reliance; from 'not good enough' to doing it all. Being a single mother can be incredibly empowering. From his conception to now, would I do it any differently? I only have to look at my son to know my answer.

Adrienne Gulliver
51 years old
Facilitator & Life Tackler
Auckland, New Zealand

59
The Choice I Made at Age Eighteen

*J*n 1961, I met David Gulliver. He was a British Caucasian male who had immigrated to my hometown in New Zealand in 1939. My ethnic background is Maori; I am a native of New Zealand. We both worked at the local telephone exchange; me as a telephone operator and David as a technician. I was drawn to David because of his smell and would find ways to be closer to him.

Our courtship began in 1961, and it was not usual to see two people from two different races in such a relationship. David's parents disliked me, and some of his friends made me feel uncomfortable. My parents embraced David and he was comfortable amongst my family. I did have some say to me that I "ended up with a scarecrow," but by and by we tended to be left alone.

In 1962, I became an unwed mother to our daughter. This may have been more challenging for others to contend with, rather than the cultural mix. I had my own internal conflicts to deal with as well as being ex-communicated by the Catholic Church.

We moved from my hometown to the city of Wellington in 1962. It was very challenging to care for a newborn without family support; we lived for a year in a flat with shared bathroom facilities. These struggles are not unlike the challenges that couples face today. The challenges may be different in form, but internal and external conflicts will still be there. It comes down to the choices you make and your resilience to carry on with those choices despite challenges you will face along the way. David and I now have six daughters, three sons and twenty-seven grandchildren.

Hana Gulliver

70 years old

Mother & Grandmother

Whakatane, New Zealand

60
Bubbles

I have often thought how everyone in a group environment is like a little bubble floating through space, and as friendships or groups are formed, they join together. As these groups grow and unite with others, they become bigger and more powerful.

One little bubble is limited in what it can achieve; however, as a larger group forms, opportunity is created. This happens in sporting teams or work places where unifying creates a community. A coach or a leader sets a path or vision for others to follow, and if the message is clear, then the group will respond positively.

A friend once told me of the time when he was coach of a country football team on the eve of a Grand Final. He took the club president up to the highest point in the town to look down on a buzzing, floodlit football ground, which had come alive with the support of the townspeople. The bubbles had united and grown, and magic had been created. Sometimes you need to look down, take a bird's eye view, to get perspective of what you have achieved.

Many years ago, I would catch the train home every night with my friend, Duncan. Duncan was funny and loud, and would be for the entire the trip home. What we noticed was that our carriage would fill up each night with the same people, because Duncan was the bubble that others wanted to connect with; his enthusiasm naturally energized them. Look around you and find the bubbles that can inspire you, make you happy, and above all, motivate you to be part of something greater than yourself. It's a great feeling, so jump on and enjoy the ride.

Rodney Tattam
57 years old
Curiosity Builder
Hobart, Australia

61
Khalil & Mary

*A*t seventeen, I left home to join the Navy; it was the most exciting day of my life! Later, I learned it was the saddest day for my mother. The day that my eighteen-year-old daughter left home, I understood my mother's pain.

A sympathetic friend gave me a poem by Khalil Gibran called *On Children*. It speaks of parenthood from a profound perspective – that our children are here for a purpose greater than we could ever understand and the world of tomorrow calls to them to fulfil their destiny. Our purpose is to share them with the world when they are ready. Khalil's poem inspired me to learn more about him and as I did, I uncovered an incredible love story.

Khalil was born into nineteenth century poverty. His talent for painting and philosophy soon made him a wealthy man and one of history's most inspiring poets. At twenty-one, he fell in love with Mary, but their cultural differences forbade marriage. Forced to keep their love secret, they shared their lives and dreams in letters. Khalil loved Mary until the day he died. When that day came, he left everything to her. Amongst the paintings and poetry, Mary discovered hundreds of love letters that she had written to him over their twenty-three-year secret affair.

Overwhelmed with grief and shame, Mary planned to burn them. But she didn't; she kept them. And many years later, she asked to have them published after she had passed away, along with the hundreds of poems that she had kept, that he had written to her. She wanted them published because, with no children, they were all that was left of their love. She wanted them published because it was a love that was finally ready to be shared with the world.

Ted Johnson

46 years old

Businessman

Perth, Australia

62
To Thine Own Self

"To Thine Own Self Be True"

William Shakespeare

It was dark, where I was. There seemed to be no hope. I sat in the summer sun quaking with fear. Two parts of my being fought, struggling to win; one with brute force, loud and demanding, and the other soft, gentle, unassuming. The battle raged, although one-sided, and flashes of blood and self-harm confronted me. From deep within the other voice ignited my curiosity, beckoning me to explore while imbuing images of my daughter's smile upon my psyche and my son's warm embrace. Fear clutched at my neck, choking and squeezing at my existence. Every which way I turned, the loud, demanding brute pulled me down, striking forceful fear, self-loathing and hatred into my being; oppressing me.

From out of the ethers, the voice of reason, soft and gentle, made its presence known. A friend called. I broke down, crying out my heart with anguish. She listened and prayed. In that presence I calmed; tranquillity descended upon me. "If you could do anything you wanted to in the world, with all your needs taken care of, where money didn't matter and you still worked, provided and were provided for, what would you do?" she asked.

The brute jolted out of its self-absorption, and within a millisecond of the stillness the answer to the question flowed from within. She asked what I needed to up-skill then told me to clean my home, leaving me with the wisdom of taking action towards the light. My life changed that day, and as all transformation occurs it is gradual. I saw clearly the brute force from within and its manifestations in the world around me. I still struggle to live my authentic life; however, where once my battles were hard, I've noticed they are falling away. Softness permeates my being.

Sandhya Porritt

40 years old

Author, Photographer & Speaker

Melbourne, Australia

63
What You Focus On, You Find

"The ideal conditions for growth may at first appear hostile."

Before February 2012, I used to have a lot of problems. You know the ones! I was running a successful property maintenance business, but things were far from perfect. My staff were punctual but not perfect; my clients were not big enough, although profitable; I had no office, although running my business from home served me well for more than eight years. The more I looked at my life, the more problems I discovered. I was certain people were causing all my problems.

When doctors discovered a brain haemorrhage (after I finally listened to my wife telling me to stop ignoring the symptoms of numbness to my left side) I found myself with a whole lot more problems, more serious than ever. During my hospital stay, I discovered that my staff did their work to the highest standards without supervision. The clients were pleased and paid their bills. And, since I ran my business from my hospital bed for a week, the office I had just rented for a year was a waste of money.

What I didn't realise on the day I was discharged from hospital, was that my recovery would take eighteen months – with doctor's orders not to return to work or be allowed to drive until further notice. All the things I took for granted previously were taken from me... and I had no control over the situation. From that day on, I promised to count my blessings, see all the good that was going on around me, never take another day for granted, and that I must make it part of my life's work to share my story, so that other people who are limiting themselves might see that there is another way.

Bill Gasiamis

40 years old

Public Speaker & Trainer

Melbourne, Australia

64
A Daily Spiritual Practice

*T*he human spirit has a profound capacity for transformation. We arrive in this world with a teachable spirit and a deep knowing of our power to be extraordinary. Sometimes we forget. We fall asleep to this knowing until a life event wakes us up, reminding us of our innate nature to heal, grow, connect, open and love fully.

One such event happened recently when the father of my baby, and friend to my two older children, withdrew from our lives, due to chronic depression, and unexpectedly returned to his home country, Ireland, to live. I experienced feelings of deep grief, rage, resentment and abandonment. In the quest for healing and freedom, I embraced the following as daily practice:

1. *Radical Self-Responsibility:* Saying the words, "Spirit, help me see and heal in me what I see in him," each time I thought of my ex-partner. This mobilised greater integrity and responsibility.
2. *Self-Acceptance:* Making space for all of my feelings to be welcomed, seen and felt. Embracing the power of vulnerability.
3. Self-Empathy: Taking sacred pauses each day and offering empathy and compassion to myself and taking rest here for as long as I need.
4. *Gratitude:* Writing in a gratitude journal helped me to see my situation with new perspective, transforming pain into love and open-hearted connection.
5. *Prayer:* Having spent most of my adult life rejecting the power of prayer, in reaction to my religious upbringing, I now felt a strong call to pray. This empowered me to reframe my experience and hold my ex-partner and self in the highest expression of who we are.

Taking care of myself in these five ways enabled me to release my past, so I am not living out of it, but learning from it, and gifting peace, love and inspiration into all my relationships.

Merri Hughes
43 years old
Psychologist
Melbourne, Australia

65
Shattered Beliefs

*F*rom childhood, I held onto a limiting belief that somehow I was broken; that there was a part of me that was missing. This belief created a deep void inside me – a persistent restlessness that was hard to ignore and drove me into depression for many years. I looked outwardly for answers, trying different means to somehow fill this growing void.

But as I began to turn my gaze inward, I discovered that this belief was born out of an image I held in my mind's eye about when I was involved in a car accident as a baby, and was covered in shattered glass as a result. Early on, I placed the meaning on this that I was broken, that I was not good enough, and that I didn't deserve to live a magnificent life.

This belief, however, left a burning desire within me to uncover the mysteries of the human mind – to put the pieces of myself back together and to lift the veil of depression. Through this journey of discovery, I learned that I was not broken, and that there was *nothing* missing from my life. It was my perception that created my reality. Every challenge and person I attracted along the way was there in some way to wake me up to this.

Our minds are vastly more powerful than we can truly comprehend. Our thoughts literally impact the very fabric of our being and ultimately shape our reality in this world; from our health, to our relationships, our vocation, and to what we truly believe is possible. When we align our hearts and minds, we can truly have a life worth living. Be grateful for all the people and experiences you encounter on your journey, as they are there to help wake you up to your own true magnificence.

Adam Gillie
36 years old
Coach & Mentor
Perth, Australia

66
Frankie

As I write my story and share my inspiration, I dig deep and have appreciation for my life. To sum me up: I'm thirty-seven years young, a hard-working, driven businesswomen, and single. I've been happy, yet something was missing: true unconditional love that inspired me to think beyond myself. This came into my life the form of a human being – my eleven-week-old daughter, Frankie. The turning point in my decision to have Frankie came when I asked two quality questions:

1. Would I be okay if I was single for another ten years? YES
2. Would I be okay not having had children in ten years' time? NO.

Both questions were game changers. I immediately investigated IVF and planned my future. I delved into the unknown of questions and decisions. I didn't tell a soul. I approached a great couple I know and they both wanted to help create my legacy! I committed to my vision and to trusting the process. Everything was on the way not in the way – including a miscarriage and medical experts criticising my decision to do this solo. I grew my savings and business to support us so I can focus on her.

My journey took just sixteen months and now I am sitting here with my divine daughter. We had an incredible home birth and Frankie is happy, healthy and a delight to be with. She is surrounded by true love with her two daddies, family and friends. I've learned so many lessons from this journey and I would do it all again, for having Frankie is heavenly. The journey isn't over yet – I am now inspired more than ever to help other women create more choice and possibility in their lives through increasing their self-worth, value and net worth.

Yvonne Hilsz
39 years old
Professional Speaker
Sydney, Australia

67
New Beginnings

*P*icture a young girl looking in her mirror, questioning the meaning of life, when suddenly in a flash her life's purpose becomes crystal clear! I had no comprehension of how I would achieve it but that moment stayed with me. Later, like many, I found myself making sound practical choices and putting in long hours to achieve the Great Australian Dream. I *loved* my family, profession, making a difference; and I'd accumulated a portfolio of properties for my future enjoyment. But outside of that, I felt limited and, at times, deeply unhappy.

However, assured by my growing nest egg, I counted my blessings and continued on. That was until I was injured on the job. The next morning I awoke 'on fire,' unable to move or walk without experiencing excruciating pain. Diagnosed with a spinal injury and nerve damage, and facing a life of disability, medication, surgical interventions and rehabilitation, pain and struggle became the norm. After decades of working to create a secure future, my world came crashing down. I'd hit rock bottom, the result was divorce. Suicide seemed easier than living with my reality. Feeling trapped, I dreamed of escaping, losing myself in a new type of freedom, and a new beginning.

I gave myself permission to explore new opportunities and approaches to life. I learned the art of positive psychology, self-compassion and practiced holistic health. Encouraged by progress, I created a new plan completely committed to changing myself and my life in order to move away from pain. As I sit here sharing this message with you, I've come full circle on my 'hero's journey' reconnecting to my authentic self, living life, fulfilled and free from the chronic pain of the past. I consciously chose to be the creator of my life story; the ending is up to me!

Kellie Anne King

40 years old

Lifestyle Practitioner & Therapist

Melbourne, Australia

68
The Power of Self Belief

*L*et me share with you my personal story of my return to Australia from South Africa in January 2005. I was engaged to be married to my future wife, who was still in South Africa. I was feeling lonely, frustrated, and somewhat unworthy to start a new life with her whilst in my situation at that time. Physically I was living out in nature, on a piece of land near Armidale NSW, Australia, sleeping in the back of my $200 unregistered station wagon by night and resting in a hammock during the day. I had very little money, no work or solid place to live, and ate only sparingly.

Emotionally, I was feeling a bit worn out from having to face starting over again. Even though I was sometimes feeling 'down and out in Armidale,' like George Orwell was in *Down and Out in Paris and London*, losing the plot was no longer an option, and I knew deep within myself that I would pull through. Spiritually I felt strong. I was meditating regularly and tuning into my spirit guides.

One chilly evening, after six days of living out in the bush, sitting all alone on a cold park bench in the middle of town, eating hot chips and watching the golden winter sunset, I made the decision that I *would* get somewhere to live and *would* get some paid work within three days — it happened in just two! Although very challenging at the time, these were very rewarding and liberating days for me, and are a great reminder that my faith and belief in myself, my daily meditations, and my connection to my spirit guides will carry me through any situation I find myself in.

Adrian Hanks
51 years old
Inspirational Teacher & Writer
Brisbane, Australia

69
Surrender

*W*hat if you surrendered to who you are, in this moment, and loved yourself unconditionally?

What if, when you looked in the mirror, you saw beauty and magnificence in that moment?

What if, when you felt that love for yourself, your heart expanded and it brought tears to your eyes?

What if you loved yourself so much that you wanted and settled for nothing less than the best for yourself, because you know you're worth it?

How different would life be, and how different would going for your dreams be, if you did it from a place of loving yourself that much?

How different would your relationships be, if you were already feeling that love for yourself and able to share that, rather than seek it externally?

How would it feel to be able to express yourself freely from this place of love, with your words and actions, and to be able to see the beauty in everything and everyone, because you see it in yourself?

Belinda Sims

35 years old

International Speaker

Adelaide, Australia

70
On The Mission

*S*ince I was ten years old, I've had a dream to travel and explore all corners of the world. As a young man in Iran, I found that achieving this dream had too many obstacles in the way. After university graduation, I had to make a serious decision: to go to the army. Going to compulsory army is a huge headache for most men in Iran; they have to serve for two years in a hard and unpleasant environment with almost no income. But, only after certified from the army, are men able to apply for their passport.

I made my decision to be 'on the mission' and started my journey. I went to army two years after, achieved my certification, and with enormous passion, on the same day, applied for my passport. A few months later, I was on the road and started travelling internationally as a gypsy backpacker. So far, I have discovered amazing people, lifestyles, and cultures and still the journey continues!

Following my trip plan, and after visiting a few countries in Asia, I decided to visit the end of the world: Australia and New Zealand. In June 2007, I visited Australia and almost instantly felt in love with the landscape and people. I found so many places touched with spectacular landscapes and couldn't believe it was real. Traveling and being in Australia transformed my perception of life and helped me to know myself in totally new dimensions. Ten years, to the day, after I decided to go to army, I chose Australia to be my home. Now, I know all dreams are achievable, even though they require effort, and an open mind and heart.

"The soul is strengthened in both good fortune and adversity, and it is these two extremes that your true nature is revealed."

Ryuho Okawa

Ali Motahari
32 years old
IT Engineer
Brisbane, Australia

71
Your Path

A year ago, I started my new job, having no goals nor knowing how I was to succeed. However, I had the strong desire and aspiration and, within seven months, I was able to do it. Most people don't understand how I got to this point and what drives me to be who I am today. You see, my life has seen many circumstances that could have led me down a very different track. That is... if I chose that track.

Some of my life experiences, that drive me to be who I am, are that I grew up with my mother and sister, living off welfare. Things were tough. I started working at the local butcher when I was thirteen to help pay the way through school. At the age of seventeen, on Christmas Eve, my sister and I left home due to circumstances beyond our control. I found a unit and completed grade twelve and three TAFE certificates whilst working two jobs to support us.

At the age of nineteen, I found my mum dead after she committed suicide. This, naturally, turned my world upside down. I had a few jobs after that, not sure where I was heading or what to do. But, my big break arrived. I was thankful, as this was my chance to go far in life. I worked hard, often seven days-a-week, learning what I needed to in order to thrive. So, my advice for you is this: "Your path is *your* path. You can't change the past, nor predict the future. But, you can do everything in your power to ensure your greatest goals and dreams are achieved no matter what obstacles you face."

Thomas Buckley
25 years old
New Home Sales Consultant
Brisbane, Australia

72
Your Soul Knows No Limits

I always had this feeling of longing in me, that there had to be something *more* to me; *more* than what my mind and body thought I was. Imagine a sleeping beauty waiting to be woken up.

You know those moments when you make a decision you think is absolutely crazy, but it feels so right you don't even hesitate? Exactly, that's what I felt that day, when I envisioned myself living on the beach in Australia, and decided to pack my belongings and move to the other side of the world. I didn't know why, something greater than me just told me to do it. It was this decision that led me to a journey of self-discovery, waking up that sleeping beauty and opening my heart up to all possibilities of all that I am.

The limitations my mind had created started dissolving, one by one. I became more aware, became more flexible, and I allowed myself to see new possibilities I had not realised existed before. My life started shifting; from just existing, to creating instead. Now, still surfing the wave of uncovering more about myself, I am stronger and happier. Each day, I experience more of the 'more' which I once longed for.

Your sleeping beauty is a vision: a vision just as real and strong as your intention to wake it up. I don't know what *more* represents for you, though I can say that you're already carrying all the *more* you can ever imagine within you. The only limits between you and your *more*, are your own mind and body; your soul knows no limits.

"You are not a drop in the ocean. You are the entire ocean in a drop."

Rumi

Mia Berglund
29 years old
Aspiring Entrepreneur & Coach
Sydney, Australia

73
The Master Within

*F*or the majority of my life, I listened to and accepted as truth, misperceptions, false information and simply bad advice from people I held in high regard, who believed they knew what was best for me. One day, I started asking questions that induced life-changing realizations:

1. How qualified is this person to judge and tell me what I can and can't do?
2. Are they following their inspired journey?
3. Is their life filled with joy and satisfaction in all they do?
4. Are they successful in what they do?
5. How well do they know me; *really* know me?

From that moment on, I have followed my heart. I constantly create inspiring experiences, attracting healthier relationships in my business and personal life. Constructive criticism is worth listening to, it shows me, "I am on the right track." Unconstructive criticism undermines, discourages and hinders true potential. But, either way, I am on the right track.

When disempowered, we live lives of "what ifs" and "I don't know." When empowered, we live lives of fulfilment with "I know!" and "I am!" Seek advice when necessary from professionals in their chosen fields, the visionaries, the trail blazers living their dream life. Be grateful to all who challenge you in life; they encourage adaptation, learning, dreaming, and they encourage you to reach further than ever imagined. Every day, learn something new about yourself and do it with purpose; invest in self-development education so you can recognise the master that dwells within you and be the expert and authority of your own life.

"Society may predict, but only I am the master of my destiny."

You are the master of your own destiny. With you, in love, health and well-being.

Marco D'Angelo

41 years old

Myotherapist, Author & Educator

Melbourne, Australia

74
Don't Disappear

Behind the outward cheeriness and pleasant demeanour, one could sense hidden eyes pleading – a soul begging to be released – to find its true meaning and purpose; its reason for being.

As time passed, the eyes dulled, the pleasantries dulled – the soul faded as hope for its release diminished. Potential, inspiration and vision, once palpable, seemed lost – and the soul, once vibrant with expectations and endless possibilities, disappeared behind endless cycles of monotony and drudgery.

The shoot that once thought it would be a tree, died never knowing what might have been...

It's a calling from within me to make sure that women don't disappear in life: to embrace all that they are, as they are... and to see the perfection of God in themselves; to have unconditional love of self and to be "the captains of their own souls."

Laura Hughes
54 years old
Director of Feminine Finance
Casuarina Beach, Australia

75
Right in Your Core

So here in the Bible of Inspiration
If you're down and happiness has left
If there's sadness running through your veins
Or maybe you're just a little bereft

If you're feeling like life's overwhelming
Or someone has broken your heart
If you're grieving the loss of a loved one
In life's journey, you've been ripped apart

If your health is not what it should be
Perhaps you're fighting for your very life
If you've done something that you regret
And you've found yourself in great strife

Life's journeys are full of emotion
The torrid seas of surviving each day
But with each test of strength and each bitter pill
There's opportunity to learn a new way

There's refuge in knowing that those with the most
Have travelled the darkest of nights
It's the appraisal of character, the ultimate test
It's just a decision to fight

You see often when you feel at your lowest
Many have been there before
Take heart in knowing that as you walk those old paths
The courage is right in your core.

Michael Spillane

42 years old

Real Estate Sales & Professional Speaker

Brisbane, Australia

76
With Challenge Comes Change

*L*ife can be so bloody fantastic at times and then other times it can come crashing down on you and you ask, "Why me?" Well my 'why me' came in 2007 when I had a hideous, life-threatening accident. Now don't get me wrong, there were reasons behind my accident and I was 100 percent accountable. I learned a damn good lesson, but all in all, life came crashing down for sure.

The essence of who I was disappeared and I felt I was a lost soul wondering whether to continue with life or end it immediately. Whilst in hospital, I was introduced to the hospital chaplain. She was non-judgmental and allowed me to debrief my life, positive and negative, with an open heart. She showed me there is life out there, and if I had a trust in my own knowledge, I would get through, no matter what.

Corny as it sounds, the light began to appear and I could see a way forward. I started to mend myself internally while the medical team worked on me externally. I learned to love my daughter, my family, my friends, my colleagues, my challengers, and supporters all over again. Most importantly, I loved myself for who I was and what I had done. I count my blessings daily and today I share my wisdom with others. No challenge is too big or too small. We all have emotional baggage that stops us from moving forward. It's time to leave the baggage behind and move forward with grace.

"No matter what you have done or not done, you are worthy of love. There is nothing but love, all else is illusion."

Dr. John Demartini

Deborah Cooper
42 years old
Demartini Method® Facilitator
Dunedin, New Zealand

77
I Am Here To Make An Impact

*M*y mum tells me we all survive things in our lives and one of the things I survived was the Christchurch, New Zealand earthquake. Little did I guess that I would be in a horrible earthquake.

It was 22 February 2011, a normal day in Christchurch, or so I thought. I went to school like any other day. My classes were average, nothing that exciting. The morning passed by like any other, everyone seemed to be moving at super speed compared to me. Lunchtime came as it always did, until it hit ...

A tremendous earthquake. All the buildings shook. I heard screams; they pierced at my head. I collapsed into a heap on the ground. The concrete cut my knees and elbows yet I wasn't feeling pain. It stopped and I looked around. The teachers and students were all sprawled out across the ground. They looked lifeless, like porcelain dolls. I pulled myself up onto my hands and knees trying to stand up. People around me were doing the same. Our principal gathered us up into our classes. The roll was taken and everyone was there.

We waited for our parents to arrive. You could feel the nerves in the air. The tension was building. I spotted my mother. A burst of relief and joy came over me. I was safe.

It was then that I realized how important life was and told Mum I wanted to move to Dunedin to be closer to family. If it wasn't for the earthquake, I wouldn't have met new and amazing friends, learned more from school, been closer to family, been able to represent my region Otago in Water Polo, Netball and Hockey. I can say I am grateful to my mum, to have survived the earthquake and what happened to me.

Sophie Cooper

14 years old

Student

Dunedin, New Zealand

78
Graduating From the University of Rock Bottom

L'ying on a cold hospital bed in April 2006, I thought my life was over. Surrounded by very ill people, I was in the midst of what I came to understand as psychotic depression, a severe form of the condition which results in losing touch with reality and imagining all manner of sights, sounds and smells. A waking nightmare that went on for several weeks. Before being admitted to hospital, my meager and hastily-packed bag of possessions was searched for anything that I could possibly use to injure or kill myself. It's just as well, because I would not have hesitated, given the chance.

In that terrifying few weeks, something inside gradually began to shift. I knew that I had much more to give to the world than I had ever given before. I knew I was here was to tell my story to inspire others who might be feeling hopeless and alone and let them know that it will all come right in the end. I realized I was here to share that the experience makes you a stronger, more caring, and more loving person who can give so much more to the planet.

Depression seems so insidious until you understand that it's powered entirely by the thoughts you choose to think. It's easy for a persistent negative thought pattern to become a habit. For about four months, I repeatedly told myself that I'd made a huge mistake in buying a house that I couldn't afford. Non-stop negative thinking literally brought me close to death in no time at all.

As a graduate of the University of Rock Bottom, I went on to discover a simple set of lifestyle habits that totally transformed my ability to deal with stress. What a blessing to know that whatever happens in the future, I will never need to experience unbearable stress or a depressive episode again.

Andrew Bridgewater

52 years old

Psychologist

Leamington Spa, United Kingdom

79
The Point of Change

*M*y life has taken many twists and turns. Finding myself married and living in Australia was probably the biggest. I've always had a taste for adventure and a sense that everything will be OK in the end. I was right about that, of course, but there have been times when I have doubted myself, lost faith in my abilities, and felt the crushing overwhelm of seemingly insurmountable situations.

One of the things I learned from facing my challenges is that there eventually comes a moment when a decision has to be made. We can accept things as they are, live with them, and accept the consequences, *or* we can decide that we want something different. I call this the *Point of Change*. It's the moment when the pain of staying the same becomes greater than the fear of choosing a new and unknown path. It's a moment, just a moment, of perfect clarity when a vision of a possible new future is glimpsed. It doesn't matter what the catalyst is, it matters that some action is taken, because there are many hundreds of ways to change a life, on a big scale or in just a small shift. But, there is only one way to remain the same and that is to do nothing.

I decided to stop accepting abuse. This was my point of change. A life-threatening situation meant that this decision was the only one I could make. I stood on the precipice of a very uncertain future, and I had to have blind faith that I would be OK. It turned out to be the best decision I ever made. Your Point of Change may be similar, or it may be a simple change in habit or belief. Whatever it is, if life isn't working how you want it to, *change it*, and enjoy the ride!

Jane Sleight-Leach
47 years old
Facilitator & Speaker
Brisbane, Australia

Beyond Fifty

J am fifty years of age. I have spent the last six months thinking about how I want to live my next forty or so years. I am not married and have no children. I have spent my life in many relationships. Matters of the heart inspire me. I am grateful I didn't succumb to society's ideals, and followed my own path instead.

My parents had the foresight and determination to escape a communist regime with me in tow. They knew we might be shot or thrown into jail if we failed, and that the rest of the family would be charged for being associated with traitors, if we succeeded. They did it anyway. They gave me that freedom. I am an adventurer of life because of that, and eternally grateful to them for their courage.

Sometimes my courage wanes because of my perceptions of 'where I should be by now.' This helps me look closely at my life. My appreciation of my gifts and the opening of my heart, which is part of my evolution, need this. I now clearly see how I get to share this in and with the world. That makes me proud of where I am now.

I feel fortunate for not having had children. I have made a business out of nurturing others. The deep love, connection and purpose mothers say you couldn't possibly know unless you have children, I have been able to find and feel inside myself. Being able to share this love and impact thousands has meant much more freedom of expression and purpose with a bigger vision for humanity for me. I believe it's inside all of us! It's just a matter of what direction you choose to focus it.

Renata Kubina

50 years old

Intuitive Coach & Mentor

Sydney, Australia

81
Finding My Mission

I believe fear is a debilitating emotion that is disempowering and soul destroying. I know that when we feel inspired to love and live our purpose we allow others to do the same. I believe that when we listen to our soul's calling and follow our heart, we can achieve anything and live and love with grace.

At forty-three years of age, I knew in my heart that I didn't want to continue working in a manufacturing company as an executive assistant. I felt dispirited, low and unenthusiastic. The politics at work, long working hours and driving in peak traffic tired me out. I thought of resigning so many times, but the fear of change and uncertainty prolonged my situation for another four years and kept me stuck in a rut.

I was afraid to make a change due to lack of confidence. I didn't feel good about myself. I was worried about money and most of all, what would happen if I failed. I knew that it was time for me to make a decision. So, I went to see a psychic reader who confirmed to me what I already knew: that I was meant to empower and help others to live the life of their dreams.

At forty-seven years of age, I followed my heart's calling, and with God's courage and strength I resigned my job to start a new career inspiring people. Today I love what I do and get paid to do what I love. Know you can do anything to master your life. Fear is an illusion, keeping you in your comfort zone. Remember, your soul loves uncertainty. Feel the fear, do it anyway, and live and love with grace.

Jackie Mortimer
60 years old
Relationship Consultant
Melbourne, Australia

82
Dedication

*M*y inspiration in life has always been the horse. Working with horses is a lot like life. It's about facing the challenges that bring the rewards. Being with horses is a lot like living life. I can remember my old horsemanship instructor would say to me start with the end in mind: just like having a goal. You need to know exactly what you want to achieve. I like to know what it is that I'm about to set out to do with my horse, just like we want know what we want to do in each venture we start.

Dedication to what I set out to do is another principle I've worked hard on. I never worry about discipline. If something is true to my heart and I really want to achieve the goal, I just dedicate myself to it. Especially with horses. I've dedicated my life to helping horses and people to discover their full potential.

As I write this piece, I've just finished an endurance ride that I complete over Easter with my good mate Drifter (that's my horse). Three hundred and twenty kilometres, four days, eighty k's each day. I had a friend tell me afterwards that every time we passed each other, she could see the dedication I had to finish what we started. We didn't need discipline. Just the resolve to finish. Keep your vision, hold that close, maintain your focus and just work with the dedication to finish what you've started. That's my message for you.

Gavin Bartlett
38 years old
Horseman & Adventurer
Sunshine Coast, Australia

83
My Path to Awakening

*T*he day I met my future husband at London Heathrow to move straight into our new home is one of my favourite personal memories. Fast forward twelve months, and we are flying across the globe to live a new life in Australia.

These are the exact moments I constantly dreamed of as a child. The school teachers named me "Daydreaming Deborah." I used to look at my feet and ask "Who am I?" I felt foreign in my body; my feet felt a million miles away.

Overcoming abusive relationships, depression and suicidal, unplanned pregnancy, financial debts and addiction to eating disorders. I came to a point where I asked myself "Is this it for me?" I wanted clarity, love and connection in my day to day experience. Since that day, by the grace of God and the love of soul family, my life has never been the same again.

Many turning points followed, including the day I looked in the mirror and saw my physical body, as it was. I was at the gym and I just stood there for ages it felt like the first time I had ever truly seen my own reflection. If I could give a gift to the younger me I would say to her: "What if life is happening for you rather than to you?"

Today I completely believe being here now, this present moment, this is the gift of living, this is it and I personally want to celebrate, appreciate and thank every one of you for being here.

Sending you love.

Xox

Deborah Henderson

30 years old

Awakening Facilitator

Melbourne, Australia

84
Say YES to You!

*G*rowing up on a small farm property in Australia in the 50s and 60s, just a scratch into the lower middle class, meant I had few influences - mainly parents, teachers, coaches, plus my own attitudes, values and beliefs. It always seemed clear that my reaction to life impacted what came next. My parents were good people who did not value themselves enough. My mother was a hard worker, careful with money, and my father was a WWII veteran whose decisions affected his health. He died when I was seventeen. I had to learn, observe and make mistakes — and I had to learn to say YES to me. This article is about what I have learned about saying YES.

You can be your own hero — just add goals, dreams and take moments to enjoy your achievements. Be prepared to manage yourself and to manage your own awareness. The emotional centre through which you process life's events requires control over impulses that direct you away from your goals. Goals are not achieved without effort — keep showing up, keep taking action.

Expect to be challenged by your moods but be driven by your values — your deepest motivators. Have faith in yourself and be truly connected to the search for, and recognition of, your true values. Every great purpose should be supported by the energy of hope and action.

Success often follows a shared passion and conviction. It is not enough to act alone — listen.

If your goal is transparently motivating to you and good for others, your capacity to succeed relies on your social skills to engage others. A wise heart communicates the shared values that drive results. Investigate SMART goals and connect family, friends, and colleagues with your passion. With these simple steps, you are saying YES to you.

Greg Pritchard
57 years old
Business & Executive Mentor
Brisbane, Australia

85
The Healing Power of Creativity

*A*re you feeling stuck in some area of life? Creative processes can help shift you out of these blockages. I've witnessed huge transformations and shifts in people who have forgotten how to have fun, joy and excitement in their lives by using creative processes.

Whilst working in a hospital, I ran art classes. It inspired me to watch people re-discover themselves through connecting with creativity. I remember one lady who had a profound fear of getting dirty due to her own mother's strict discipline. She even found it difficult to touch things of differing texture. I assisted her through finger painting exercises. At first her hands were tense; she was only able to put small dots on the page. I could see her pain and watched her whole body stiffen.

My intuition told me to stick my hand in her paint and smudge it across the canvas, which instantly brought her back to the present. She glanced at me, then thrust her whole hand in the paint, smudging it all over. She revelled in the play and fun it brought to the moment! She could hear her mother's voice telling her not to get dirty, and felt liberated by defying the voice as she got messy. Months later, she confided that she was able to play in the dirt with her daughter, and actually enjoyed connecting with her daughter in this way.

If you're looking to shift some area in your life that feels stuck, then try re-engaging in a creative art to access more joy, fun and freedom. You can start by doing what you did as a child and re-connect with these activities. Remember the joy and fun you had in building sandcastles, finger painting, dressing up as your favourite star, dancing, and singing!

Chafica Heseltine

37 years old

Mother, Leisure & Health Consultant

Sydney, Australia

86
Celebrate Your Magnificence

I was frustrated.

What was missing? I'd been practising affirmations, visualising and writing my goals daily. I worked hard and took advantage of every opportunity. But still, my new business just wasn't growing quickly enough.

I took a long walk in nature to clear my head and this gave me the opportunity to reflect back and have a massive eye opening moment.

A few years earlier, I'd just become a single mum of a three and five-year-old and was struggling to pay the rent. I'd lost touch with my career and my days were spent in a cloud of despair, my heart gripped by fear around money. I threw myself into personal development and set a lofty goal to achieve a five-figure monthly income. At the time, it seemed like a Utopian dream.

I compared this to my life now. I smashed that lofty income goal out of the ballpark years ago, and not only did I achieve my financial aspiration, but I also managed to create an incredible life as a result of it.

I smiled to myself. How had I managed to completely lose perspective of where I'd come from? The thing to remember about frustration is that it's like driving with one foot on the brake. It simply slows down the unfoldment of your goals. Overcome with a wave of gratitude and pride, I promised to never berate myself again and focus only on celebrating how capable and successful I was. Magically, the brakes came off and everything moved forward at warp speed. That missing ingredient had been: Gratitude.

Please remember to reflect on your past achievements and celebrate your magnificence. With gratitude, anything is possible.

Miriam Castilla
43 years old
Author & Speaker
Adelaide, Australia

87
Wish Granted

J had been looking for work to supplement my business income for several weeks, but it was becoming a thankless task. I was tired, and life was becoming a serious struggle. *It's not supposed to be this difficult!* I thought. As I lay there pondering the futility of it all, soft tears began to fill my eyes and stream down my cheeks in little salty rivulets. I considered what I wanted instead.

My business was not working. Why? Marketing was not my strong point, *I thought, I need some training in marketing and advertising. Maybe I could get a job in an advertising company where I could learn that skill. And I could really do with around $50,000 paid in weekly increments to help get me solvent. Yes! That's what I need right now!*

I brushed my tears away, threw the covers off and got out of bed. On my way to the kitchen, I stopped at the office and turned on the computer. Off to the kitchen to boil the kettle and make a cuppa. Back in the office, steaming tea in hand, I started scanning through the endless offerings in my in-tray, looking for anything to spark my interest. The phone rang.

My recruiter was on the other end. "Morning, Allison. Would you be interested in a twelve-month temp contract at a large marketing and advertising company?" My heart skipped a beat. "Oh yes, please! What do I have to do to get it?" I asked. "If you want it, it's already yours!" He answered. I couldn't believe my ears. "Yes! I want it. Just curious... what would the income be over the life of the contract?" "Hmmm. Just a mo. $50,000, give or take."

Wish granted – in the time it takes to make a cuppa!

Allison Walker
58 years old
Personal Empowerment Facilitator
Perth, Australia

88
Inspiration

*I*nspiration is a word, which used in the physical sense, refers to the expansion of our lungs with an intake of breath. The life-giving force of oxygen infuses every cell in our body, sustaining our very being. With the expansion of our hearts and minds, comes the inspiration from our soul. It is the receipt of an infusion of desire and deeply driving motivation, sustaining our very spirit. Inspiration is the catalyst for change in the lives of others, and we each receive inspiration from those around us.

The most inspirational people prove that what may be deemed the impossible by many is in actuality a possibility. Achieving the amazing, the awe-inspiring and unbelievable, ignites a spark in the souls of others, awakening the flame of their own intrinsic desire to be more, to achieve more, to go further, and to reach higher.

An abundance of limitless potential surrounds us. Inspiration allows us to see it. Opportunities beg to be acted upon, stretching our boundaries, and pushing us forward to reach our utmost potential. When we strive to overcome our most stifling of challenges or difficulties, we discover the key to many doors. The magic of life unfolds before us when we ignore our innermost hesitations, cementing the belief in our own ability to leap over previously perceived improbabilities. Courage collapses our invisible fences, diminishing unseen barriers. Those same barriers, which previously might have constrained us, threaten to contain us and prevent the attainment of our highest purpose.

When we live with fearless determination, we uncover our innate ability to rise above any treacherous territory arising along life's path. It is through adversity and pain that we develop strength and tenacity, enabling us to endure. Through this example of endurance we may then become an inspiration.

Elizabeth Sayers
46 years old
Nurse & Chiropractic Assistant
Geelong, Australia

89
Dad's Dead

*S*tanding outside my office, suitcase in one hand, phone in the other, I heard the words I hadn't expected. I was on my way home to New Zealand to spend time with my nana who was dying. As I waited for my taxi to the airport, Mum told me Dad had collapsed of a heart attack and died, hours before I was due to arrive home.

Instead of a relaxing time with Nana, I flew home to a dead father, a family in pieces; a mess. This was just the start as my family went through six deaths in four months, starting with Dad and ending with Nana. It was like life kicking us in the guts again and again.

I spent months in a state of numbness, moving on to a most painful, desperate, and confusing couple of years. I was told I could come to accept it, but that the pain would never completely go away. I was told that I would never stop hurting. Despite hearing this from every voice around me, the voice inside me knew that true healing was possible, that my dad deserved a better legacy, and that I deserved a fuller life.

I turned my back on conventional ideas around grief, counselling, sympathy, and on my own psychology studies. I found my way into coaching and vast human potential... to the realisation that total healing is possible and achievable. This is not my opinion, or just an idea I like. This is my truth. I found my way from pain and loss to gratitude, real connection, inspiration, empowerment and freedom from pain. I reached a place I was told (and am ironically still told) didn't exist, where only love is left. The worst events in my life became the best, and I will be forever grateful for them.

Kristie West

35 years old

G.R.I.E.F Specialist

London, United Kingdom

90
Listen To Your Inner Voice

J spring out of bed. I am continually amazed at the ease of this as my alarm sounds at 5.00 a.m. I have an appointment at the gym. The client is me.

Ten months ago, life was extremely challenging. Six months earlier, I had broken a bone in my foot and it had only just healed enough to run. One evening, I was running around the Botanic Gardens in Melbourne. I noticed a fitness trainer. A little voice inside suggested that I approach him and ask for help. I turned away. *No, he wouldn't want to talk with me.* But the voice was insistent, so I ventured over. His voice of passion and kindness inspired me so much that I gave him a big hug.

He suggested that I join his boot camp. I trained three times per week. My heart was happy. Next, I was training two times a day. Up the hills we would go singing, "We love it!" It changed to five sessions per week, then six. I found new friends, a whole new community, leadership and a new strength within me. And, I found my voice. Never before had I thought I could influence a group, as I had always shied away from public speaking. The group provided the opportunity for me to be myself, and for that I am eternally grateful. A new excitement about life came over me that hasn't left since.

With enthusiasm, movement, conscious eating and connecting with community, we can thrive and reach our full potential. The magic of one man connected with my heart and changed my life forever. When your little voice speaks, honour it, take risks, and reach for the stars! Opportunities are endless!

Andrea Cooper
49 years old
Personal Trainer & Natural Foods Chef
Melbourne, Australia

91
How Taking a Bath Changed My Life

*I*n 2001, I travelled to India for the world's largest festival—the Maha Kumbh Mela, held on the banks of the sacred Ganges River. At the time I was a free hippy, with dreadlocks, sari-style skirts and a carved wooden staff, bejewelled with crystals and feathers, which I carried with pride.

Over 100 million pilgrims attended the festival, intending to bathe in the river in order to purify themselves for the coming year. Sadly, the Ganges isn't the world's cleanest river. Dead bodies, sewage and rubbish are often dumped in there, which is why I refused to even dip my toe in it.

On this particular day at the Mela, it was my twenty-fourth birthday, and it happened to be the most auspicious day to take a bath. As I stumbled along the road with millions of other pilgrims, my ribs being crushed and gasping for oxygen, I looked up and saw a guru on an elephant gesturing at me. I forced my way over and was pulled up on the elephant to sit behind this holy man.

"I will take you to where the two rivers meet, where the feminine and masculine become one," he said.

At last we arrived and people were running towards the water in joy. I knew it was time to put my resistance aside: I walked into the river. Bolts of energy coursed up my legs, through my stomach and up my spine until an explosion of light danced out the top of my head. This feeling bound me to that heavenly moment forever.

These days, when I find myself resisting change, risk-taking and letting go, I remember the Kumbh Mela. I tell myself that even though things may look hard or unpleasant, even dangerous, as long as I have trust in myself, there will always be bliss on the other side.

Emma Kenyon

37 years old

Entertainer, Speaker & Entrepreneur

Melbourne, Australia

Your Life is Your Message

J believe we are all here to connect with each other, with nature and with the Universe. We get so 'lost' along the way that we forget our true nature, which is LOVE. We lose ourselves in the jungle of distractions that are available to us all. Now, more than ever we are literally saturated with connection, whilst remaining truly disconnected from each other and our self.

To have awareness that we are looking for a way back to that part of our self, our true nature, that seems so elusive, connecting back to our *heart*. The truth is, nothing is missing; the connection has been there all along. We've just been blinded by our current illusion/reality.

"To those who seek, a way shall be shown"

"To those who want to know, knowledge and wisdom shall be given"

"To those willing to risk it all, more will be given"

"With Gratitude, the kingdom is yours"

"To thine Own Self be true"

"Know thyself, Be thyself, Love thyself" – the three keys to Life

Deep inside you there is greatness so huge it will shock you. Hopefully, it will shock you enough to wake up. You can hide from this greatness for a very long time, but what a disservice we do this world and ourselves. Can you imagine getting to those very last breaths of life on Earth and wishing you had done more? It's a very real risk we all run in this lifetime. Your life *is* your message, and when your life's message is as big and as beautiful as you can possibly make it, you will discover you have been as much of an inspiration to others as those who have inspired you. What a fascinating journey life is – it's all up to you. That *is* the wonderful responsibility of life!

Rachael Claire Heart

41 years old

Demartini Method® Facilitator & Mother

Christchurch, New Zealand

93
The Perfect Balance

*T*he world is a place for human beings to love each other and to live the best life they can. But most importantly, it's a place to learn and love everything in your life.

Everyone gets a perfect balance of love and support, hate and challenge. You can dwell on the hate and challenge, but while you're doing that, you will be ignoring all of your love and support. There will always be someone playing every role you need to grow. Remember to let people and things be a part of your life, but not rule your life. I believe that everyone in the world can make something great out of their lives. It's up to you how you choose to live. There's nothing wrong with trying to fit in as long as it serves you. For teens: you've got the rest of your life to feel grown up, why start young? Be happy, be different and just be you!!

Any memories you have are either perceived to be good or bad. Memories: your brain either stores them, or ignores them. You might vividly remember being seriously hurt, or the time you went on an amazing holiday. That's because you're perceiving the events to be one-sided and you're not seeing the balance. Look for who's supporting or challenging you in every situation.

Everyone has dreams. Would you believe that every single dream and idea could become your reality if you believe in it? Make an affirmation, believe in it. Say it at least 200 times a day. See it, feel it, smell it and believe in the power of your mind. Your mind is the most amazing, most powerful tool in the Universe. You can do anything and everything, if you believe you can. The only thing that's always perfect is the balance in your life.

Jennifer Lewis – Rachael's daughter

14 years old

Singer & Student

Christchurch, New Zealand

94
Awaken to Your Magnificence

*D*o you know who you truly are? From spirit unto human form you personify life itself. The entire Universe dwells within you, and you are one with its essence. Your magnificence is an aspect of the divine and reflects that you are truly made in the 'likeness of God.' You are stardust embodied beloved, so awaken...

The four elements of creation are your very being: *Earth* herself is your beautiful body, and you are inspirited with every breath of *air* that you take; *water* streams through your arteries and veins; *fire* ignites within your luminous heart, so awaken beloved, awaken...

Even though you may still slumber, you might ask yourself: Does a flower know of its own exquisite beauty, even whilst its silent presence uplifts every soul who beholds it? Does the grandeur of a mountain's peak ever proclaim of its own exalted heights? And does the flow of a mighty river's course ever consider its own path as it deeply carves through the unyielding red earth before her? All this is within you my beloved, so awaken...

Are you afraid beloved? Then allow life to take you by the hand within trust. Unfold and open to the radiance of the incandescent sun. Stand tall and stand strong; permit your magnificence to shine. Push off and out into the steady flow, knowing that the river has its destination. And upon reaching the vastness of that ocean's expanse, your eyes will open, and your heart will soar, for you will remember why you have come here.

For you were born to manifest the glory of God, to open your heart, embodying heaven on Earth, knowing that life is yours to choose for the living, so awaken beloved, awaken... Know who you truly are, for you are blessed; you are loved, and so it is...

David de Warenne
47 years old
Awakening Facilitator
New Plymouth, New Zealand

95
Trust and Follow Your Heart

*I*n 2010, I made one of the best decisions of my life. Australian year-ten students had to make a choice about their final study years of school. I had two options:

1. Traditional – examinations that lead to University.
2. Apprenticeship and no examinations – this option generally perceived as leading to less opportunities in life.

I was determined to prove this perception wrong. My heart wanted the second option. It was a hard decision to make as my family and friends were strongly advising me to go with the first option. I knew in my heart that university just wasn't for me. Thankfully, I trusted my heart. What a difference it made. I decided to live my dream. What is your dream? How can you impact our world in a positive way? Life is literally all about peace and love. We know this but how often do we practice it? Too often, we get caught up in our everyday lives.

I saw world speakers such as Richard Branson. I began meeting people who believed in my abilities. I discovered what I wanted to do in life, which is helping people in their lives and spreading positive energy to all. I have always wanted to make a positive difference in our world. When you change to a positive outlook on life, happiness amplifies. It doesn't matter what age you are.

Despite what others say, you have the power to live life on your terms, according to your heart. Give yourself permission to listen to it. It will guide you in the right direction. I also love spreading joy on the streets through dancing and giving away free chocolates. I love experiencing the positive connection between all humans. No matter who they are, we can all share a smile. ☺

Renee Wilton

19 years old

Founder of Positive Connect App

Melbourne, Australia

96
There is Only Love

A change in consciousness will transform the world. It is only through unconditional love and compassion that we can be healed. As we search for the meaning of life we need to ask the questions: Who am I? Why am I here? What is my purpose? Where are we going? These are challenging questions but they need to be asked. In all the great teachings of the world there is a great truth. We are all one, and we are all love. If we learn to explore the inner dimensions through meditation and prayer we will learn that All is One, and One is All.

We live in challenging times where we face extreme weather patterns, wars, economic collapse, starvation, corrupt governments and corporations. We are taught to hate those who are different from us, and fear and violence is fed to us daily on TV, the Internet and in newspapers. There is, however, a glimmer of hope on the horizon as people all over the world awaken to their Divine Higher Selves and take back their power. A good example being the *Inspiration Bible*, inspired by Emily, to uplift many people who have perhaps, lost hope.

My two children died in road accidents. As I overcame my grief, I was guided by them both from spirit. They came back to prove they still existed and gave me unconditional love, and inspired me to uplift and give hope all those who have lost children. For, unconditional love reaches you from spirit, embraces and uplifts you. You are never alone and your loved ones are with you forever, for the spirit never dies – ever.

"A man with outward courage dares to die.
A man with inward courage dares to live."

Tao

Di Gordon
69 years old
Naturopath & Healer
Rotorua, New Zealand

97
Hope

*T*hree months shy of twenty-four, while my surroundings are filled with heartbeats only just beginning their story, I feel like mine should be near completion, or at least have a substantial interlude in the foreseeable future. I believe that the consuming, consistent battle will subside, and the breakthrough will come. I believe it because I've seen it, and felt it. I think I've always been blessed with too many burdens, but thankfully, my blessings reach the same amount of strength to overcome each individual tribulation. I think I've always struggled, and I think, to an extent, I always will.

The world becomes a war, and my armour becomes my daily uniform – but sometimes a helmet of protection isn't enough. Actually, I guarantee you it won't be enough. In those moments of crushing clarity; in those moments of destroying reality; 3 a.m. has only loneliness to offer you. I promise you that. But, when the darkness steals your breath, and hijacks the life out of your eyes, you don't have to be imprisoned in your own personal temple turned tomb. You don't have to brave the seconds until the sunrise, alone.

Find hope in your 3 a.m. friend. Find hope in the person who has hope enough for the both of you. Find hope in the words of a kind stranger. Find hope in simply a smile, or a supportive embrace. Find hope in the Universe, and its plan for you. But, above all else, find hope in your own survival. Find hope in your fight; find hope in your destiny. Before it gets better, the darkness will get bigger –but remember, for as many days as you've been alive, the sun has risen to greet you. Find hope in the sun rising, because with it comes the relief of waking up one day closer to your breakthrough.

Grace Blevins-Hunt

23 years old

Administration

Adelaide, Australia

98
My Sister's Gift

*I*n April 1995, my sister Michelle had a near-death experience and spontaneously entered a state of peace and bliss that lasted six months. For the next eight years, she researched and developed tools to help her get back into this amazing state, which she calls 'the Zone.' She subsequently distilled her findings into a coaching program to help others access this state.

Not long later, I needed Michelle's help. As an A-type perfectionist, I'd begun parenthood with high hopes and expectations. Unsurprisingly, I was soon stressed-out and miserable. My biggest issue was my daughter Lara's rebelliousness. Even though she was only five, I felt like a total failure as a parent! My mind couldn't seem to stop the spiral of anger, guilt and fear.

Michelle taught me that what was disturbing me wasn't what was happening. Rather it was my thoughts *about* what was happening and why. I started to question my belief that I had to control what should happen in each moment: "Can I really know what should happen in each moment for our lives to be wonderful? Can I read the future?"

When I debunked these thoughts, I finally saw Lara's innocence and my own too. A crushing weight lifted from my heart and love flooded in. I hadn't felt such love in years. When I'd been judgemental and guilt-ridden, there was little room for love. Coming home that evening, I gave Lara a cuddle and she asked, "What's happened, Mum?" Startled I said, "Nothing's happened." But Lara insisted, "Something's happened. You're different!" Somehow she'd sensed the unconditional love I was feeling for her. I'm sure she'd also noticed its absence. Now seven years on, Lara is still my Zone barometer, reflecting instantly my inner peacefulness and love.

Joanne van Ravenswaaij
50 years old
Zone Coach
Melbourne, Australia

99
A Chance Meeting

*F*riday evening I was running along Southbank, past couples dining and strolling along arm-in-arm. I ran onto Story Bridge with its thin rails you can see-through, feeling giddy looking at the swirling waters below. Something was leaning against the rails lifelessly, facing below like a discarded doll. It was a young girl. I couldn't go past, so I interrupted her contemplation, "Are you OK?" She glanced up listlessly and then away. "I'm alright," she sniffed with tear-stained cheeks. She whispered, "I'm tired." "I'm also tired," I replied as I stood there sweating, "but from enjoying this run." "You don't have to stop," she mumbled.

We talked and she told me she loves running and that feeling you get, but now she is sick, and needs a cane to walk. She confided in me that she threw it away tonight and didn't want to go on living because it's "too painful." My heart went out to her, and I decided I wasn't going anywhere until she was off that bridge. I shared my love of the beautiful cities shimmering at night and that fresh tropical air.

"Those lights look beautiful!" she sighed, "... I need time to think." I told her I'd walk her home, but she wouldn't agree, falling back into her cloudy contemplation. We spoke on and on and like the dappled sunlight streaming through clouds, she gave me the occasional smile and small laugh.

"Come on Alex, let's get off this bridge," I insisted helping her to her feet. We then started walking when four police officers (called by passing motorists) ran up sweating profusely and out of breath, gasping, "Stop and sit down!" Another officer asked Alex, who I was. "He's the guy who talked me out of it," she said smiling at me.

Michael Dempsey
45 years old
Social Media Manager
Melbourne, Australia

100
Travelling the Journey
of Adoption

Compassion and honesty are so important to me, having learned when I offer both, I experience people in a whole new light. I grew up in the wrong family after being adopted at birth. My adoptive parents had serious illnesses. My father had open-heart surgery and my mother needed a heart and lung transplant. Both had died by the time I was twenty-seven.

Family provides reference points to forge my identity, they remember my birthday and tell me they care about who I am. For me, family imparts stories and memories to grow my life. Losing one family in a lifetime is hard enough. Losing two families, at such a young age, was a tragedy and affected me deeply.

When I found out I was adopted, kids teased me, telling me my parents didn't love me. It erased the truth of my story, that I was lovable, offering instead a stigmatised identity. Being adopted has meant questioning the way things are, where other people just follow along. I am careful what I listen to, take on board and allow to shape my decisions. Etched on my soul is the importance of being an individual and expressing myself in ways that are truthful and right.

Travelling the journey of adoption hasn't been easy, it has required holding courage in both hands and saying "yes" to its call. Yet, I am lucky in so many ways; I've been gifted with intelligence, creativity and determination. I am proud to have used these qualities to educate myself, achieving multiple university degrees, where I discovered my true identity is expressed through the power of art. I hope to make a difference in the world by using the lifelong legacy of adoption to practice suspending judgement and live my life with a heart that is tender, kind and wise.

Lisa-Maree Botticelli

42 years old

Creativity & Life Architect, Artist

Sydney, Australia

101
Venturing into Possibility

*J*drifted into a career in banking at age eighteen. Back then, I didn't really know who I was or what I wanted to do. I cared more about what others thought of my choices than finding my own path. It wasn't until twenty years later, coinciding with a second round of redundancy, that I stepped back to evaluate my life and career.

It was 2012 before I finally took a leap into the unknown. Within two weeks, I met an inspiring entrepreneur who introduced me to the ancient Greek ideal *Arete*. Its origins can be traced back to Homeric times, almost 3000 years ago, and later through such figures as Socrates, Plato and Aristotle. Arete is associated with timeless character qualities such as virtue, excellence and valour, and being all you can be – especially in service of something larger than self. It has affinity with Aristotle's notions of a *good life* and *eudaimonia*.

Living off savings, I explored how I could find my 'flow,' embody my own expression of Arete, and make a difference. A willingness to be vulnerable, and be ok with finding myself lost, helped me lean into the unknown and develop a capacity to sense and respond to what intrigued me in the moment. Separating constructive feedback from outright negativity, reading, learning, reflecting, and meeting wonderfully diverse interesting people doing things they care about, helped me find a path that feels right. I didn't, and still don't, have a 'master plan,' which I sense would only get in the way of embracing what is emerging in a new (ad)venture I'm co-stewarding from 2014.

My hope is that anyone who reads my story, at whatever age, can find inspiration to explore, experiment, and find their authentic path. Because by doing so, the Universe will conspire to offer support, challenge and reflection along the way.

Gavin Peacock
48 years old
Conscious Business Entrepreneur
London, United Kingdom

102
Permission to Win

*A*t twelve years old, I finished a tennis match against a weaker opponent. I had destroyed him 6:0, 6:0 losing only five points in total. It was a strong, focused and dominant performance that clearly stated my number one ranking. As I exited the court, my mother asked, "Did you know he was crying when he came off?" "No," I replied. *What the hell did that have to do with me winning?* I asked myself. "It would have been nice of you to give him a game or two," she responded. I suddenly felt like I had done something wrong.

The following week at training we were doing sprints. I had won the first three, so I decided to let some of the others boys win the last two. My coach noticed, and pulled me aside afterwards and implored me not to hold myself back. But, it was too late. I was now more concerned with being liked than winning all the time. My match results suffered and, within a few years, I walked away from tennis.

I spent the next twenty years seeking approval by trying to be nice to everyone. In the process I became depressed, lost and weak. I felt dead inside. It wasn't until my partner saw an old tennis photo of me I had hid in storage that I had my breakthrough. "Wow look at your face in that picture, you are so confident," she said. Her words almost made me cry as I realised that was the last time I could remember loving myself and being happy. "Yeah, back then I didn't care about what anyone else thought. I just loved competing and winning," I quietly replied. It finally hit me. Only I could give myself approval and permission to win. My competitive spirit stirred.

Andrean Patkas

38 years old

Sports Mindset & Performance Coach

Melbourne, Australia

103
Facing Failures

It was the year 2000, I barely had any food to eat for the past several months as there was no income for my family. I was nineteen years old, attending college. Most of the time I skipped lunch, as either I didn't had the money to buy lunch, or I wanted to save whatever was left. I was lucky to have friends who shared their lunch with me. Then I had to step up to get my family out of bankruptcy. I decided to drop out of college and get a job, which is one of the toughest decisions I ever had to make. At an age of nineteen, with no graduation and with no money, I started my career with a salary of twenty dollars per month.

Being a college dropout, I knew I had to keep learning and work harder. I wanted to win, not just survive. Even at the time of bankruptcy, I used to dream of a good life. I had no idea on how to get where I wanted to be, but I was committed to reach there. A few years passed; I was twenty-four. It was a big day for me as I was being appointed as Managing Director of a UK-based company in India. Soon after that, I got invited to the same college I dropped out of, to take a workshop on management for the postgraduate students there. And, my business life grew from there.

With the way I started my career, I found failures could be motivating. Then onwards, what drove me to success was my understanding that every failure is an opportunity to rise up as a better person. If you are facing failures, then you are on the right path to success.

Prabhul Sankar

32 years old

Entrepreneur

Kochi, India

104
The Warrior Woman

I am a Warrior Woman. I am unafraid to face my fear.
I live with my heart on my sleeve. I am real like you.
I stand for your rights. I accept your imperfection.
I understand your challenge.
I expect you to fight for you, with the same dedication I will.
I love you.
You are deserved of your joy. Your potential is infinite.
Your heart is strong
You must DECIDE there is a way.
You MUST fulfil your dreams.
You have 'this ONE life' right now - to do it!
So Live!
I believe in you - I believe in you - I BELIEVE in you!
YOU believe in you!
You shine! You soar!
Success Is Yours
I sing in your honour.
I stand and applaud your achievement
You are extraordinary!
You never give up...
You BE the hero of your own story.
Bravo!
For the Warrior Woman in me
− Sees −
The Warrior Woman in You!

Alisse Bradley
41 years old
Business & Wealth Coach
Toowoomba

105
Courage

*G*rey skies outside. That's what I saw staring out of the classroom window. Daydreaming was my hobby. Everyday things seemed worse. They were constantly dragging me there and back. You would be lucky if I talked to you. I hated the fact that I was forced to stay someplace where I had no choice and didn't like. I was upset, angry, hurt and emotional. I knew this wasn't right, but I didn't know how to get out of the sadness, hurt, and fear, or how I could improve my life so that things could get better.

I was the black sheep: constantly bullied, teased and unable able to fit in. I never gave up hope, though. Despite these emotions rumbling inside, in all of six years, I hardly ever skipped a class. There must have been courage inside me somewhere. When the time was up to finish school, I couldn't believe I had made it. Me? I? I didn't think I had it in me. At the time, to face another year felt so long. To say the least, it was an absolute relief to know I had finished my time. For all the bullied words that had stuck for a while are now a distant memory of their own battles and insecurities.

If you are reading this right now and are finding it hard to see the light, feel like you are all alone, not being heard or understood, frightened and scared to speak up, lost and lonely, just know this: you are not alone. You will get through it, even if it seems no one cares. Keep your faith that things will work out, even if you are just clinging on. Hold on to the one positive thought and keep remembering and reminding yourself of that to get you through.

Kathryn Perry

28 years old

Placements Officer - Recruitment

Melbourne, Australia

106
One Question That Will
Change Your Life

*H*ave you ever had a dream that hasn't been realised because you thought it was too big or crazy? Perhaps people told you it won't work. Most dreams die with us because of the stories we tell ourselves. People love playing when-then games with their life: "When the kids leave home, then I'll have more time. When I retire, then I'll travel. When I have a job, then I'll be more confident. When I lose weight, then I'll be happy..." We tell ourselves we're too old or too young, not qualified enough, not good enough, that 'little old me' can't make a difference or that there's still time to dream. Is there?

I've also used these stories in my own life to avoid sharing my special gift with the world. And so have many of the people I help, and possibly even you. *"What would you do today if you weren't afraid and knew you couldn't fail?"* This simple question has changed my life countless times, and I know it can change yours too.

How would your life change, if you had the courage to speak up, put yourself forward or try something new? You could take a risk, get out of a loveless relationship or start a business. Who could benefit if you were less fearful? Every person has a special, unique talent that comes so naturally, it's like breathing. I call it the magic in us. It gives your life meaning and makes you feel happy and fulfilled. The biggest contribution you can make in this world, in our lifetime and beyond, is to discover the magic in you. Stop being afraid and call on your courage to take bold moves towards your dreams.

"Life is an adventure, be courageous and dare greatly."

Alicia Menkveld
40 years old
Speaker & Author
Perth, Australia

107
What the Bully Didn`t See Coming

*J*used to be that kid who would fade into the background. I never used to be able to speak, or stand up for myself. I used to accept everything that came my way. Some days I felt like it was me against the world, that everyone had it out for me. Some days I felt that no matter where I went, someone always had a problem with me. I felt like I was carrying around a bunch of emotions that I couldn`t shake. It just stuck.

Bullies were a problem for me; a problem I dealt with on a daily basis. One day I went to school, and I had a really bad feeling about going. Turns out my instincts were correct. I was in the gym, having a weights session, when a group of people came in and started threatening me. I got up and went to my classroom, and they followed me.

I felt scared, afraid and frightened. There was a teacher inside the classroom when I came in. I barely had enough time to explain before they started to come through the door. As they were coming in, the teacher went to the door, and physically put herself in front of them, grabbing each side of the doorframe, to keep them out. The teacher put herself at risk to protect me. Eventually the group gave up, and one of them said a few 'nice words' to me before they left.

Being subjected to bullying has led me to train in MMA. At first it was for self-defence, so I would feel capable of defending myself. And now, it is professional because my goal is to be UFC champion of the world. Remember your strengths.

Brenton Torrens

16 years old

MMA Fighter

Adelaide, Australia

108
Aiden's Fight for Life

*I*t was six weeks early when I gave birth to my second son. They rushed him to the ICU because he had trouble breathing, but after twenty minutes he was breathing on his own. Being early, he needed to grow so he stayed in the hospital for a month. One day, before I went to visit Aiden, I received a call from the ICU saying I needed to come in immediately as he was very sick. Breaking down in tears, I rushed over there, and after doing some tests, they told me he has hydrocephalus due to a brain haemorrhage.

After leaving the hospital in a stable condition, he had an MRI, which confirmed shortly after that he had brain damage. After months of hospitals, Aiden screaming 24/7 and doctors telling me I was paranoid, he was sleeping twenty-three hours-a-day, and after a five-hour wait they told me it was nothing. The following day I took him to the children's hospital and had six doctors fighting over his case. He had emergency brain surgery the next day.

He had a shunt in his brain, draining the excess fluid into his stomach. Since then he has had three severe seizures that left him unconscious, a few other minor seizures, three shunt failures, four brain surgeries, and endless amount of headaches, throwing up, passing out and brain bleeds. He has almost died twice, but he will always be my little trooper.

He is now going strong, and he has taught me to be strong and to stand up for what I believe in. He's taught me to not just believe what people tell me, but to trust myself, to raise my voice to be heard, to live life with no regrets, and that it's okay to cry. He has taught me how to live again.

Rhi Butler
28 years old
Author & Project Manager
Melbourne, Australia

109
The Protector

J'm at school in grade three, and I see kids getting hurt all the time. I see this happen a lot. They hurt each other with their words and by pushing them around. This scares me, because it might happen to me and I have been bullied before, so I know how this feels. It hurts me seeing my friends go through this, as I want to help them, but I'm afraid. I'm protective of kids because my brother had a brain injury when he was born, and I look after him. I am terrified that he won't be here one day.

If I could tell the bullies anything, I would tell them how much what they do hurts people and how it will affect them for a very long time. I would also tell the bullies that there are consequences to their actions, because it's not the right thing to do.

When I see that people have been hurt, I tell them to stand up for what they believe in. I tell them to get help if they are scared of being hurt. You shouldn't be afraid to ask for help, because it will keep happening if no one knows that you are scared or getting hurt. When I am older, I want to be a protector so that I can protect people as much as I can. I want to change the world and make it a better place. I want to teach others and help them so they have a better life. I want to do this by starting right now.

Sebastian Butler
8 years old
Student
Melbourne, Australia

110
2.5 Kids, a Hunky Husband and a Happy Life!

*M*y story doesn't begin with a phoenix rising from the flames. My story begins at my white picket fence, a hunky husband and 2.5 kids (the half is our dog, a male boxer).

I had all the classic accompaniments of being a traditional Kiwi girl. I grew up with love, food, warmth and more opportunities than I could ever imagine. But I was playing small. I was bobbing along in game of life until I had a *huge* realisation: I wasn't grateful for anything I had. I was unhappy. Life was becoming a dress rehearsal – an utter drag!

How did I lose myself, my identity, and begin sweating the small stuff? I blame our fellow grandmothers and mothers who were the *real* Super Mums. They were the new era of divorcees, single woman who were working to provide for their latchkey kids. They made a secret code that you were successful if you were the cleaner, cook, best friend, immaculate wife, textbook mother, and so on. Now here comes me: the modern woman, mortgage, three jobs, kids, self-employed husband, social butterfly, and budding entrepreneur, working out, staying healthy, cleaning, and making the lunches. Before I know it, I was burnt out on an epic scale.

I made a commitment to myself. Ditch wasn't working for me. I started using my heart and trusting my intuition. To get started, I kept a gratitude journal. This simple yet profound daily task turned my world around. It showed me just how amazing my mind and my life was. It was time to stop trying to be everything to everyone and choose to do what fulfilled me, alongside helping my fellow woman to create new rules for success and the new kind of housewife: happy!

Natalie Tolhopf
37 years old
Modern Woman Career Advisor
Auckland, New Zealand

111
Confidence Counts

*H*ow would you live your life if you knew you only had one year or six months to live? Who would you spend your time with? What would you make sure you did before your time ran out?

In 2006, when I was twenty-six, I learned that I had an abnormal growth in the right temporal lobe of my brain. I had to undergo surgery to remove it so that the doctors could examine it and work out what it was and how I could best be treated. The risk of the surgery was that I could go blind, or lose my mobility, but if I didn't have the surgery the risk was far greater... I could lose my life.

So I asked myself – did it make sense to continue working in an unfulfilling job where the work hours continually got longer, the expectations to deliver greater, and whilst it appeared from the outside that I was climbing the corporate ladder to success, deep down inside I felt that my soul was suffering? What was the point of acquiring money if the trade-off for that money was less time to do the things that I wanted and not having anyone special to share it with?

After some deep soul searching, I arrived at the conclusion that life is meant to be lived, that fear and love are friends guiding us to be the best versions of ourselves, and I learned that chasing those butterflies in my stomach, instead of running away from them, opens up the doors to daily magic in our lives. Live confidently and passionately.

> *"Don't ask yourself what the world needs; ask yourself what makes you come alive, and then go do that. Because what the world needs is people who have come alive."*
> **Howard Thurman**

In memory of my mother, Somchan Chansamooth (04/06/1955 - 22/04/2009)

Anfernee Chansamooth
35 years old
Philanthropist & Career Consultant
Bonnyrigg, Australia

112
Reading Creates Leaders

*M*y story is about the youngest of my four children. This story begins with my experiences in primary school and with the knowledge that my family did not place a high value on books. Being a good student, I mostly came first in every subject; well, almost every one. I was relegated to second in English, in *every* exam, by a boy who, in my perception, seemed to have his head in a book whenever he could. When it came to essays, he would be well into them and I would be still trying to write the opening paragraph. It was such a painful process. At this point, I decided that it was his reading of books that gave him the edge, leaving me to wallow in second place, and I made the decision that when I became a mother I would read to my children. This I did.

So, for my youngest child, this meant that by birth, this child had listened to me reading for over 400 hours and by the first day of school... over 3000 hours. Three times a day, every day, even if we had been out, I still had to read, even if I was tired or busy, the reading was still done. One and a half hours, each and every day. I continued reading chapter books until my youngest was in year three, so the 3000 hours is really only a conservative estimate.

So, where did all these hours of reading take this child, you might ask? What benefit was all this reading? Well, this child is now twenty-six years old and, at times, has been described as amazing, empowered, brilliant, talented, beautiful, and gifted – and an inspiration. This twenty six-year-old is a writer, mentor, speaker, author and a publisher.

You all know her as... Emily Gowor.

Rae Antony
65 years old
Healer, Artist & Author
Brisbane, Australia

113
Self-Doubt Vs. Self-Belief

*S*elf-belief is connecting with your truth and self-worth. Self-doubt is your very own prison; a false sense of security. Like an anchor weighing you down, your self-doubt will drown you if you let it, or you can simply cut the rope and rise to the surface.

After a lifetime as an employee, I now enjoy a life as an entrepreneur. I was offered the opportunity and said "Yes," being more afraid of missing out than of what I might find. My transformation would be about my own self-belief and not being ruled by fear. My self-doubt was a crippling secret I was hiding from the world. I had everyone fooled, including me, but eventually realised my true happiness relied on how I could change.

I went to a global conference on the other side of the world to stop myself from quitting. My suitcase weighed a tonne but somehow airport baggage control still let me check it through. Surrounded by so much incredible energy, I discovered there that quitting was not an option for me, no matter how tough it was going to get, and I needed to 'take care of my junk.' Just when I thought it was going to get easier, my self-doubt found a way to grow bigger. There was still a part of me that didn't *really* believe I could be successful; I was afraid of success and everything I didn't know.

Embracing the unknown and being honest set me free. With honesty came clarity and the pathway ahead unfolded. Arriving home, I got straight to work. Build your belief like a house, one brick at a time, then stand back and witness the transformation. It will take courage, effort and persistence but the reward is connecting with your true self, abundance and true happiness.

Lili Csongrady

41 years old

Network Marketing Professional

Stirling, Australia

114
Six Months to Live

*H*ow would you react to being told you had six months to live? Not sure? I had no idea either, but that's exactly what happened to me in the oncologist's office as I was told I had terminal abdominal cancer in November 2005 – a staggering nine years ago.

I am happy to tell you I am alive and beaming with good health and have been ever since. It's simple: always remember you always have a choice. A choice to choose your own thoughts, your own actions, your own results, for *your* body. Just like I chose not to have any chemotherapy or radiation treatment, not a drop, because it was my choice not to. It was always my choice to choose what treatment I wanted or didn't want in *my* body, no one else's.

Did I want to go through chemotherapy and radiation and become another statistic like both of my parents? Did I want to be a victim of circumstance, a victim of someone else's decision about *my* health? No! So, I chose to follow my own instincts and knowledge base of natural medicine, and began having potent TCM – Traditional Chinese Medicine (plant-based), combined with other non-invasive natural therapies and meditation twice a day to re-train my brain.

I chose to power on, and to think positively and focus on being well, single-mindedly. Something deep inside me, a profound sense of knowing that I wouldn't die, drove me to a point of wellness. I have achieved complete wellness of every cell, with my unbeatable spirit to live my life differently, with a completely healthy body, mind and spirit... so that I can tell my story one day, to inspire people. And that day is today.

Deborah Johnston
41 years old
Well Being Speaker & Author
Melbourne, Australia

115
Live with No Regret

*T*here are many times in our lives when we have been consumed by a situation that scares us and is rapidly approaching. I know I'm not alone; we have all been through circumstances like this. My first real test of manhood was when I had to ask my future father-in-law's permission to marry his daughter. I was twenty-one years old and wow, what I put myself through building up to this.

It was just the start of what was going to be a life's journey: learning how people manage when making decisions, or facing a situation that they think is beyond their ability, or above their pay grade, so to speak. My big test came in 1994 when I was told by a surgeon I wouldn't work again after a back injury. But two years and seven months later, I was back on the job doing what I loved. I also lost the use of my hand for nine months after a mishap during an operation on my arm in 2007.

Knowing, of course, that other people have been through much worse and having a faith in God and a loving wife, has always helped me keep things in perspective (yes, we did get married in 1982 and she is still the love of my life). We have six wonderful, grown children; three girls, three boys, in addition to three great son-in-laws, and seven grandchildren. I've learned to be grateful for what we have, even if it's not as much as others, it's often more than most. Have a go at every good opportunity that's presented; it's important to always encourage others, discern right from wrong and above everything else, make sure that our integrity is above reproach to live with no regret.

Peter Owen
54 years old
Structural Landscaper
Sydney, Australia

116
When You Love Yourself, You're Free

"*The* only reason I would ever take offense is if I didn't love myself." The words of my partner hit hard. We had been teaching Unconditional Love courses together, helping people embrace and love every part of themselves. I realized quickly that he was right. I rarely ever take offense to what anyone says or does, but every so often I feel the sting of harsh words poking at my past wounds. Even something as simple as my boyfriend's request to be alone at night can still set off a battery of worry.

"Did I do something wrong?" I wonder. "Why would he rather be alone than with me? Is he seeing someone else?" Thankfully, it doesn't take long now before the bigger 'me' realizes what I am doing. I then recognize it's often as simple as him honouring himself and having some solitude. How many times have I rejected those very same feelings of needing solitude, in order to please others? I reject myself, because somehow it's more important that the other does not feel rejected or offended. The ultimate form of betrayal is self-betrayal.

I think, "Why is it so easy for him, and I struggle with it?" I immediately recall that comparison is the thief of joy, and I impress myself with how quickly I am able to let it go. I am grateful for these little lessons and to finally be able to step back and laugh at myself, "Me and my need to be liked... again. Isn't that cute?" If I really loved myself, would it even matter what anyone else thought? I think not. Back to the drawing board to find and nurture those little wounds that still need some loving attention. It's not always easy, but it's definitely worth it. When we love ourselves, we are free.

Jeri Tourand
44 years old
Self-Love Coach & Trilotherapist
Spruce Grove, Canada

117
You Are Loved

L ove. We want it, yearn it, crave it, desire it, search for it, kill for and even die for LOVE. No matter your experience of love so far, if you look, you'll find it naturally evolving within and without, in the people, moments and experiences we cherish. Always evident.

Love is etched in the memories of events past, of idyllic childhood days, the healing powers of a mother's kiss, time with dad, building sandcastles on the beach, rolling in lush grass, diving in the surf, sun-kissed in summer, a nuzzle from a pet, the enduring significance of a home. It's in your future, the longing gaze shared with a lover, the scent of the woman you'll love, embraced in the strong safe arms of your man, lips and fingers caressing skin, the heat of insatiable passion, the miracle and scent of your newborn baby, wet kisses from the children, family memories, secrets shared with friends.

Love is all around you, within a colourful sunset, the awe of a star-studded night's sky, the value of an art piece, the beauty of Earth, flowers, creation, and the reverence of a sacred place. It's in the birthing of your dreams, giving hope, inspiring others to give birth to theirs.

To feel *love*, remember that unrequited love can lead to deep love, leaving you abandoned and a soul mate appeared. Heartbreak awakened you. Break up – the catalyst from which to learn forgiveness and unconditional love. If you're feeling unloved right now – you fear love, are closed to it or focused on being broken hearted. Heart break after all is your heart breaking open to allow *greater love* within. Love is limitless – just count the ways.

Love is limitless – just count the ways.

Terai Koronui

46 years old

The Love Connector

Toowomba, Australia

118
Breathe Deeply. Live Fearlessly.

"*L*isten, are you breathing just a little and calling it a life?" Mary Oliver's poem summed up my beige existence. Despite every success – career, marriage, and lifestyle – profound discontent overwhelmed me. I weighed almost 100 kilograms. Gyms, diets, trainers, shakes, and weird infomercial gadgets – nothing worked. The issue was not my body, but my soul. Food and alcohol were an anaesthetic. In my heart was a dream, smothered by fear.

I despaired most deeply for my daughters. Fifty-one years of living and I could not truly say to my girls, "Follow my example." I was a cowering cliché, buried in suburbia. No leader. No father. Teddy Roosevelt pointed the way, *"Do what you can, with what you have, where you are."*

For twelve months, a solitary question propelled me forward. How can I do more of what I love with my body, my mind and my service to others? A year of living dangerously and stripping fear off my dream. I lost twenty kilos, learned, taught, and started a business. I became inspired, discovered wealth, forged a path worthy of my daughters' footsteps. But most of all, I breathed deeply. And lived.

It's never too late. Ask Marianne Williamson. We serve the world by shining, not shrinking. As we liberate ourselves, we inspire others to do the same. There are seven billion people on the planet; you are the only one qualified to be you. There are no mistakes, only miracles in the making. Keep going. There are no limits. You have a dream. Whatever it takes, be that person. Don't fear change. Change fear. Follow your heart, it knows the way. Breathe deeply. Live fearlessly. Listen again to Mary Oliver.

"So every day, I was surrounded by the beautiful crying forth of the ideas of God – one of which was you."

Bruce Conrad Williams

54 years old

Author, Consultant & Speaker

Noosa, Australia

119
Ignite Your Life

*J*t's been a wild ride to aliveness over the past forty-two years, but nothing compares to the love, courage, inspiration and gratitude that I have experienced in the past five years. It has been a journey of blood, sweat, tears, support, challenges, messengers, a giant leap of faith and belief in myself that has led me to living an inspired life with the love of my life in the house of my dreams with four amazing children and a fulfilling career.

I'd have to say that I've lived a colourful life, filled with many highs and lows, successes and failures, of which I have become eternally grateful for. I immersed myself in personal development courses and literature, healed my soul, and supported others. I was in my element; I loved what I did and did what I loved!

I remember the actual moment that my spark emerged, however I ignored it at the time. I scribbled some notes and pictures down on a napkin: it was "just an idea" that I thought I wouldn't ever act on. I never dreamed I would be capable of what emerged from that day, but when I finally surrendered to my calling some years later and to what was on the napkin, my life changed.

I must ask... Do you have an idea that's tucked away and neglected, a dream that is still a dream? Are you clear of your purpose and living it with conviction? I urge you to find your light, purpose and passion, search your soul, listen to your heart and take the time to discover your own brilliance... I dare you to find your divine spark and ignite your life, as it's your birthright to shine!

Deborah Grice
41 years old
Inspirational Entrepreneur
Redland Bay, Australia

120
Time Is All You've Got –
And Time Is Running Out

*T*hese ten words are to me some of the most powerful motivational words I have ever heard and have brought great change in my life. Throughout my life, I have attempted to commit suicide twice and also had a long case of depression. With caring family and friends, I was able to overcome my suicidal and depression times.

It was during these times of change that I started studying about what causes people to do and behave in such ways and have had the pleasure of meeting some great spiritual and influential people from around the world that study and teach these things. I came to realize that TIME IS REALLY SHORT and to hold onto pain and hurt can and will destroy yourself, your family, friends, people around you and your view on life. As you look at yourself right now;

Have you accomplished what you want in your life?

Have you made peace with people you have wronged?

How is your health?

What plans or ideas have you let slip by because you have used a simple phrase *"Oh, I will do that tomorrow"* and yet many years have now gone by and this thing or task has still not been done. Life is fleeting and you will never know when your time is up. Trust yourself and do what needs to be done and get it done NOW. Do not waste your time on small things or on repetitive tasks that you could get someone else to do or let go totally if they do not serve your wants or needs. After all, time is all you have... and time is running out.

Live Your Life Till The Wheels Fall Off.

Phillip Manfredi
52 years old
Coach, Counsellor, Author, Speaker
St Leonards, Australia

121
The Simple Purpose
of Humanity

J never felt my life was perfect and complete. Being brought up in a strict household with two half-brothers, I felt alone. I had a childhood of loneliness. I was bullied and I did all the wrong things to fit in. I grew up fighting with my father. My brothers felt that I was the spoilt one, which I came to believe. My parents passed away in my early twenties, which altered my world completely.

I experimented with drugs and lied. I was used and abused. I then met my twin flame: the person that accepts me, all of me... and there is a lot of me, believe it or not. I now have three gorgeous children; my first has a disability, which changed my whole life. There was a part of me that wanted to die. I felt unworthy. One day it all shifted and I got myself out of my darkness. I realized I am worthy. My inner child spoke to me. I started my spiritual journey in June 2001. I have and still do work through my stuff. I am pure light with DNA fragments of others that I allowed to filter through me. I began to believe, "I am strong, courageous, supported and successful. I am love."

Today, I make sure that people know we are here on this planet to make a difference. We all have a purpose. You *are* worth it. Without my experiences, I would not be who I am today. I own my thoughts, my body, my DNA. This energy then radiates outwardly to help people to find what I believe is the simple purpose of humanity: to *love* and be *supported*. I got through it and so can you.

Margaret Ioannidis

45 years old

Healer & Spiritual Teacher

Melbourne, Australia

122
With Great Power Comes Great Responsibility

A parent's power to inspire and their responsibility for raising their child is one of the greatest examples of, "With great power comes great responsibility." You see, I was very nearly not born. As loving as Dad was, his alcoholism often fuelled violence. So, when I was six months old, Mum chose to shield, but also never reveal, this aspect of him to me.

After twenty-four years of holidays with Dad, I confronted him about his alcoholism—he lunged, hands up and around my throat — and I made the choice to never see him again; this is when Mum revealed her story. To Mum, her choice was not a difficult one, because it was her responsibility to ensure that I have the best chance at developing and having my *own* relationship with Dad.

Six years, two reconnection attempts, and a stroke later, Dad passed away. Dad wasn't a great man, nor did we have many memorable moments together, so I was shocked by my immense sadness and grief. But why? Then, it occurred to me: I, like many sons, had grown up with the dream, the *hope*, of having the kind of relationship with Dad I always wanted. But my hope had disappeared. It was gone.

Three weeks after Dad's service, I found myself at an event being asked, "What is the one message you want to tell the world?" and, without conscious thought, I exclaimed, "Every son deserves a dad!"

While the full story behind this revelation may be interesting to many, it's less important than what actions, and who, enabled it to occur. It was that simple, loving act by a parent with great responsibility, and the greatest power of all, to ensure her son grew up knowing his Dad: my Mum.

Nathan J. Burke
33 years old
Author, Teacher & Facilitator
Brisbane, Australia

123
Willpower for the World

*T*he first forty years of my life were physically and mentally abusive. It began with my family and evolved into an abusive marriage, which almost ended my life. I managed to break free, but by that point, I was just a shell of who I am today. Although I was walking around in a body, I felt empty and hopeless inside. I had no self-esteem, no self-respect and certainly no self-love. I became an alcoholic, smoking two to three packs of cigarettes a day. I was a mess.

One night while driving home drunk, I almost ran through a red light. That did it. I knew that if I kept on going like that, I would end up hurting or killing someone. There was no way I could live with that. The next morning, I made my decision to change my life. I looked at it this way: up to that point, I had experienced a lot of 'bad' stuff so why not just do the opposite and choose to experience the 'good' stuff.

I made the commitment to myself to change, so I quit drinking and smoking, and for the first time in my life, I felt like I was in control. From that day on, everything shifted. My life became better than I could have ever imagined. For the past six years, I have done a lot of self-journey and discovered some amazing things along the way. I am now happily married to the man of my dreams and I am the co-owner of my dream business. Every day now, I remember my own story of coming out of the darkness so I could shine my own light – it inspires me endlessly, as I now live from a place of peace and joy. And so can you.

Carmen Braga

49 years old

Personal Growth Specialist

Sherwood Park, Canada

124
A Letter to the Girl with a Broken Heart

*T*his is a note to every girl who's ever worn a broken heart. I feel your pain and have cried your tears. Sometimes for days, sometimes for months, sometimes for even years. I know it hurts now and you have tunnel vision. You wonder how this could happen; how he could do this to you. I know you gave so much. So much love, so much time, so much of you. I know you feel that you will never love anyone like this again or maybe that you aren't worthy of love.

I'm here to tell you that sometimes, a broken heart isn't such a bad thing. It can allow more love in than you ever thought you were capable of. Sometimes it gives you the needed time to spend in solitude and form a relationship with yourself, perhaps for the first time ever. Sometimes we must suffer heartache to open us up and let out all the magnificence we have within.

I want you to realize that you *can* live without him. Realize that you are worth someone loving you just as you are. Realize that you deserve someone who won't cause you tears and pain. But, most of all, you are worth loving yourself; who you are, where you are. As a broken bone grows back stronger, so does the heart.

Remember this: love doesn't hurt, loving the wrong person does. So open your mind and shift your thoughts. Perhaps this heartbreak is just preparing you for the right person. The one who will love you the way you deserve, who will love you with as much love as you give to him. The pain won't last too long. I can promise you that. So, take care and heal fast.

Love always,
Been there, felt that.

Jenn Scalia
33 years old
Love & Confidence Coach
Hammonton, United States of America

125
Finding Happiness
after Losing a Son

*F*ather's Day will never have the same meaning after losing my son on Father's Day 1994. Imagine: the last day of a six-week overseas family holiday, your nearly fifteen-year-old child drowns on a river excursion that you, as a father, had organised. We nearly lost his mother in the same drowning accident caused by flash flooding, whilst touring Pagsanjans Falls south of the Philippines capital of Manila.

I had many sleepless nights dealing with the awful pain of a broken heart, the feeling of guilt, walking the streets, swearing at the gods, trying to makes sense of why the creators (who are espoused by most religions as all loving) would give us the ability to feel such pain, and trying to rationalise whether I had been punished for some misdemeanours in my life. The grief was so intense, I considered suicide on more than one occasion. If it wasn't for the love of his mother and my daughter, who knows, maybe I might have done so.

To deal with our grief and to understand the journey ahead, I connected with other bereaved parents. The majority of these people agreed they had become better people because of their loss; more compassionate, more tolerant, more forgiving, more loving. All were in agreement too; this was one hell of a way to learn these lessons. I could have remained a victim, but chose to find a way to be grateful and happy with what life has to offer.

It took many years of soul searching and personal development, but eventually I came to feeling blessed for the nearly fifteen years I got to have with my son, and despite the pain of grief, I would do it all again. I'm a happy man again.

Steve Lyddy
60 years old
Mindset Coach
Melbourne, Australia

126
Use Every Breath

J was the full-of-life girl. What I was really doing was building up the tension I carried in me, that I pushed aside. I didn't want to grow up and deal with life, until one day it hit me. I woke up one morning and wasn't the same girl. I was full of strong feelings and an overload of stress I didn't know how to handle. I was over-exhausted and burnt out, isolating myself and attempting to self-diagnose which made life ever-so-daunting.

It lasted for weeks, showing me that something wasn't right. I was fading, and I didn't know what was wrong. I was on this trip alone, thinking it was never going to end. It wasn't: because it changed my life forever. My previous life was dying and birthing a new one. Some call this a life crisis, burnout, or psychosis. I felt like I was slowly suffocating, only to learn that nothing else mattered except breathing; reminding me to use every breath to live a magnificent life.

Isolating yourself from the world just means you're making time to be with yourself. That's the blessing of breakdowns. By going through them, we find what we are missing in ourselves because we gave it away. Still breathing, reminding us that it's never too late to change your life.

Out of all the experiences I've encountered in my life, this memory sticks with me, reminding me to do something with what I experienced, share it with others who relate to it to see the amazing outcome it brings. Obstacles are an opportunity to do something great. Something I can be honestly grateful for. There is always a new beginning with an ending. You will see the light at the end of the tunnel. It's a bright one.

Diana Emma

31 years old

Nutritionist & Yoga Teacher

Toronto, Canada

127
Tyson

*J*nspiration hasn't come back into my life as a sudden bolt of lightning. It has been a gentle reawakening to life, showing me the beauty in all that is around me, the reconnection to my energy form, my spirit, which has taken place ever so slowly over the last seven years. Like climbing a ladder out of a deep dark hole, each rung with its own gifts.

You see, in October 2006 my thirteen-year-old son Tyson was diagnosed with stage four Ewing's Sarcoma, a rare bone cancer that is found in young children and adolescents. I promised myself when I heard his diagnosis that I would either drag him through this kicking and screaming to good health, or I would give him the best death experience I could possibly give. In April 2007, he died in my arms, surrounded by a family that loves him.

For several years after, there was little or no inspiration in my life, the world was dark. I breathed in and out, simply because I was held by a group of people who loved me more than I loved myself. I went to work; pretending to live a life. There was no particular 'dark night of the soul' for me, no pivotal moment where I said, "Now is the time to make changes." I was climbing the ladder, one rung at a time, finding small things to be grateful for on each rung.

It was this decision, to start to look for simple things that sang to my soul that started to transform how I looked at the world. I now see the beauty in all that is around me, and choose to find strength in the gift of Tyson's journey, honouring him and the incredible impact that he had on his world.

Kym Lawn
49 years old
Energy Coach & Trainer
Gladstone, Australia

128
Freedom Arrived

*S*uddenly I was a single mum with three babies under two years of age, feeling lost, angry and alone, and suffering extreme depression. Anxiety had overtaken me; I had burning sensations in my hands and arms. My mind was out of control. I was clinging to life by a thread, scared and under attack, a broken woman with a broken family. My inner voice berated me in daily mantras; I felt abandoned; I was in total reaction to life: full of rage and despair. I felt I had failed at the highest possible level. Life was too painful to bear... I no longer wanted to be here. I felt powerless to change my situation as I fell deeper and deeper into self-loathing, distrust and negative thoughts, buried in chaos, and struggling for air as I faced the daily struggle of caring for my children.

What happened next changed the course of my life. A powerful conversation ignited a huge moment of clarity. I realised that I had a *choice*. It does not matter what circumstances I am faced with, my responsibility is how I *choose* to react. I then set a strong intention for my life, to only respond with love, while allowing my feelings to be felt internally, without judgement.

Every decision, I now ask myself, "Will this action bring peace and joy for all involved?" This question allows me to stop in any moment and get in touch with my feelings and intentions. As I take positive action, everything changes. I feel like I am in the driver's seat of my life for the first time. Just by honouring my feelings and making conscious choices I now feel joyful, my children are peaceful, my relationships have deepened, life flows more easily and my heart has cracked open releasing a deep compassion and love for all. Freedom has finally arrived.

Lucy Phillips
35 years old
Travel Manager & Intuitive Mentor
Adelaide, Australia

129
If You are Not Following Your Heart, Where are You Headed?

*T*he irony and wisdom of this timely whispered question, which popped into my awareness one day, was not lost on me. It was a gentle reminder from my best friend as I stumbled through a lingering inner turmoil. My head had tried in vain to work out my next move. No joy there.

My heart had been 'whispering' to me for some time, but I hadn't paid attention. Thus I had lost my way and a cloud of uneasiness seemed to slow down my natural momentum. My life wasn't as vibrant and vital as I had come to expect. This chasm deeply troubled me. Surely life had more to offer me... and surely I had more to offer to life.

In the spirit of collaboration, I asked my heart how we could serve each other more fully. It replied simply, "Let me lead you..." It offered to lead me to a more deeply connected and expressed life – exactly that which I was missing and seeking. So we made a deal. I ask and listen, and my heart guides me. Now my heart leads and my head follows. In return, my heart has taken on the role of 'life navigator,' 'magical connector' and source of deep peace and comfort. My inner relationship with my *heart intelligence* has led to a deep and profound understanding of myself and what brings me joy, peace and fulfilment.

Perhaps you have been asking yourself similar questions. Maybe you are becoming aware of an inner disquiet...of something not as it could be, of something not yet expressed in your life. It could be that your heart is whispering to you, wanting to get your attention. It may have something of profound importance to tell you. And it's only a heartbeat away. Shhh... listen.

Bill Lee Emery

64 years old

MBIT Coach & Trainer

Gold Coast, Australia

130
Life is an Open Book

*T*ime to look, friends, the Universe is an open book. Have you ever wondered why some people are always happy and smiling? Why do others always seem to get the lucky breaks while the rest seem to do it really hard in life? Well it's time to listen up! You, my friend, are the master of your own destiny. You are the director of your own movie. You are the writer of your own book. You are the creator of your dream life.

With the Internet and new technologies connecting people at the speed of light, there simply are no more excuses for not living the life you dream of. Earth is the most awesome school in our Universe – and you should jump with joy that you were accepted into life. If you are not happy with where you are in life right now, archive that book and start a new one. Create a new chapter right now. You, my friend, are *unlimited* in how many chapters you can create in your new adventure book.

We were born to create or destroy: so stop destroying the awesome magic and gifts you were born with and start sharing them. Make a difference to someone every single day using your gifts. There is only one of you in the multiverse and we need you to start shining right now. Together we are transforming the planet into the dream life that you, me and everyone else is wishing for. But it all starts with you: you need to be that inspiration and light for everyone else. My dream is to watch this kindergarten planet of humans be accepted into the galactic race of universal beings before I leave.

Now that is my dream, folks. What is yours?

Clayton Johnston
43 years old
Internet Entrepreneur
Perth, Australia

131
There Is Always Hope

*J*am renowned for my big happy smile to the outside world. I am taking this opportunity to share a minuscule part of me. It may possibly resonate with you or inspire somebody out there who is going through incredibly difficult times at the moment.

A long time ago (it feels like a lifetime ago now), I had to return to my home country, where I lived for two years in a stressful environment; every waking hour was riddled with anxiety, fear and grief, cold, leaking roof, not an inch to move through the cluttered ramshackle house, and constantly having that 'walking on egg shells' feeling. I thought I would never be free to return to Australia and live my own life ever again. I had no bed to sleep in. I kipped on two sofa cushions on the floor. One night, I scribbled these four inspiring words on a scrap of tissue paper: *"There is Always Hope."* I kept it on the floor where I slept for two years. It gave me something tangible to focus on.

I have recently learned, since discovering yoga, that when you say positive words you are actually setting an intention out to the Universe. It's similar to a prayer (but not religious); you're planting a small seed. It's a glimmer that there is always hope, no matter what. Set your powerful intentions and let the Universe know, otherwise how can it help and answer you?

Now I am back in Australia and exercising through yoga. I find yoga to be a daily inspiration in many dimensions: physically, mentally, spiritually, and emotionally. This has helped me to learn to drop my armour and let go. To be true to yourself. Never quit no matter what; because *there is always hope.*

Rachel Pilgrim
44 years old
Yoga Teacher
Perth, Australia

132
When Being Strong Is Your Only Option

*I*t's frightening when you hear someone you love has cancer. But when it's your mother, the whole world stops. You don't matter anymore, only she does because you're too afraid of losing her. It was February 2009 that doctors diagnosed my mother with Acute Myeloid Leukaemia – a rare form of blood cancer.

You quickly learn how much you can do, as her needs became more important than your own. You refuse leaving her hospital bed, so you don't mind sleeping in the only chair that nurses could spare you. Your family tells you to go home because you haven't slept in days. You oblige, eyes flooded as you leave her behind in hospital. When you return, you pull everything together to replace fear with belief, and sadness with hope, because you knew she'd lost all her hair that day, and chemotherapy had begun taking its toll on her fragile body. You don't know how strong you really are, until being strong is your only option.

Parts of your life that were on pause will one day play again. Following multiple rounds of treatment, my mother's determination and strong will brought her to remission. It was a second chance. We had to endure to learn what we can rise from, and we're not the same people we were five years ago. We're stronger. I am grateful for every new day my mother and I still have together.

You can live without a lot of things, but hope isn't one of them. So, listen to the quiet whisper of your inner strength when it tells you that this is only temporary. There will be many challenges, setbacks and dark days but keep perspective. You've had beautiful days before and they will come again. You will get through this.

Jenny Nguyen
23 years old
Pharmacist
Brisbane, Australia

133
Your Agreement With Life

*B*eauty grows from decayed matter (of fact). My mother only knew how to hurt. The pain she held within, burrowed and borrowed another timeline. That little girl, mighty in her tiny, emphasized "Mama... my heart doesn't want to grow your pain, this world doesn't need more sores." With deep knowing, I no longer pressed 'play.' I no longer pressed 'record.' And with confidence, I opted out of pressing 'repeat.' Instead, I edited the imprint that would otherwise be left right in my consciousness.

What you perceive as silent, in reality, is amplified. That not-so-secret inner-dialogue plays on speakerphone to the entirety of existence. It's not self-talk; it is your agreement with life. It is the nectar that lingers to fuel your ensuing action, reaction and interaction. Life is not only an exemplary listener; it is an agreement facilitator. Agreements are always fulfilled, affirmed by the observable laws of nature, cause and effect. Whether misaligned (pain-inducing) or aligned (joy-inducing), life supports every agreement you make. Science describes these laws well; experience demonstrates them without fail.

"I found a letter on paperless sound; for reading, for feeling, for being light crowned. I danced with a freckle who knew its own place, a forbearingly miniscule void in space. I held onto nothing never so tight, I stood up and am walking, towards my own light."

Mothered by creation, I live the 'now' in truth, deep love and non-resistance. My paintbrush dances in purposeful motion, as my heart endlessly delights in each new unveiling of inspired growth. No amount of decay will ever inhibit your growth capacity, rather the contrary. I invite you to explore your creative reality as empowered children. What will you cultivate and inevitably grow?

Lavida Rose

35 years old

Creative Consciousness Facilitator

New York City, United States of America

134
Letting Go

He sits before me.

Eyes lowered. Unsure, yet determined. Wanting more for his life.

Limited by his beliefs. Proud.

Pain etched on his face, subtle, masked.

Regret for a life half-lived.

Rapport. Trust. A willingness to surrender.

And now we are raw. Now all can be revealed.

I reach out and allow. He gives over. We gently place the past to one side.

Where to now? What if?

Can the greatest of dreams be possible?

Is there another way?

Beyond this. Beyond what has been. Beyond.

Change, real change. The desire compels him forward.

Enticing.

Small, tentative steps, offer reassurance with every forward motion.

Momentum builds. Ambiguity fades. The veil lifts.

Clarity revealed like a flawless gem.

A future. Potent.

Surrender comes. Tears of relief. Joy.

Eyes wide, windowing his soul.

The sense of a new beginning. Real. Authentic. Profound.

Inspiration, self-belief, a conscious knowing – his new companions.

My honour. My privilege.

Gillian Skeer

53 years old

Master Coach, Speaker & Author

Perth, Australia

135
A Search for Meaning

J was born during an air raid at the end of the Second World War. My mother thought I was a good baby, since I hardly ever uttered a sound. Little did she realize that when I arrived into this world, I was filled with terror and couldn't understand how I had landed here: a place of conflict, turmoil and chaos. I began seeking answers to the meaning of life, to the meaning of *my* life and the part I played in the grand scheme of things. The answers did not reveal themselves for years.

With a desire to heal those in pain, I became a medical doctor, discovering the powerful connection between the mind, body and spirit. However, it was not until many years later that I had a profound experience of my heart awakening: not the physical heart but the essence of who I am.

I began the relentless pursuit of trying to understand why my life and the world was the way it was. It became a search for hidden treasure, which I soon discovered was not buried under the ocean or in some spot marked X on a treasure map, but was deep within me. It had been there from the moment I was conceived: I brought it into this world.

I also realized each one of us has a treasure chest of gifts, talents and attributes that make us special and that the world needs to fulfil the purpose of life. My deepest wish for you is that you find your purpose, your treasure chest of unique abilities. You don't have to go anywhere or do anything; you already are all that you could ever wish for. If you listen, your heart will lovingly guide you to lead a meaningful and inspired life.

Dr. Erika Yeates

69 years old

Corporate Strategy Consultant

Sydney, Australia

136
Everything is Possible

*W*hen we come to know the greatness of our whole being and start living from it, we free ourselves from the things we think are holding us hostage.

There is joy in everything. You knew this before you were human, and you will remember this when you discover you are all aspects of your being – human, soul and spirit. Act as one.

Your body is amazing. When you feel unhappy it is telling you that you have lost touch with the voice of your soul. Happiness just is. If it isn't, you knowingly or unknowingly have found a way to block it.

Know that you are meant to feel good, all the time if you want to. Learn to listen to your soul again. Your soul is infinite and forever. Be brave and dare to let it guide you.

It is time to include your heart in your decision-making process. Don't believe the mind's reasoning that the heart makes blind decisions. Through your heart you have access to the part of you that knows all. It communicates with you all the time, and its message is always direct, pure and clear. The only reason people experience a negative outcome is because they are following a distorted translation of their heart's messaging.

Your heart is a gateway to your soul's desires. Seeing with your heart is seeing clearly. Seeing with your heart is seeing from your soul. Your body and mind are your soul's extensions and are necessary to experience physical life. Your soul chose this human existence to experience how it feels to live a life shaped by fear and then to experience the joy that is found when we find ways to move beyond those fears.

Love life and your world will love you.

Herbert Bossaerts
40 years old
Project Manager
Vancouver, Canada

137
The Spirit of Horse

"Show me your horse and I will tell you what you are."

Old English Proverb

I grew up learning life lessons from the herd. Horses are my inspiration. They have been partners with mankind for thousands of years and feature strongly in our collective consciousness. The shamans believe the horse is a message carrier and the carrier of wisdom, associated with myth and magic, representing power, stamina, strength and freedom. We can learn much about ourselves, who we are at the deepest level, what our gifts are and how we can evolve the world, by listening to that ancient collective wisdom.

Horses have many lessons for us. They are social and authentic beings that seek harmony and balance. They have huge hearts, bringing endless love and compassion in relating. They help to heal the soul by guiding us to see new possibilities, along with providing pure, non-judgmental and non-biased feedback.

Horses are innately honest. They don't lie, wear masks or ignore, repress or bury their emotions. Becoming more horse-like means we take the time to stop and tune into the subtle sensations in our body. Horses teach us the importance of communicating with all of our intuitive senses, aligning, integrating and honouring our head, heart and gut intelligence. In doing this, we get the messages underlying our emotions, so that we can respond mindfully and wisely, rather than simply reacting to life.

Perhaps the greatest gift horses bring is the importance of living fully in each moment. They re-connect us to the natural world—an integral part of our being—evolving our awareness, consciousness and sense of deep heart-felt connections to both our internal and external environment. I've saved horses and hence horses have saved me. They've taught me to live my passion, liberating my spirit and guiding me in times of deepest and darkest need.

Cheryl Cruttenden

52 years old

Equine Guided Learning Facilitator

Monbulk, Australia

138
Our Nature Is Love

We are all life, and the attempt to fragment is the challenge that, when taken on, draws us farther from our connectedness from all that is. We are beautiful pieces that come together, each with our unique and special gifts, yet if we attempt to place ourselves into a box, we miss the point of life, which is unity. We are ever expanding beings and our world is expansive beyond comprehension. We are the microcosm of the macrocosm. The duality of life is within us, which is why at any given moment, we can be open loving light, or closed down fear creatures.

Our journey is to explore all of it and come to love, because it all ultimately comes from a good place, and that is love. Even someone who hurts another, at some level, however deep, the act of hurt comes from a desire for love that went awry in our very human world. We are to love anyway. Yes, this can be hard to do, especially when we feel wounded. Honour yourself and those feelings. Then, when you're ready, move back to a place of love. That is the space of our truth. Our nature is indeed love.

There is no need to compete, to harm, to dwell. Just love and keep moving. Or, stand still if the moment grabs hold of you. Breathe. Feel the flow of life beneath your feet. Let it permeate your gorgeous healthy cells. And as it fills your heart, notice how your heart's tickled pink to have so many joyful opportunities to love and be loved. Focus on what *you* want to give and share with the world. Then create around that in a way that sustains continued giving. Find out what's meaningful to someone, and help them with its development. This exchange contributes to global sensitivity and unity.

Trina Gauri
41 years old
Human Experientialist
Toronto, Canada

139
Pressure to Prevail

*M*y ten-year-old daughter, Nicola, was quietly crying as she lay in bed trying to go to sleep. She was worried about school because she was struggling with some of the difficult work in class. I told her she was lucky; luckier than other kids. She looked at me confused.

I told her how her mum, who has been sick for over ten years with mercury poisoning, had studied healing, nutrition and used herself as a human guinea pig to help her body heal from the damage. She would ask, "Why is this happening to me?" when she felt weak, and continue to fight to help her body heal. Then her dad was diagnosed with cancer. I explained to Nicola: "If Mum wasn't sick, she would have been no help to Poppa. Because she is now an expert in disease prevention, she knows what to do."

I talked about how we lost a lot of money in a business, along with our house and car, which drove me to turn to mining: a huge transformation professionally. I told her stories about famous people that have suffered life-changing traumas then went onto make a differences to people's lives. She started to smile and understand that she has to work through some hardship now, which will make these challenges easier later in life. With an almost determined look in her eye and a grin on her face, she peacefully went to sleep.

My daughter was born with a very different heart from most. She has been through two major heart surgeries and is doing well. My vision in life is to help people unlock their true potential and use their difficult times to leverage them to a truly rewarding future.

Jason Ryan
36 years old
Entrepreneur
Whyalla, Australia

140
Dear Mum and Dad

J wanted to thank you for the decision you made when my sister Brenda was a baby. You raised her at home, even though society said people with disabilities should be locked away in institutions. This one choice you made, without hesitation, had a positive effect, not only on us as a family, but on our extended family and community.

At school, I felt isolated as I was teased for many years. However, at home we were four girls who laughed, played and fought like any other normal family. I felt nurtured and loved Brenda like my other sisters. Mum, I watched you persevere when others said it was too hard and saw that your devotion endured any judgement.

Thank you Mum and Dad for sending me to health camp for eight weeks when I was eight years old. No one knew my history, so I wasn't teased. Although I was very insecure and shy, I had an opportunity to allow the essence of who I am to shine brightly. I had an opportunity to learn without judgement and felt I could really breathe freely. This gave me hope for a bright future.

Brenda taught me perseverance, courage and the compassion to accept people for who they are. It has stayed with me as an asset to my ongoing career. When Brenda died in August 2012, I saw all the hearts she touched in our community, heard their stories and felt their loss for this beautiful woman – my sister. The splendour of her spirit stays with us, even though the beauty of her heart has left us and returned to God.

So, thank you Mum and Dad. I feel so blessed for the gift of my sister Brenda.

Your loving daughter, Angie.

Angie Johnston
42 years old
Coach, Trainer & Author
Toowoomba, Australia

141
Life Can Change in an Instant

J had it all: gorgeous wife, two adorable children, five bedroom house with a pool, spa, sauna, an expanding business and a lifestyle to die for. What could go wrong? Well, life can and does change in an instant. I don't mean slight bumps. I mean life-altering single or sequence of events. Mine hit me from 1998- 2013.

1998: Sitting at the traffic lights all calm, a car behind me stops. We wait. Lights turn green. We move forward 100 metres. Tyres screech for what seemed like an eternity. Bang! I am thrown forward in my seat. I immediately feel the pain in my lower back, as if someone has hit me with a sledgehammer. It took me three years to manage the ongoing pain and to get back anywhere close to where I previously was physically and financially, but I did it.

2007: Firmly established again, enjoying life with our children, my soul mate was diagnosed with terminal cancer and given three months to live. Previous life challenges paled into insignificance compared to losing my soul mate. The grief, financial stress and ongoing health challenges brought me to my knees. I was admitted to hospital suffering major depression, complete nervous exhaustion, and I lost my family home, income and self-esteem.

2013: G'day, as the sun streams through the window on another beautiful sunny morning in Perth, Western Australia, I begin the first day of a self-imposed two-year challenge to create jobs and opportunity in the local community. You see, despite all the heartache and challenges, there is always *free will*, and combined with the flicker of *hope*, they can be a catalyst for restoring your *why* and making the continued journey of success a legacy for all of your loved ones both here and on the other side.

Al Connolly
53 years old
Whealthpreneur
Perth, Australia

142
My Anxiety Tree

*I*rrational fears, sudden panic, lost concentration, and pounding heart triggered by unknown causes. Dramatic and ridiculous! Or so I thought until one day I found myself scared to death to go outside, sickened by images on T.V., and unable to make decisions. I couldn't eat more than five bites or sleep more than an hour; and driving my car caused physical trembling. Every thought was another monster that filled me with fear. What had happened?

Feeding my fears, I had developed symptoms that became anxiety. It grew out of control. I decided each fear was a leaf on my anxiety tree. I traced the branches to the root. My fear of television came from my fear of doctor shows which came from my fear of illness that stemmed from my fear of death that triggered my fear of driving that started with my fear of losing my daughter to a drug overdose. There, we have it. The root was found. It was all based on a night she came home from the hospital after an actual overdose. I fed that seed until it grew into a giant anxiety tree that ruled my life. Once I knew my root fear, I looked for the hidden blessings.

Still afraid to let go for fear of what might replace it, I realized this was a test of faith. Facing the risk, I cut the branch. Instead of falling, I was elevated. Blessing! I found that ninety-nine percent of my worries were never realized because I had avoided them. Blessing! I could advance forward after having first failed. Blessing! Clarity was obtained after confusion. Blessing! Baby steps created the anxiety and baby steps diminished it. Blessing! I began to look at what I was grateful for daily. Blessing! I gained compassion for others. Blessing! I reclaimed my life. Blessing!

Stephanie Fleishman
48 years old
Artist & Ezechiel Method Trainer
Dallas, United States of America

143
The 8-Trak To My Life

*J*ntravenous opiate drug use is one of the hardest addictions to overcome. It affects everything. I'm here to tell you that you can still love life even after an opiate drug addiction.

Having used since thirteen, I made attempts to stop. Physical withdrawal was followed by overwhelming emotions. Guilt ruled my thoughts, which drove me back. I had lost time, did things I never wanted, and acknowledged hurting those who loved me most. It was overwhelming. I lost a fiancé, my best friend, mom, brother, dog, friends, home, health, education, teeth, hair, possessions, morals, sanity, confidence, trust, respect, spirituality, God, everything. I felt I knew nothing and my life meant nothing. Even death was meaningless.

Out of pure desperation, I sought to redefine life. Starting with the colour blue, I recreated life as I would love it to be. I created a vision so fantastic that I found myself laughing out loud. I delved as deep into this new fantasy as I had been lost in the drug fantasy. When I created this mental balance, time and space disappeared and my heart opened. I no longer needed motivation from outside. I received inspiration and direction from within. My heart guided me to teach, travel, and share my love helping other young people globally. Details poured in clearly. I found who and what I was meant to be, do, and have. My fantasies had morphed into a new reality of inspired thoughts and goals. In that moment, my guilt and desire to use drugs was no longer perceivable.

That was two years ago. Feelings and memories of my past are altered with each day I live this new life. I appreciate colour, flowers, birds in flight, children laughing. I've been reborn to a world alive with clarity and love.

Cassandra Shrader

24 years old

Student

Dallas, United States of America

144
Let's Chant

*A*t four years old, I awoke to a voice inside saying, "What if there was nothing?" As an adult, it changed to, "Who am I, and where am I going?" My life felt like a continuous soap opera I couldn't escape like the movie *The Truman Show*. I knew I was a seeker but I didn't know what I was seeking. My wake-up call came through years of severe bullying at school. Bullying had a traumatic impact on my well-being. In my teens and twenties I turned to drugs and alcohol to relieve unbearable low self-esteem.

Then, I was a professional actor in a West End musical. I played a Victorian drug addict and opium seller. I sang her songs *The Wages of Sin* and *The Garden Path to Hell*. The lyrics resonated with my own dark and hedonistic existence. A cast member followed a spiritual path where 'chanting' was a main practice. I was drawn to her energy, and by grace I too began to chant, which led to a life-changing 'Kundalini awakening' or 'spiritual emergence.' I experienced the bliss of oneness in an urban park. I cried tears of joy at being alive and feeling at one with strangers. I knew in my bones this was the real deal.

Days later, I had a vision. I felt this immense vibration expanding inside. A shimmering radiant being appeared in translucent blue with ebony shiny hair and blue eyes. The being spoke with deep compassion: "Nikki... all there is, *is love*. This love is the purpose of your existence!" My spiritual questions were finally answered. I have since been clean and sober for twenty-five years. I will always remember the blue being. Let's chant!

Nikki Slade
52 years old
Chanting Leader & Author
London, United Kingdom

145
Inspiration Through Self-Love

*A*fter a tumultuous childhood and early adult life marked by health problems, surgeries, heartbreak and a futile search for self-worth in external circumstances, I began to understand that the source of all this was my lack of self-love. It led me down many dark paths of judgement, as I often deemed myself 'incomplete.'

Socrates said: *"The unexamined life is not worth living."*

Taking responsibility for everything I have created in my life has led to profound self-healing. I have learned to tap into my intuition and inner wisdom. I would describe this as a place of self-love, the place I come to when I let go. When I release my ego's falsehood of who I am or ought to be, I surrender to the truth. Through self-forgiveness, I have been able to let go of fear and false perceptions. I have been blessed with inspirational people around me, including my best friend and my sister, who have supported me every step of the way.

My spiritual exploration has made me realise that when we love ourselves we love the world. My self-healing journey has guided me to the best in ancient and modern wisdom in the fields of natural medicine, environmental activism, mindfulness and conscious living. As our world is starting to change and breathtaking transformations are being created globally in the fabric of many societies, I have felt the need to respond to the call of our planet.

I consider myself very fortunate to be able to connect with my purpose in life and take a stand for the change in the world by taking inspired action. Feeling inspired is the first step. We all need to move to a more profound level of our humanity by awakening the intelligence of our hearts.

Bianca Madison-Vuleta

39 years old

Health Coach & Environmentalist

London, United Kingdom

146
Life is a Mystery – Unfolding: There are No Mistakes

*T*he people and events we encounter in life are for our higher purpose, but we have to be consciously aware to receive the wisdom of the experience. In 2011, my career as a teacher was taking me in a different direction I was powerless to stop. I didn't know where, what or how this change of direction would occur, but deep in my heart I knew it would happen. An experience in 2012 left me feeling unappreciated, frustrated and angry. But instead of remaining in that state, I asked the question, "What is the higher purpose of this experience?" My intuition said, "It is time to leave teaching; your talent and skills are required elsewhere."

The year 2013 proved to be a profound experience. By the end of the year, I realised I couldn't teach anymore. I also realised I had no control over my life except for my thoughts, the actions I took and my interpretation of life's experiences. As I changed my career, I discovered:

1. Let go of control: the more you try to control things, the less control you have.
2. Surrender: the more you surrender and allow life to naturally unfold, the more peace you find.
3. Accept: that the people you meet and events you experience are for your higher purpose.
4. Be open: By being consciously aware of your life's experiences, life unfolds in ways you never expected.
5. Receive: In a state of gratitude, you are open to receive the riches and messages the Universe has to offer.

Rumi's words are so appropriate here: *"The grapes of my body can only become wine after the wine maker tramples me. You can deny me if you want, you have every excuse, but it is I who am the Master of this work."*

Leon Beaton

59 years old

Spiritual Teacher & Mentor

Koroit, Australia

147
Every Body is Beautiful

I learned when I was a tiny child that there was something very wrong with how my body looked. I was a healthy, happy, but really skinny kid. I learned that other people could talk about my body, say anything they wanted to, and my objections meant I was "too sensitive." I learned that my opinion about my body didn't matter and that I should compare my body to other women. It was like a secret language and life of women; striving to have *her* body is what women do.

I learned that some food was 'good' for making women thin and some food was 'bad,' that calories, fat content and carbs were far more important than how my body felt eating diet foods. The mantle of 'good' from being thin was everything. I learned that weighing my body daily was a priceless virtue, second only to wearing clothing that had a single-digit label inside.

I learned that women only reach their full adult growth around age twenty-two, long after I'd drowned in depression about my double-digit clothing size and a number on the scale that seemed beyond my ability to control. I started to wonder. I learned that pushing myself for 'the burn' for hours every single day and counting every single calorie that passed my lips was disordered behaviour. I never knew that. I thought it was normal. I wondered some more.

I learned that my body, like yours, is awesome. It can make perfectly-formed whole humans beings. It can heal itself from debilitating illness and devastating injury. It is beautiful. I learned, slowly but steadily, that I could give myself permission to treat myself like my own best friend, and relish life in double-digit clothing and without knowing my weight. It took forty years.

I learned I'm worth it.

Sandra Ross
52 years old
Spiritual Counsellor
Brisbane, Australia

148
The Visit

*I*t was spring of 1993 when I got my first visit. I was fifteen and having a tumultuous time trying to make sense of it all when an inquisitive voice from deep within surfaced and started pulling my life into pieces. It was my own soul's voice, and it wanted me to start making meaning of what was worth valuing and loving. The process of deconstruction I was put through ended up leaving me exhausted and quite vulnerable. What was worse, I was not getting any answers. It was slowly killing me on the inside.

Fast forwarding fifteen years, and following the end of an intense work stint in the psychiatric wards of a London hospital, I entered a dark depression again. It was at that time that I had the same visitation yet again, picking up from where we had left off, and I got to be asked yet again: *"Why in life is worth living for?"*

It was then that I started looking deeper into my experience, and I finally realized the significant truth that depression held about life. And that truth was: It's hard to try and carry life forward on our own. And it's because we're trying so hard to do so, that we end up depleted and disconnected from one another and ourselves.

Life is one of unity and connection. We simply need to allow and trust source/ God, as well as each other, to help carry us forward. We don't have to do it alone. Since realizing the truth about my depression, my life has transformed. Nothing has felt unmanageable since. I feel immensely grateful for life: for work that gives me joy, for true friends and a beautiful son. I'm grateful to my soul for being my greatest and wisest guide.

Samaya Adelin
36 years old
Spiritual Counsellor
East Sussex, England

149
Healing Designs

Whenever I'm in need of inspiration, I take myself out into nature. There is a beauty, harmony and flow that I haven't found anywhere else. Nothing in nature is pushed or forced. Each season happens effortlessly by letting the previous one go, without resistance. Have you ever given a flower your full attention? *Really* looked at it like, like you were seeing it for the very first time? Looking deeply at the colour, the shape, the proportion, texture, and really smell it? I believe nature's rhythm and geometric patterns harmonise our body and mind to bring us back in tune with who we really are. As William Blake says:

"To see a World in a Grain of Sand

And a Heaven in a Wild Flower,

Hold Infinity in the palm of your hand

And Eternity in an hour."

Water has a deeply healing effect on me. I can look at the reflections in water for hours on end. The colours, patterns, movement and sound, all working in harmony deliver an enchanting and mesmerising show. Most of the time, this natural awe-inspiring beauty goes completely unnoticed in the busyness of our day. Whenever I stop and look at a flower that I am passing, I cannot help but be amazed, inspired and moved by its perfection and beauty. And somehow, feel more connected to myself.

No pushing, no pulling, no wanting, no needing; just being fully present in the now. This is the lesson I have learned in nature and that I call 'healing designs.' Beauty is all around us all of the time, all we need to do is open our eyes and let it in so it can inspire and reconnect us to ourselves. Take yourself out there and who knows what mystery you will uncover.

Marianne Hartley

44 years old

Branding Designer

London, United Kingdom

150
From Stress to Inspiration, Vision and Mission

I was bankrupt in 2007 and grieving over the sudden loss of my mother when stress knocked my health backwards and I ended up experiencing all manner of unpleasant symptoms. My stomach felt like it was on fire, no sex drive, flat energy levels, roller coaster moods, poor quality sleep and awful dandruff. Then came the inspiration!

I contacted a doctor who'd been practicing 'functional medicine' for many years. He sent me some lab testing kits that told me I had a stomach infection called *H. pylori, Candida* and intestinal parasites. My hormones were way out of balance. When I removed the bad bugs and rebalanced my hormones using a one-hundred percent natural approach, nearly all my symptoms melted away inside ninety days.

I was truly inspired by my outcome. It was a life-changing experience that enabled me to once again live my life free from the confusion, fear and anxiety I'd experienced over the previous three years. My self-confidence began to return, and people noticed a sparkle in my eyes. I asked myself how many people around the world were also suffering and could benefit from improving their health the way I had. I also began to wonder why all this had happened and what the deeper meaning was behind it as I had experienced such a profound transformation in my body and life.

Inspiration often emerges from strange places and has a habit of appearing when one expects it least. When I was bankrupt, grieving heavily and feeling depressed and unhealthy, I could never have dreamed such a surge of inspiration might emerge and expand so rapidly. So, no matter where you are or how you feel right now, please know that true inspiration is just around the corner.

David Hompes
39 years old
Functional Medicine Expert
London, United Kingdom

151
Creating a Ripple Effect

*L*ike me, many of us have grown up with some form of sexual trauma and low self-esteem. Feelings of shame, fear, and isolation were common. These feelings were mostly due to a variety of reasons but the two main ones for me were religious and personal. I grew up needing desperately the security of knowing that my parents were good, trustworthy people who would protect, and nurture me. Not being protected by my parents left me believing that I'm not good enough, I felt abandoned by them and in turn how can I believe a partner, or anyone could love me?

The belief system that I created was, that relationships were fake. However, I was fortunate to marry a kind man who became a great father, but sexual activity was a major issue. I had shut myself down physically, emotionally and spiritually. I was a prisoner within myself. When I became a mum, I realized I had to change my thoughts about intimacy. I found that thinking negatively about sex had become a habit and it was a very strong barrier to creating safety and intimacy in my relationship.

My 20-year relationship with my husband ended and personal development work followed. What I had was a lack of understanding of my own body and issues accepting pure love without conditions on it. I now support people in becoming free of what holds them back and help them heal. My mission is to teach and inspire people to live with an open heart and create a ripple effect. The energy that we create is amazing. If we love ourselves then we become responsible for our being.

> *"Loving ourselves through the process of owning our own story is the bravest thing we'll ever do."*
>
> **Brene Brown**

Debbie Barker

41 years old

Ka Huna Bodyworker

Toowoomba, Australia

152
Remembering

*T*o my dearest Ray,

You have been gone over four years now. While the pain of emptiness has faded a little, I still feel your echo in my life. I need to thank you for being in my life, for the nineteen years of friendship, companionship and the intimacy we shared. There is no one on this planet that is as unique as you were.

Your passion for music still lingers in my heart, mind and soul. You were my biggest teacher of unconditional love, patience, cooperation and trust. Sharing the journey with you was to expect the unexpected. Your love for life was an inspiration to all of those you touched with your presence. You showed resilience, persistence and flexibility through the many health crises and trials you endured. Your sense of humour and your worldly vision was creative and benevolent.

As the seasons change and with each breath I take, I become more of myself just as you would have wanted me to. While the journey has not always been easy without you, I have learned to stand in the truth of living life from within my heart, just as you once did. Integrity was your motivator and truth was the creed you lived by.

The feeling of being lost and broken by grief through your loss has made me aware of my own vulnerability and impermanence. I am especially grateful for the support of my wonderful sister who understands the process of grief through the death of her own partner. My learning journey is continuous. I can only expand and express the essence of my being more fully. That is the knowing and integrity that you have instilled within me.

With my whole heart, thank you for sharing your life with me.

Maryika Welter

57 years old

Artist

Toowoomba, Australia

153
Held At Gun Point

While visiting relatives in Africa, we were tourists. We were reversing out of their garage in Parktown, Johannesburg without a plan when BAM! We were set upon by two men wearing balaclavas and wielding guns. Time stood still. I clearly remember my mother-in-law saying, "Oh yeah, I forgot to tell you what *not* to do if this happened."

The gunman was at my door. He shoved the revolver at my head. I was thinking, *What do I do?* Panic immediately followed. Grabbing my phone, I threw my handbag on the ground outside the car. He went for the handbag. Attempting to get out of the car, I was upright and ready to run. I felt his guns in my ribs. I froze. He grabbed my left hand that clutched my iPhone, gesturing for me to give it up. Stupidly, I challenged him. Bad move. He hit me. The phone flung violently away.

Fearing for my life, adrenalin kicked in. I bolted and hid in the garden. The gunmen escaped with the car and our belongings. PTSD immediately set in. I was a mess. Posting my ordeal online Facebook, Deborah Cooper suggested visiting The Demartini Institute for help. Driving to Sandton, I was a nervous wreck with horror stories and flashbacks mulling in my head. Stopping at traffic lights was torturous. Consulting with Clarissa Judd forever changed my perception of that event.

In Africa, an IPhone can feed a family for two years and provide a child annual education. Carjacking, holding people hostage, and robbery is a way of life: a simple business transaction, an act of survival, no different to mine and how I do business. It was simply in a different form! Inspiring me from that day forward, I now share with others the simple truth that if you fill your day with a plan, the Universe will!

Kellie Stewart

45 years old

Equinologist

Bakers Hill, Australia

154
Forgiveness is Empowering

J had a perfect childhood in the 60s: good parents, scouts, nature, lots of friends. Or so it seemed. But there were those moments in my adult life when I would cringe in front of an angry male. Cringe, cry, and disappear inside: completely disempowered. After divorce, job-loss, and a move, I went on a journey – to find myself. To find my power.

I discovered there were some dark grey scenes in the pink movie of my childhood. Grey, as in punishments; dark grey as in violence. Physical. Psychological. So I got angry – boy, did I get angry at those horrid parents. In anger I found power... but, I still cringed in front of a noisy boss. I had not made peace with my life´s story. People advised me to forgive them, for they knew not what they did. "Yes, they did," said a part of me. I could not 'simply forgive,' even though part of me understood: forgiveness is needed to heal.

I attended a shamanic weekend; early rise was at 5:00 a.m. It was a cold, misty morning. Birds chirped in the forest. There was magic: we passed, one at a time, through small crevices, really close to Mother Earth. The final passage led through a narrow opening into a little cave, barely high enough to sit, barely long enough to stretch out. I lay on a bed of dried leaves, comfortable, like a mother´s womb. There it struck me: I am whole.

I am who I am today, because of my path. And today, I am whole.

Yes, it happened. I know my story, I know how I came to be here. It is like reading a book: you know its content, you put it back on the shelf – and go on with your life, empowered and aware.

Wiebke Hansen
50 years old
Speaker, Healer & Coach
Munich, Germany

Igniting Your Love Intelligence

What is love to me?

- ♥ It's the feeling when your lover looks into your eyes and sees your pain, and gives you the most heart-warming smile.
- ♥ It's the feel of a child's hand on your cheek when they try to get your attention.
- ♥ It's the worrying phone call from your parents when you haven't called.
- ♥ It's what you feel when you see an elderly couple holding hands.
- ♥ It's a phone call from your bestie when they know you've had a tough day.
- ♥ It's a warm pie that your in-laws drop in when you're sick.
- ♥ It's the invite to the wedding of an old friend who you haven't seen in years.
- ♥ It's the snuggle on the couch with your pet when they just won't leave your side.
- ♥ It's the look you give yourself in the mirror when you are feeling good about yourself.
- ♥ It's waking up to the whole family bouncing on your bed.

My personal commitment to love started as a little girl. I wanted to know what it was like to have someone who truly loved me for who I was. Growing up for me was a challenge. As a youngster in my home, I was exposed to alcohol, drugs and violence. I always wanted to be the centre of attention in my parent's world, but it was not to be. After years of grappling with the desire to be loved, I became a mother myself, as well as a lover, a daughter, a sister and many other important roles. I have been so blessed to truly know what love feels like in my way. And I have fallen in love with... *love!* They do say that love makes the world go round – I say love makes the world!

What is love to you?

Jacque Opie
42 years old
Entrepreneur
Warradale, Australia

156
I Think I Can

*H*ave you ever questioned your own ability, whether it be sport, skill, hobby or a promotion? I certainly have. I know how frustrating this can be — aching so badly to achieve something and yet that little (or not so little) voice inside doesn't believe in you. Well, no more limitations. If I can overcome it, so can you! I'll share with you my favourite analogy that I relate to whenever tempted to give up. Find your own true inner grit!

For years, I was an avid cycle tourist, venturing off with fully loaded bicycle, self-sufficient with clothes, tent, stove and cooking gear loaded into front and rear panniers. As you can imagine, this was no light load. In every Australian state and in New Zealand, there were gruelling hills to climb. At first they stressed me out — until I had a change of perspective that enabled me to enjoy the other delights associated with this kind of touring.

It began one day with a mantra to distract myself from sore and tired muscles: *I think I can, I think I can...I know I can...*until successfully reaching the top. Once realization hit that climbing hills gave rewards of magical views whilst taking a breather, this became the carrot for long arduous rides. Eventually I adopted a positive attitude about hills no matter what the gradient.

Life's challenges are like pushing pedals uphill one slow stroke at a time. When you reach the top (the goal), take a rest and admire the view (fruits of your labour). Coast downhill before you reach the next challenge, gaining strength with each one. The life obstacles I've experienced have helped me become a much wiser, more balanced person. Don't give up: keep persisting and work towards achieving your dreams. Discover the amazing soul you really are.

Gael Nicholson
56 years old
Mind, Body Wellness Coach
Brisbane, Australia

157
My Lie

*I*n my early twenties, I felt out of love with my dad, often listening for his appreciation and seeking words of approval. I had a restless nature and was not comfortable in my own skin, often finding self-destructive ways to deal with the bad vibe.

One drunken night, I told him that I had been diagnosed with HIV. The morning after reassuring him that it was true, he cried and held me in his arms... I felt terrible, since it was all a lie to make him express his love! To make it believable, I told my mother. "I'm not surprised!" was her reply, and insisted that I get tested again. At a party, I told close friends and my ex-girlfriend, suggesting she should get tested. At the new HIV test, to convince the doctor, I made-up a story about how I had been tested!

After the results came back negative, I insisted that it all had been true and the hospital explained it with a possible lab fault. The following decade, my family relationships fell apart. The self-contempt was growing inside me like a cancer, every passing year made it harder to come true, to confess! The intensity and consequences of my self-destructive behaviours increased, leaving in its wake abused friendships and an ugly divorce.

Age twenty-nine, after my third drug overdose, I left Sweden, friends and family, cleaned up and started fresh. I travelled the world, making friends with incredible people who finally helped me hold myself accountable. Ten years after lying to my parents, I told the truth. It was amongst the scariest moments of my life! My dad embraced me without any resentment. The moral of this story is best summed up by my mothers' reaction: "We all lie, Magnus!" Confess your lies and live today!

Kram Magnus Robinson-Wolrath

46 years old

R.M. Therapist & Spiritual Surgeon

Brisbane, Australia

158
When the Gift in the Challenge is Revealed

J grew up in a typical English family, the youngest of 5 siblings. I expected to get married in my early twenties, have kids and settle close by, hopefully with a good job. All of that changed one evening when I was 16. My parents announced a sudden divorce. It was my first day of college, I knew no-one and all my siblings had fled the nest. I turned to my boyfriend, Mr. Right, who was going to be my saviour.

Abuse can creep up on you like a stealth bomber. For me, it started with him ridiculing my friends and family so that I withdrew, then followed the emotional putdowns so that I would feel grateful to have him in my life. The physical beatings came later and, though excruciatingly painful, it was the emotional scars that cut the deepest and took the longest to heal.

I reached a point where I knew I had to leave and I made the bravest decision of my life. At 20 I moved to another country to make a new start. That country was the Netherlands.

Fast forward to 2012, thirty years later. I am living in Australia, reflecting on my life so far and I've come to an inspirational realisation that resulted in my being so very grateful for what happened to me.

Had I not been abused I would not have fled to Holland and learned the language. Had I not become fluent in Dutch I wouldn't have secured the corporate job that provided me with a stellar career. Had I not had this career I would not be living my vision as I am today.

I waited 47 years for the real Mr. Right, marrying in 2009 and it was worth every minute.

Clare Edwards
52 years old
Speaker, Author & Coach
Sunshine Coast, Australia

159
The Rock

A terrible car accident transformed my sister's life and the lives of all those people who were close to her. After that, I understood I had been taking many things for granted, and that if you can't change something, you have to accept it. We all have one thing in common: we don't have control over our lives. Even if you know where you want to go, you may end up somewhere else. I always remember my father's toast during my sister's fifteenth birthday party. At the end of his beautiful toast, he recited a beautiful poem I'd love you to have. It was a very special moment in my life, and this poem has been always in me, helping me to make big choices in life. He said:

Piu avanti!
Do not give up, even defeated,
Do not feel a slave, even enslaved;
Trembling with fright, think yourself brave,
And assault fiercely, when badly hurt.
Have the tenacity of the rusted nail
That old and ruined, is nail again;
Not the coward stupidity of the turkey
That shrinks its feathers at the first noise.
Do like God who never cries;
Or like Lucifer, who never prays;
Or like the oak grove, that in its greatness
Needs water but does not plea...
May it bite and clamor vengeful,
Rolling in the dust, your head!

The author of this poem was a very humble schoolteacher from a little Argentinian town. His nickname was "Alma Fuerte" which means "strong soul." All expectations, all pride, all fear of embarrassment of failure, these things just fall away in the face of death, leaving only what is truly important.

Alexander Salcedo

33 years old

Business Strategy Consultant

Melbourne, Australia

160
Love Yourself!

*D*o you ever beat yourself up or judge yourself harshly? I spent a lot of my life doing this and now discovered it's actually not arrogant or conceited to love yourself. Self-love and self-belief are essential for true happiness and success. For many years, I drifted along aimlessly and it wasn't until I actually gave myself permission to work out what I wanted that I was able to get it. I needed to forgive myself for all the things I did wrong or badly which became easier when I realised there is no right or wrong, we just label things that way.

What I really want to say to you is: you can be, do and have what you want! Especially if you make the decision to create a habit of practicing self-love. There are plenty of ways to 'Love Yourself' including the reminders you might like to play with below. Remember, even though self-love is an inside job, it's a great idea to ask for help. So, go on – Love Yourself some more every day!

Let go of judgement of yourself and others.
Observe your feelings, allow them to guide you.
View yourself through complimentary loving eyes.
Everything about you is okay (no matter what you have or haven't done).

You truly are a magnificent miracle.
Only you can be responsible for your happiness.
Utilise your gifts and discover your personal value.
Regularly nurture yourself with self-love habits.
Stop comparing yourself to others and telling stories that don't feel good.
Every moment you can choose a fresh thought to make you feel better.
Listen to your heart; it always gives you the best answer.
Follow your intuition and inner guidance, it is always right.

Deb King
41 years old
Happiness Ambassador
Sydney, Australia

161
The Quake of Transformation

*H*ave you ever experienced a quake of awakening in your soul, so electrifying that it shook every atom of your being?

It was 2010. I was a new graduate chiropractor volunteering in the Philippines when news of the Haitian earthquake that claimed over 300,000 lives took over world media. Next thing I knew, I was on a plane from Sydney to Port-Au-Prince, feeling out of my depth yet determined to serve in what was to be a life-changing journey that lay before me.

Port-Au-Prince was completely in ruins. The air was filled with tragedy and suffering, yet one could also sense glimmers of hope amidst the chaos. I was the only chiropractor amongst a group of dedicated medical personnel. Together, we tended to patients in a makeshift hospital equipped with basic donated medical supplies. There were at least three deaths in the hospital every day. Internal trauma, breaks and fractures, spinal cord injuries and encephalitis were common. Adults and children underwent amputations almost daily. My heart shattered many times over.

I remember adjusting a young girl who was bed-ridden. She never smiled or spoke to me. I worked with her daily. One morning, as her mobility was improving, she looked at me and quietly said, "I love you." My heart lifted. Within a week, we all witnessed her walk out of the hospital on crutches, smiling for the first time in months. I want to thank this brave girl and the people of Haiti who were my source of inspiration. In every heartbreak there is an opportunity for us to access a vortex of infinite love to bridge the gap of each other's weaknesses and differences, to better help humanity. And perhaps in the process, we can rediscover our own humaneness in this beautiful journey that is life.

Dr. Alice Nguyen

30 years old

Chiropractor, Humanitarian, Yogi

Sydney, Australia

162
Your Health is Your Inspiration

*S*truggling with my weight from the time I was young meant I was ripe for teasing. My peers were full of taunts about me being fat and ugly, and I believed them. With low self-esteem and no self-worth, I became a people pleaser and yearned to be liked by everyone. Who was I? I didn't know. I spent so much time focusing on my weight, and the ugliness I saw in the mirror, I lost sight of the woman I hoped I would turn out to be.

Diet after diet, failure after failure, I came to the conclusion that I would never be a model, nor would I become that woman I always looked up to with the perfect body. I couldn't become her because I was placing me in someone else – a better body, a prettier face. After a bad relationship and realizing I put so much energy into loving someone that didn't respect me, it dawned on me I had a lack of respect for myself.

Carefully, I stitched together the broken pieces of myself and learned to love every single part of who I am. I now believe and see my beauty on the inside and out. I discovered that my health is my inspiration and focus – not a perfect body. When I became in-tune with my body and listened with intent to what it had to say, I heard this:

Forget dieting. Fuel and energise me with a nutritious balanced diet. Working together, we have the power to achieve a healthy weight and maintain a healthy body. Speak tender kind words to me that are positive and full of love, focus on my beauty, not my faults. Most of all, love and embrace me for all that I am, right now.

Your Health is Your Inspiration.

Louise Ginglo
41 years old
Author & Weight Loss Consultant
Central Coast, Australia

163
The Three Questions

*L*ooking at my own life with all the experiences I had, good and bad, I realized: all experiences teach us something. So I used my own life to educate myself with these three simple questions:

Why do good people suffer?

I longed to understand the suffering and pain I saw in my life and in the world, until I was humbled to understand that we all have moments in our lives that shape us. It is how we perceive these moments that build character: My greatest challenges and sufferings made me who I am today.

Who is making the rules?

By accepting academic and religious authorities, I created a lot of false ideas and beliefs in my life, but this also created opportunities for growth in my life. They helped me to take ownership of my own life and to build my own philosophies. I discovered my life is far too precious to let an outside authority decide if I am a genius and how I should live my life. I learned to be attached to nothing and open to everything.

Why am I here?

I would have gone the end of the world to discover this answer, because a life of just existing is not worth living to me. It took me twenty-six years of blood, sweat and tears to discover that every moment of my life reveals my purpose. I was fanatic at finding my mission, in such a sense that I was missing my life that was already happening. The difficult part is not discovering your gift — it is rather to own up to your unique gift and to give yourself permission to go share it with the world. You don't have to find anything. You are *already* it. May you have the courage to know the truth, patience to accept the truth, and the wisdom to live your truth.

Emile van Biljon

29 years old

Life-Style Entrepreneur

Cape Town, South Africa

164
Important Life Lessons to Date

J have to start with the most important lesson I have ever learned. It is: I am responsible for everything I do, say, think and feel, and this is my power (thank you, Mum). With this power, I am able to be aware of how I live my life and take in learnings from lessons given to me through stories from books, movies, music, and especially, conversations with elders who have come into my life and taught me to always be awesome. Some important lessons I learned by stumbling into the abyss where challenges were thrown at me. Eventually, they turned from misery to enlightenment in the end and others just came drifting into my mind...

I am alive! What has happened, has happened (move on).
Forgive rather than fight back. Live in the moment.
Act on your gut feeling, not on hours of calculating all possibilities.
Playing small only lets down the world and I.
There's always a reason to smile and be happy.
I'm perfect to be imperfect.
To speak my mind is like singing aloud on a bus.
An ocean isn't an ocean without every drop of water.
Like a drop in the ocean you could change the world.
Live as I want others to live.
To accept losing means knowing I can do better.
I can beneficially impact a person's day every day.
I'm alive to learn from mistakes, not victories.
Nothing is lost, everything will always exist. Expect the unexpected.
Everything I do, I either create, preserve or destroy something.
If I want the truth to be spoken, I must speak the truth.
The children *are* our future, so teach them well.
The only true enemy is the ego. We are love.
May we converge as one people in love and peace
and lead ourselves out of the path of ego.

Samuel Kanaan-Oringo

15 years old

Life Enthusiast

Sydney, Australia

165
My Knowing

*A*s far back as I can remember, I had this knowing in my gut that no matter what, God loves me unconditionally, no rules, obligations, exceptions and expectations.

Growing up, this knowing gave me the courage to stand up and be true to Who I Am despite familial, religious and societal rules and conditioning. This knowing gave me the courage to go through my challenging life experiences to date. Challenging experiences without which I would not know what blissful ecstasy feels like, for if I have not felt and experienced gut-wrenching despair, I will not have known such ecstasy that every pore on my skin comes alive with electricity!

This knowing gives me the courage to love with my heart fully open and to keep my heart fully open even when my heart has been torn apart. This knowing also gives me the courage to let go of relationships that no longer serve each other's highest good.

This knowing gives me the courage to trust, be uncomfortable, jump off and take that leap of faith...and magic happens serendipitously... and those times when I don't listen to my gut and fall flat on my face, this knowing gives me the courage to pick myself up, dust myself off and rise up once again.

This knowing gives me the courage to love myself unconditionally first and foremost. I cannot possibly love another the way I want to be loved if I do not give that love to myself first. This knowing gives me freedom, freedom to be who I am. Who am I?

There was an awesome man who lived amongst us to show us who we truly are and his message to us is, "The kingdom of God is within you." I am God within. You are God within. This is my knowing.

Zinnia Oringo-Hantos
48 years old
Agent for Bodacious Beings
Sydney, Australia

166
A Single Step

They hey say a journey of a thousand miles begins with a single step. What they don't say, and should, is that it not only starts with a single step, but also passes the halfway mark, the finish line and every point in between with a single step. Really all it ever takes then is a step. So, if that's all it takes, then what holds us frozen in place, endlessly going in circles and never getting to that slim, healthy destination?

What if, we paid attention to our focus? What if where you look, is what you automatically start moving towards? How far would you go at 80 kmph looking out the back window? How erratically would you drive with your focus constantly moving from the road ahead to the road behind? What if a thought that feels slim and sexy like "Wooo, I look good tonight!" is you driving *towards* being healthy? And, a thought like, "You fat slob, eating whole tin of chocolates!" is you looking out the rear window?

What if, when we set ourselves up to expect perfection, we actually set ourselves up for failure because of the grazes we get from the inevitable falls off the wagon when our old habits kick in? What if we focused a little more softly and, instead of beating ourselves up for falling off the wagon, we just brushed off the dirt and got back on?

What if I stopped expecting perfection and made a year commitment to find a way where I could balance everything in my body and train myself to focus on where I want to go? Eight kilos down, muscles defined, body balancing and abundant energy, I found the system that worked for me, and five months later, I'm getting better at it, one step at a time. That's all you'll need, too.

Dee Shelton
31 years old
Personal Development Coach
Perth, Australia

167
Rani's Rampage of Appreciation

I love flowers, I love unicorns, I love zebras and sparkles.
I love smiles and cuddles, my dollies and teddies
and I love you too!

I love Mummy, yes I do and the things you do make me,
like dinner, fruit and shakes
like rice and worms (spaghetti) and my cakes,
I love you, that you do!
All the things that you do!

I love silks and Gabi and Isaac
I love being nice and strong
I love my curly hair and big blue eyes
I love the doggies eyes too Mummy
aren't they nice and yellow?

I love rocks and crystals, playing games, dancing and being happy,
I love being happy, isn't happy so good? Are you happy too my mummy?
When I feel happy, I smile really big on my face and in my body,
and my feet want to move lots more

I love showers, baths and being clean
parks and slides and swings
I love stories and my bedtime cuddles
loads of teddies all piled in.

We are ready for bedtime, ready for sweet dreams,
It's like little stars are in your eyes.
Te Quiero, I love you, Buenos noches, goodnight,
I will see you in the morning Mumma.

Rani Shelton

3 years old

Child

Perth, Australia

168
Anchoring

*T*oday I want to share with you something I have accomplished, something that changed my life: confidence. Confidence is feeling happy and relaxed. It's where you stand up tall, welcoming things into your life with ease.

I used to be petrified of public speaking. I never would have chosen to do it. Yet now, I comfortably enjoy myself. Being comfortable doesn't mean I'm perfect or getting it right all the time. It does mean that each time I improve. It does mean I have the confidence to get up, so that I can improve. You do have choices. You can, like I did, go from fear to confidence. So how?

Anchoring... that's how. The easiest way to explain anchoring is to tell you about a scientist called Pavlov, who was curious about how learning happens. He created an experiment with his dog, a bell and food. When he gave his dog the food, the dog drooled and he rang the bell. He did this ten times and on the eleventh time he just rang the bell and the dog drooled! The dog would not have drooled when the bell was rung before. But now, the dog drools because it anchored the bell to the food which makes the dog drool.

You can drool too. Have you ever smelled a yummy smell and had your mouth water? It's the same as Pavlov's dog; we anchor and learn in the same way. Only we have the gift of being able to use this knowledge deliberately without drooling most of the time!

So, remember the last time you felt confident and link it with an action like rubbing your hands together. Do that enough times and you can access that confidence anywhere. You can change what you learn; it's your choice, so choose what makes you happy.

Gabrielle Loschi
14 years old
Student
Perth, Australia

169
Your Inner Ninja!

*T*o me, inspiration is bringing out the inner ninja! Your inner ninja is what makes you feel pumped, ready for life and proud of yourself. It's what helps you know you can bring down any obstacles in your path and know you are in control. Like when I did a martial arts board-breaking exercise and broke the board, not with brute force, but with focus and ninja moves.

It amazed me how one moment the board seemed so impossible to break through, even to the point of physical pain, the next it broke with ease. I could feel the difference in my focus; I had discovered my inner ninja.

We *all* have an inner ninja that can accomplish anything if we believe in ourselves and know how to bring it out. When I broke that board, bringing out the inner ninja was getting myself pumped up. It was feeling like it was already broken; I was energetic and focused. A true ninja knows that your focus becomes your destination, so focus on what you want.

You can do simple things, like exaggerating how you feel when things go your way or remembering a time when you felt amazing. Imagine what it would be like to have arrived at your dream destination. This develops a relationship with your inner ninja.

So, if practised consistently, bringing out your inner ninja can be done with ease. Enjoy your moments of success; celebrate them. Do not fear your moments of failure. For a true ninja knows that failure only means there is more to do and learn, and impossible is really "I'm possible" in disguise. This is the key to the ninja. With this you cannot be defeated or overwhelmed. You only grow stronger. If you fear failure, your inner ninja will be locked away forever, never to see the light of day.

Isaac Loschi
12 years old
Student
Perth, Australia

170
Pay it Forward with Unconditional Love

*T*here has been one woman in my life that loved me more than anybody else. She never put me down and never once scolded me, yet in her own way set boundaries and disciplined me to respect and serve women and people in general. She is my hero, and you may have guessed, she is my mother, who passed away last year.

We sometimes undervalue the power that a mother's love has on her offspring and how it positively impacts long after they pass away. Looking back on it, I guess I took her love for granted, thinking it was normal; however, it was not the norm. Her love for me was so strong that I even remember asking her one day, "Mum, why do you love me so much?"

I have soared to great heights and achieved many extraordinary feats in my life both professionally and personally, but my greatest achievement is my eight kids and the positive impact that my mother's love, through me, has had on them. It has not always been an easy ride but good things are always worth persevering with, as my mum would say, "Never give up son, you can do it."

Mothers can have a very strong influence, and the unconditional love and support they give seems to transfer and multiply in others, like a 'pay it forward' sort of thing. Unconditional love seems to multiply when given in the world. Live and love fearlessly and unconditionally and pay it forward to make a better world come true with each generation.

Peter Kritas
52 years old
Business Owner
Sydney, Australia

171
The Magic Of Time

The old saying goes, "Time heals all wounds." I have yet to find if it does. Some wonderful things have happened in my life. Although some were bad, all these things make me who I am today. I have lost loved ones in my life; I have watched others suffer and battle. But here I am, telling you this now. I am telling you that we can overcome anything and everything. We can find our own peace of mind, get through and overcome our obstacles in our everyday life.

We do things for ourselves and we do things for others to make them proud, whether it's our parents, grandparents, friends, or children. We have the magic of time to change ourselves and mould who we want to be; to inspire others; to help when one is down. We can listen and change the lives of others. If we truly listen, we can give someone a lending hand and let them know it is alright.

The magic of time is something we all have so we must use it wisely. Let's make our mark in the sand, so our names can echo on through the decades. When we leave something behind, long after we are gone from this Earth, our name echoes on. We live on in all that we have done, all that we do. We are all we can be and more. We choose our goals and the path we walk on. We should help others along the way, in any situation that we can.

So, be inspired; inspire others. If you ever feel down, look within yourself and find your self-worth. You are someone and you should be proud of yourself.

Elizabeth Blade

32 years old

Author & Poet

Adelaide, Australia

172
Wisdom = Develop Your Health, Fulfil Your Purpose

*O*ver the years, I have witnessed the distraction that poor health causes for people. Many would otherwise be living an inspired and adventurous life of purpose and contribution. Your body is an incredible gift. No matter whether you're thin, not so thin, weak, strong, able, disabled, beautiful or plain, your body is more than capable of being the 'vehicle' necessary to deliver your unique gift to the world as an expression of your divine purpose. However, your health still requires self-responsibility and care. Here is what I call the A, B, C's of health:

A. Continually address Your Five Pillars of Health:
1) Exercise (find a new sport, or step up your exercise program)
2) Nutrition (supplement with the essentials; vitamin D, probiotics and fish oils)
3) Adequate Rest (standardise your sleep time, or use a contoured pillow)
4) State of Mind (meditate daily, or keep a gratitude journal)
5) Optimal Nerve Function (get checked by a chiropractor, or practice good posture)

B. Live an 'Innate Lifestyle:' This means eating, moving, and thinking in a way that matches the human genetic requirements for health and wellness. Remember: despite our world having changed radically, the human genome hasn't changed significantly in nearly 40,000 years. The closer you can mimic these conditions by reducing modern day stresses, the better your body will serve you!

C. Find a Health Mentor: Find someone you trust who can always be a source of guidance and inspiration.

Health is your greatest asset. Guard it well. Do whatever you can to proactively develop and build your health, rather than reacting to it once lost. It will pay you back a thousand times over.

Angus Heseltine

41 years old

Doctor of Chiropractic

Sydney, Australia

173
Waves of a Clear Heart

*T*he rolling waves create a sense that everything quietens, though my heart speaks louder than ever. A sea doesn't judge itself; it trusts its direction and constantly flows, moving in each moment, simply beautiful being what it is. Sunlight allows the ocean floor to be seen as the water naturally purifies, so little debris contaminates it, flowing harmoniously with the current and all that resides within its depths. A smile and tears flood my face simultaneously. Its beauty is ecstasy; a feeling unable to be taken and created simply by connecting. This authenticity encourages me to share what my heart speaks; my truth.

Being 'unique' was always a strength and weakness. Part of me loved it and part felt so alone. Havoc forms inside when we fear acceptance of being authentic. We become numbingly cold, immobile and starved for life, not unlike iced water. But when the sun warms the sea, like self-love warms the heart, it's inevitable that we begin to melt, soften, and expand. Love drives us in a way that fear never can. Lovingly expressing our truth, we are raw and this is worth loving. Our vulnerability is exposed and that's ok. Truth is felt, breathed and lived by so life becomes clearer. We are purified from self-love.

A current never sailed before may reach uncontaminated waters, bringing peace, harmony and beauty; similar to the ocean before me. Connecting authentically and developing self-love creates tidal waves. Sometimes it's necessary to sail the storm and go where you can't see. We are nature and get to expect miracles. Sailing the tides, while keeping lessons and love, helps clear the ocean in our heart, as debris washes aground at the coastline. May the moon cycle your tides, the sun expose your ocean floor and the wind carry you in a loving direction.

Angela Joy Johnson
35 years old
Holistic Mind Body & Energy Coach
Gold Coast, Australia

174
Practicing Gratitude

I believe the most inspired thing you can do to change your life is be grateful for the problems you're currently facing. Learning to appreciate your problems as much as you appreciate your successes creates a paradigm shift in your mind and heart, which provides the inspiration to find new solutions and processes to change your life in powerful ways.

Practicing gratitude for my problems saved my life. There was a time when I was dealing with major issues. At twenty-one, I was discharged from the army with post-traumatic stress. This led to several years of severe depression; I became a drug addict, ended up homeless, in debt and contemplated suicide every day. I craved change!

I read somewhere that changing your perception was the key to changing your life. So, I began seeing my problems as challenges and as gifts that were there to teach me deep wisdom about myself and life. I began practising gratitude for everything in my life including all my problems. I began to appreciate everything, good and bad. It was hard going and a slow process, but I kept at it and developed discipline. I said positive affirmations every morning. Each day, I was becoming more conscious of my thoughts and whenever I noticed a negative thought, I would replace it with a positive.

I began producing dramatic changes in my life. I gave up drugs and exercised daily. My depression was replaced by moments of inspiration. My self-esteem grew. Friends started to notice the changes and my newfound genuine enthusiasm for life. I took small steps every day and those small steps have compounded into a deep belief that I am blessed. Everything happens for a reason – even if we cannot at first understand what or why that is. There are no mistakes, only lessons.

Allan Kleynhans
47 years old
Professional Speaker
London, United Kingdom

175
Once You Realize

*T*hey say once you know where you're going, the steps to get you there suddenly become visible. Well, I challenged that idea for almost a lifetime. I realize now, at fifty-one, that I lived in the fear of not knowing that I am good enough. Sadly, I held myself back, because it wasn't anybody else holding back. Then I realized that the people around me, whose comments I took seriously, were only saying what applies to their own abilities and beliefs, not mine. Therefore, living my life according to what others say or think is, in itself, a fear based on a non-reality. Once I understood this, I was free. Free to think the thoughts in my head, speak the words in my own mouth, and do the things I once dreamt of. Free to live the life I deserve!

I released the voices that dominated my thoughts, the words which filled my ears, the societal and the cultural demands, to which I conformed my deeds, and the ideals that dominated my femininity and existence as a woman, belonged to someone else. I thought I could be content within my role as mother and wife, but what I found was that I was so much more than that. I am more and so are you!

There is a yearning inside for purpose. There is a search to quench the passion that lies deep within; to follow the path unfolding before me. You see, it's not just about the 'where' I want to go but the living in the 'how,' the journey that will get me there. This is my path. So now, find yours. See the bigger picture of your purpose, your mission and go be the 'more' that is deep inside you. Nothing can hold you back... once you realize.

Chris Georgopoulos
52 years old
The Diamond Diva
Melbourne, Australia

176
From 'Not Enough' to Self-Worth and Self-Love

*D*uring a meeting at work, I felt my heart thud. My energy slipped away, leaving me feeling extremely weak. This was the beginning of my journey through burnout, forcing me to leave the company I had been with for seventeen years. For an entire month, I slept twenty-three hours a day. I struggled with feelings of anguish, shame, guilt and resentment. I felt that I had failed. I felt I had betrayed my company.

I lay in bed one night and felt my breath getting short. I thought that night would be my last. Flashes of past and future family events (which I would miss out on) and faces of family members appeared in my mind. Then, my mom's face appeared. I couldn't bear the thought of her losing me; she had done so much for her children. I gasped for air, and vowed I would do whatever it took to recover.

The two-year recovery process was similar to rebooting a computer and loading all new software. I discovered and sorted through my emotions, beliefs and habits, determining whether they stayed in my life, or whether I would replace them. This process was extremely uncomfortable. I felt vulnerable, alone, and misunderstood.

I read, researched, attended numerous workshops, listened to audio programs, and worked with coaches. I discovered pieces of myself, my gifts, I hadn't recognized before. I realized the underpinning of my being, from birth, revolved around beliefs that I wasn't good enough, worthy or deserving. Everything had to be better, faster, bigger and stronger. These beliefs held me back from being authentic and truly grateful for myself.

It has been eleven years since I burnt out. I love myself exactly as I am. I am grateful for the journey and the lessons I continue to learn about myself.

Sandra Corrado

49 years old

Performance & Wellness Coach

Richmond Hill, Canada

177
The Game Changer

My vision for the world has always been that there are safe homes and safe schools for every child everywhere in the world. I had on other occasions attempted to make this vision come alive... and I had very successfully found ways that do not work. On the last occasion, I lay in a heap, not able to move, paralysed.

Then one day, I was cleaning out my filing cabinet and found the picture that I drew when I was five years old. The picture was of the safe homes and safe schools for every child everywhere in the world. I looked at that picture and began to cry. I knew at that moment I had to get up because the kids needed me. My heart reached out and connected with the dreams, visions and hearts of all the kids in the world. I got up!

Sitting in meditation, I asked the question, "How do I build these homes and schools?" and what came to me was that the projects already exist, the people already exist, the passion already exists. I am not to invent anything new, my purpose is to bring everyone together. The projects are the wheels and I am the axle that keeps the wheels turning.

The only way I was going to engage in making this happen was in knowing that every single element of our world is taken care of: the Earth, the plants, the animals, the people, the water, the community projects, and the visions and dreams of the children. I have never ever given up on this dream and I never will. I am one-hundred percent committed to my vision.

Stacey Huish
30 years old
Game-Changer
Toowoomba, Australia

178
It's Not Over Till You
Say It's Over

*D*uring my thirty years on this planet, I have had to cope with setbacks, change and loss several times. Sometimes I wanted to give up, give in or run away. I have certainly cried a little (okay I cried a lot) when I thought no one was looking.

The truth is, life is tough. And it is tough for everyone.

It took me a while to realize this. Financially, I was secure but bored. To escape my boredom, I became obsessed with acquiring material possessions e.g., luxury handbags and shoes. I was shallow but I thought my life was good. I didn't realize how fragile my veneer of happiness was until I came home one day to find my Russian fiancé cheating on me. I threw him out expecting him to come crawling back – but he didn't. I was devastated. Life lost its meaning.

Even in the darkest moments, light exists if we choose to see it.

I was a wreck after my engagement fell through. I didn't leave my apartment for days. My feelings of loss and betrayal were so great that one afternoon, I swallowed all the Paracetamol I had at home. As I lay in bed hoping that I would die from toxic poisoning, I thought of all the things I would never do and suddenly I realized:

I'm in control of my life. Nothing is over until I say so.

I survived that afternoon, but my old beliefs about life died. I made a decision to live life to the fullest, to make my time on Earth meaningful. Oh... and I'm engaged again. To a much nicer man this time!

Karen Chow
28 years old
International Speaker & Coach
Johor, Malaysia

179
Inspired Beings

*W*e are quite literally inspired beings. Our breath does more than keep us alive. It is the driving force for inspiration. It's perhaps a natural misconception that inspiration is generated internally. All inspiration has an external source. The dictionary definition gives the first clue as to why:

Inspiration [noun] :
- an inspiring influence, person or notion
- the output from be inspired
- the inhaling of air into the lungs
- a divine influence on the mind or soul
- the divine quality of art and science produced by someone so influenced

The latter definitions are the most telling. The etymology of the word inspiration gives the second clue. Inspiration is based on the Latin word 'spirare' which means 'to breathe.' The life breath is the Ruach from which all creation was invented. Most people speak on an out breath. This is the aspirational phase of the breathing process. The inspiration phase is where we stir up the universal mind-stuff, such that ideas percolate into our conscious mind from the Collective Mind. As we have to breathe anyway, it makes sense to utilise our breathing to increase our creativity. Our diaphragm is our inspirational generator here.

At the start of each day, or before embarking on a creative task, sit upright with your hands on your belly with the middle fingers touching. First, breathe in deeply so the middle fingers just part. Next, breathe out fully about four times as long as the in-breath. Repeat this process three, five, seven or nine times. The number is important. As you become more comfortable with this technique, start to pay particular attention to the thoughts that arrive between the in and out breaths. Be mindful of your aspirations and dreams as you breathe out. On the in-breath, be open to being inspired.

Tom Evans

56 years old

Author

Surrey, United Kingdom

180
Biography Is Not Destiny

*B*iography is not destiny. We all create stories about our life that determine why we are the way we are. This is one of the most important things I learned at a Tony Robbins conference. The memory of losing my father when I was three remains as permanent as a tattoo, yet invisible as a ghost. And that ghost haunted me for over twenty years. The eerie sound of sirens pierced through the stillness of the night. The red and blue police car lights blinded me as I peeked out the window and watched my dad get handcuffed and taken away.

For years, I blamed my mother and sister for the pain it caused me. I believed that they took my father away from me. I blamed them for the bad things in my life: my post-traumatic stress disorder, severe anxiety, a series of unhealthy relationships, my lack of boundaries, a constant feeling of worthlessness, profound self-hatred, agonizing guilt, and most of all, the irreplaceable hole in my heart.

During the conference, we were asked to dive into our past, pick out a memory and attach a new meaning to the experience. I had the startling realization that my mom did not "take my father away." This was the night that my mom saved me. She saved my sister and I from suffering any more abuse from our father.

Although my childhood memories seem painful, I now choose to rewrite the story of my life and attach a new meaning to it to the experiences. I am no longer a victim. I now focus on the positive that came out from it. It gave me a drive, a passion and a desire to succeed. It has given me the courage and audacity to speak my truth. When you change the meaning you attach to your childhood, you change your life!

Brittany Hammond

25 years old

Branding & Communication Stylist

Nice, France

181
My Commitment Ring

*G*rowing up reading fairy tales, I always imagined that a prince would come on a horse and whisk me away to a happily ever after future. And he did on a horse at our traditional Indian wedding and for me, my fairy tale did come true, or so I thought. But, the happily ever after future wasn't how I had imagined it. My fairy-tale marriage turned out to be a roller coaster ride that seemed to speed up and slow down at random intervals when I least expected... and I seemed to have no control.

The part I found the hardest was that, in my perception, my wedding ring symbolized commitment and unity; my husbands' and my definitions for that were different. This was something I had to come to terms with. My wedding ring had, for eighteen years, symbolized commitment to my marriage. It seemed to weigh heavily on my finger, so I decided to take it off. This was one of the most confronting and challenging moments of my life, as symbolism had always meant a lot to me. As I looked at my bare finger every so often, I felt lost and confused, until one day walking into a shop I saw a beautiful Blue London Topaz ring.

As soon as I put it on my finger, it felt right. Looking up the definition of blue topaz, I learned that one of its properties was to assist in living according to your own aspirations and views in truth and wisdom. It also assists in seeing the scripts you've been living by and to recognize where you have strayed from your own truth. As soon as I read that I came to the realization that, first and foremost, the person I needed to be committed to was myself. That's how I chose to live from then on. I now call that blue topaz ring my commitment ring as it's taught me my most valuable lesson: commitment to one's own truth.

Wandna Suri Tucker

45 years old

Intuitive Counsellor

Adelaide, Australia

182
Lost Voice and Innocence

When Reggie was thirteen years old, he made a life-changing decision that forever reshaped the destiny of his life. He was forever challenged from the events that took place at an earlier age when he was five years old. He was the witness to the family destruction when his father committed suicide in front of him and his mother. This was the foundation that Reggie had to build his life from. By the age fifteen, he left the violent and abusive home life of poverty and welfare, and faced the unknown bitter challenges of life without resources and no privileges of social upbringing.

Without high school and college, Reggie gained 40 years of life's experience through the disheartening trauma of restarting his life over five times. He was a last survivor, he has overcome three capitol economic recessions, four marriages (two domestic and two international), two bankruptcies, a DUI, foreclosure, and when the doctor declared he was dying and had no medical reason, Reggie had to learn how to 'live life over again'! With wealth of wisdom in his mind and heart, sharing his truth with everyone inspired by him, "If he made it through all of these catastrophic events, so can you."

From stepping up and out of poverty, self-learning how to change outcomes of catastrophic events, his courage to love, see, hear and feel the truth has driven Reggie to become a highly accomplished and extraordinary man. His gift of gratitude and un-conditional love authenticates him as a self-made person. He's making a difference in other people's lives, being on purpose with inspiration in serving a bigger impact on the world with his life's experience and extraordinary story: "Un-Conditional Love, Loves Everything!"

Reggie Lacina
51 years old
Master Builder & Life Architect
Los Angeles, United States of America

183
A Moment of Clarity

We all have it – that moment of clarity. When the vision we'd dreamed of falls into place. That moment for me was in February 2008.

I was the kid who dreamed big. I did my first personal development course at fourteen, and had enough vision boards in my teens and twenties to wallpaper the Great Wall of China seven times. But... on my twenty-fifth birthday I cried myself to sleep because I was not a millionaire yet. How could this be? I'd visualized for a decade and did the 'perfect day' exercise a thousand times, yet here I was nearly bankrupt. I felt like such a failure. Maybe those teachers were right: maybe I wouldn't amount to anything.

Then it all changed. I was thirty. My daughter was a few weeks old. I was rocking her to sleep with one foot, mouse in right hand doing business, using my left hand for the express pump (sitting on my printer) to get enough milk to feed her when she woke up. I screamed to myself: "This is not living!" That's when realised that you have to drop the story and create the actions. Figure out the big picture, set the actions and put one foot in front of the other. On the days that are the toughest - is when you have to push through. Those are the days winners are made.

That defining moment changed my life. I now get to have fun working with clients. I take my kids to school and pick them up and take them on amazing holidays. Visualizing, vision boards, personal development... doesn't mean anything without the action. You just have to decide and do it. Drop the story and get it done. (With love, of course!)

Jody Jelas
39 years old
Online Business Strategist
Auckland, New Zealand

184
To See The World

J grew up amidst the chaos of tumultuous family dynamics and learned to 'survive' by immersing myself in books and study. One book in particular opened me to a whole new world: *The Magic Faraway Tree*. With its many different lands at the top of the tree, and a dad who had a 'foreign accent,' I was intrigued to learn more about different places, cultures and languages.

My burning desire to travel, however, was constantly quashed by, "We can't afford that." I was told, "You have no voice in this house" whenever I expressed opinion, and when I said I was leaving the UK to go to Belgium I was told, "You don't have it in you."

I'd pushed through adversity to achieve a scholarship to one of the best schools in the country. I'd worked and saved up enough money to support myself. When only a week before I'd been told in front of several hundred students that I couldn't work for the Foreign Office because I had, "Too many relatives on the other side," I vowed nothing would ever stop me from the desires I'd dreamt about for years.

Within a week, I arrived in Belgium after a long journey of buses, trains and a ferry. A few days later, I had my first full-time job – 'International Representative' for an American State Office. After years of applying 'powerful creativity' and assigning power in consciousness, I was now travelling on business every second week throughout Europe and the States. Despite being told as a child that I could never travel, I haven't stopped! I've lived, worked and raised a family in various countries worldwide; visiting many more. I strongly urge you, therefore, to always focus on the end result. Feel the emotions of that and it will certainly manifest.

Susan Dellanzo
56 years old
Emotional Well-being Specialist
London, United Kingdom

185
Free To Be Me

*A*s a child, I was inspired to empower people and always scheming about making a difference. At nine years old, I got elected as year level captain and honoured my election promise by implementing a composting and recycling system into the school. I was so proud, but I felt like I needed to play it down. There were two parts of me: the part that wanted to do my best, and the part that wanted to hide and keep myself small. I was bullied for being such a bright spark, and slowly I hid how insightful I was. I shrunk to fit in.

My own beliefs about myself and my own self talk became my worst enemies; and I didn't think anyone would ever find me attractive. I felt undeserving of love, but at the same time I craved it. At sixteen, my first real boyfriend was emotionally, verbally, physically and sexually abusive. It confirmed my beliefs, "I am not deserving, and love hurts." I stayed with him because I felt like I could help him, while I further shut myself down.

Three years later, I came to life again and broke it off. I realised that who I really am and the stories that I'd told myself about who I needed to be in order to be loved were very different. It was exhausting pre-empting what would gain me popularity and then adjusting myself to fit in.

I chose to love myself and enjoy the experience of being me. By being myself, I draw the people into my life who I love spending time with because they are just like me. I am perfect, whole and complete just the way I am and just the way I am not. My life's purpose is to empower; and to do that I must trust in who I am and be willing to stand out.

Rachel Anastasi

31 years old

Speaker, Coach & Psychosomatics

Melbourne, Australia

186
Rise and Rise Again

My name is Will Engelbrecht, and this is a snippet of my story.

I have had to learn a few invaluable lessons in business at a young age, and I see it as a privilege to share some of them with you. First of all, don't wait for second chances to come around. When you come across a concept or an idea that can turn into reality, grab it because it won't be there forever. Being able to see opportunities when they come along is a valuable skill, but even those who do, often fail to fight for their dreams because they think they're never going to happen. We keep thinking success is the guy in the Ferrari – when in reality that is only the product of success! True success starts in the mind!

Second, life is a series of choices. When you boil everything down, you either choose to win or to lose. Believing it's possible even when no one else does, and having the determination to wake up every morning and rededicate yourself to a cause much larger than you, that is success!

Finally, stumbling blocks or, as I'd like to call them, stepping stones are going to happen. Once again, you have two choices: this trial will either build you and your envisioned future, or you'll undergo an unpleasant learning experience that you will just have to try again at a later stage, as life's lessons tend to keep coming back until you conquer them.

The future gets brighter with every step. I hope that this very brief insight into my life has encouraged you in some small way. I leave you with my life motto:

"Rise and rise again, until lambs become lions."

Willem Engelbrecht
27 years old
Founder of MIA Sportswear
Townsville, Australia

187
Moving Past Heartache

While it's true to say that my life's work was borne of my own personal heartache and devastation, it's also true that I have been richly blessed on my journey of healing. I exhausted every avenue in my search for profound wisdom and insight, which led me to study with some of the greatest teachers. Today I share all that I've learned with many around the world, but I never forget that it's not what we do that matters most – it's who we are.

We've all had our hearts broken at some stage in a relationship. But, what we often fail to grasp in those painful moments is that the deeper the heartache, the greater the invitation to transcend all our inner obstacles to loving ourselves. Consistently filling up our own cups and ensuring that we expand each area of our lives is empowering. But, the key to being truly irresistible at every age comes from a much deeper commitment to continuously catch and cradle those things that hold real value for each of us as individuals. It is when we do this that we feel on purpose and radiate a beautiful and magnetic light.

The most pivotal thing I can share about relationships is that we have a tendency to see others as we are and not as they are. Understanding this leads to a profound shift in awareness as you recognise that how you label each encounter is actually a reflection of how close or how far you have moved from your true centre of love. We are the ones who give each person the meaning they hold for us. Each new encounter graciously gifts us with another opportunity to look within, take ownership and make a higher choice. Self-love is the key to enjoying successful relationships with others.

Desiree Marie Leedo

44 years old

Author & Founder of Invisible Goddess

Binfield, United Kingdom

188
Beyond Despair

*M*y past experiences have made me who I am today, and I love who I am today. My father started to abuse me when I was five-and-a-half years old, which went on for seven years until he was found out. During that time, he emotionally blackmailed me to keep quiet. He destroyed the bright sparkle within me. I grew up full of shame and guilt. When I was eight years old, he told me that when I grew up I would be working as a prostitute. I knew what a prostitute was and I was scared of what might happen. However, the seed was planted in my mind, and in my early twenties I was attracted to a man who introduced me to that profession, and I worked as an escort girl for many years.

I never gave up looking for ways to get out, and finally after overcoming many difficulties, I made it. My process for changing my life was to find a way to accept what happened to me. I'm not saying that what my father did was right, but accepting it helped me to move on. I stopped fighting something I couldn't change. It freed my mind, body and soul to look into the future instead of hanging onto the past.

I learned to change my negative beliefs to positive ones. I started to like myself, and I found self-acceptance and worth again. I knew I had a choice. I could either stay in a past that could not be changed or find a way to move on and make the changes. The hopelessness and despair was painful at times but it was exactly what made think in a different way. If we don't change what we think and do, we will always have the same outcome.

Angelika Breukers
57 years old
Author & Speaker
Wantage, United Kingdom

189
You are the Gift

*R*eflecting on entering my sixth decade of life, I asked myself what I wish I had known when I was younger. Three things came to me. First, I wish I had known how to love myself. Second, I wish I had known early on the importance of choosing a career path that inspired me. Third, I wish I had realized that there is divine perfection in everything that happens.

Looking back, I've had a wonderful life. I have learned these three things through much pain, depression, swimming upstream, and finally getting out of my own way. I know now that all along it was up to me. It wasn't because my dad died when I was five, or that I thought my mom was emotionally unavailable. It wasn't because no one told me about possibilities in careers or options to relocate.

It was all divine perfection, guiding me to find it all in me. I am grateful for the pain of careers that did not inspire me. I see how what I learned in corporate America benefits to me today. I see how what I learned during the time I spent trying to make my mom happy benefits me and others today. I no longer spend time trying to make other people happy. That is their responsibility.

I am grateful for the lessons and the letting go. I feel like I finally know myself. I have learned that it is not only okay to love myself, but it is necessary in order to love another. And only by being authentic can I offer my real gifts to the world. My words of wisdom no matter what age you are: Know, love, and be yourself to live your unique inspired life. The world is waiting for your unique genius.

Susan Kennedy
60 years old
Coach & Homeopath
Plano, TX

190
Bella's Theme Park

*C*olourful lights flashed. Carousel music played. Children smiled, laughed and cheered. At a distance, Bella faced the rides before her and held her father's hands, "Daddy, there are so many, which one do I choose?" Her father replied, "Explore and experience, sweet Bella, you have absolutely nothing to lose."

Bella inched towards the mouth of an ominous ride. Nervous she said, "Daddy come with me, with us two it's much more fun." Her father replied, "Darling, discover the magic for yourself. I'll be here waiting when you're done." Minutes passed, the ride ended. Bella walked out, shivering cold in fear. With tears streaming she cried, "Daddy! Where were you when I called?" The gentle father hugged and kissed Bella. Yet Bella pushed him away, scared to place her trust.

Decades passed now, and Bella is sitting at that familiar scene. Her daughter says, "Mummy, I want to go on that special ride!" Bella resists the request, in fear for her little daughter's life. She feels nervous, visualizing that memory of decades passed. Looking at her daughter's innocent request, Bella, through her own eyes, finally saw what her father had meant: to give her the freedom to choose her experiences.

Humbled, Bella set aside her fear, "Go have fun my sweetie, I love you. I'll be waiting just right here." Her daughter hugs her, grateful for her consent. And in that moment, love flowed both ways. Bella wondered, "How might have been different for me?" as she reflected on her days. Bella whispered to herself, "Raising a child can be a mystery, that's what I am often told." And with a sigh of acceptance, "I guess I'll wait to see what happens, as more of this mystery unfolds."

Mario Pirotta
41 years old
Wealth & Mindset Consultant
Melbourne, Australia

191
Awakening to Self

*"If there is something missing from your life and relationships,
there probably is... and it's probably you."*

$\mathcal{J}$ was born with an awareness of spirit and a deep inner knowing that there is more to life than what we believe. Raised in a broken family with an angry father, an abusive stepfather and a loving but lonely frightened mother, has navigated me on a journey of recovery and healing. If I were to share one thing from all that I have learned on this journey that has made the most difference to who I am today, it is this: before all else and all others, cultivate a loving relationship with your self.

You see, the relationship you have with your self will determine the quality of the life you lead. It will determine your ability to love, your ability to learn and grow, as well as the ability to let go of things that no longer serve you; this may include people, situations, habits and thoughts. It will also determine the quality of your relationships.

So, where do you begin? Simply by cultivating a daily practice of mindful presence through focused breathing, you are able to connect to the larger part of who you truly are – an ever-present glorious radiant being that is infinite and divine. This practice of conscious awareness creates an opportunity for you to bear witness to your mind stories, and, it is in this place that you awaken to your true nature, accept all that you are and love yourself no matter what you have or haven't done, no matter your life experiences. It is through taking this path to self that you may discover true joy and peace.

So, if you seek a deeper connection in your life, go within. If you seek joy, wisdom and peace, go within. With love.

Mandi Cloete
45 years old
Healer & Transformational Coach
Perth, Australia

192
The Rose

When our life is not working, why do we continue pushing, fearing failure, ignoring our intuition, only to find when the load has been too heavy for too long, that our lives collapse? I found myself in this situation in May 2013, broken physically, mentally and emotionally, wanting to end my life. In despair, I let go and painfully walked away from my life, existing for three months in a turmoil of darkness. Knowing the only way through was responsibility, I began questioning my thoughts, feelings and judgements, pleading for insight, when unexpectedly, my call for help was met by the beauty and fragrance of the rose; a perfect metaphor for the blooming of my authentic self.

As her spirited voice guided me, I listened, and as I looked within my answers emerged. What a sense of relief as I began to own my pain. A deep inner peace replaced my fear, and joy with a new sense of wonder, my hopelessness. My life lit up with a profound self-acceptance and freedom. Unaware at the time, my courage to let go was the beginning of an empowering experience of self-discovery, leading to a beautiful book of poems to share with the world. So please, embrace your fears, surrender to the whims of your mind, listen to your heart and share your fragrance with the world. You are unique!

Taken by the Impulse
A Rose does not shrink nor holds anything back
Is not shy or afraid to stand up or stand out
She does not question her beauty or why she is here
But gloriously blooms for all to admire
She is saying, I am life and I am living
My impulse is guiding my way of being
So bathe in my beauty and perfume divine
And allow your impulse to guide you as thine.

Carol Phillips
57 years old
Author & Retreat Facilitator
Adelaide, Australia

193
An Inspirational Dad

*J*t was a cold morning in January, in the high altitude of the Colombian mountains, in a room with nothing but a blanket and the companionship of a woman, when a new baby boy was born. A baby who would have to leave his home at the age of eight, just to be able to survive on his own. Moving hundreds of kilometres away from his parents and having to overcome a way of slavery at a young age: milking cows and feeding pigs, sometimes just to get by for a day or so, and in some cases getting close to starvation. With no chance to attend to school or play like any other kids, this man overcame poverty, pain, misery and illiteracy.

After all of this and much more over the years, that baby who is now sixty-two, has been a man of dreams, hard work, inspiration, generosity and endless love, a hero, a supporter and the person who planted the seed in my mind to dream big, try hard, be fearless, go the extra mile regardless of the circumstances, lead by example and help the people around me.

This man, at the age of eighteen, created an indescribable desire to become a professional one day, and he took action and committed himself to achieve it. And guess what? It would take him just over fifteen years of discipline, persistence, endurance and sacrifice to see his dream materialised. The best advice I've got from this man has been: "Inspiration and motivation is within yourself, no matter how old you are, the opportunity to be the best version of yourself, the dreamer, the achiever, the happier, whatever you want to call it, it's within your heart, so go slow and steady son but never stop and you will reach your destination."

Eduard Acosta

33 years old

Property Advisor

Brisbane, Australia

194
An Example for Others

*Y*our past does not have to dictate your future. You have a choice. I am writing to all those that have been the subject of bullies, to those with low self-esteem and limited confidence, because that is where I have come from. I spent quite a few years at school being on the receiving end of a bully's torment, and it breaks my heart to hear how much of it still goes on. I am here to tell you that it doesn't have to define you. As difficult as it can be, school makes up such a small part of our lives, and once in adulthood it all changes.

My lack of self-confidence followed me into adulthood, and it has only been recently that the tables have turned. Twelve months ago, I was feeling lost and a little empty when I went on a search to find more in life. To my amazement, I discovered a whole new world I never knew existed. With one choice, I was propelled into the world of personal development. I became connected with positive and supportive people that, rather than pull me down, actually encourage me to succeed. These people do still exist. I know that by making a choice I am capable of creating a better world.

I cannot express enough the value that there is in personal development and spending the time on ourselves. All I ever wanted was to be a great example, not only for my children but to help and inspire those that have come from the same place I have; to show them that there is a light at the end of the tunnel and a better way of living. By simply opening my mind to new possibilities and immersing myself in personal development, I am achieving just that. I finally believe that I am worth it, and you are too.

Kimberly Bennetta
29 years old
Entrepreneur
Normanville, Australia

195
Living My Purpose

*T*here I was: in a career helping people to climb the corporate ladder. The majority of my time was spent listening to their concerns. The words they were using were demotivating: "stuck in a rut," "not making a difference," "burned out," "stressed," "exhausted," "suffocated," Even worse, were their reasons for choosing the career: "My parents wanted me to do it," "the money," "I didn't know what else to do" or the most worrying, "I fell into it"; like they had no control over what they were doing: a victim of circumstance in their own life.

The even bigger irony was that I was providing career advice to clients but didn't feel that I was in synchronicity with the advice I was giving. I wasn't living my purpose. How could I truly help others to do the same? Many of the concerns resonated with me on some level, but the biggest realisation was that in between all this I was lacking inspiration. I was working to build someone else's vision, building their dreams, and putting my own on hold until the time was right. I didn't know what inspiration was, that I needed it, or that it was the oxygen for my soul.

It hit me when I got on a plane to the other side of the world. I saw that inspiration was everywhere. I had just been too busy living my logical life to see it. My life changed. I could no longer do something that was not my passion. My mission ignited. Life was too short to spent precious days in unfulfilling jobs. Today I wake up excited to work and be alive. Most importantly, I seek inspiration everywhere. It is, after all, the oxygen for my soul.

Tasmin Sabar

35 years old

Career Coach

Manchester, United Kingdom

196
Positivity – People, Passion & Persistence

*T*o be or not to be positive, that is the question.

We live a life of emancipation, not isolation. We are completely free, yet some of you choose to hold onto people and past experiences that keep you trapped. This is your chance to let go.

Surround yourself by the things that matter. Every single person in your life, and I mean every single person, needs to add value and be positive. By being overwhelmed with positivity and support, you naturally have a more empowered, vibrant and rewarding life. Your experiences are enriched by the amazing people you share them with. You are attracted to the best and open to being in the presence of greatness. In turn, you become great.

Make a list of the people who matter to you most and go spend time with them. Make another list of people you want to get to know better and pick up the phone to see how they truly fit into your life. Most importantly, make a final list of the people who bring you down. Those people who go out of their way to make you feel bad, who complain about everything, who saturate your life with negativity and take their frustrations out on you. Make that list and put a line through their name. This line signifies progress, it represents a future you and a stance on what you want your life to be from this day forward. Do not accept mediocrity; only accept positivity.

Positivity is the fuel to your heart. Identify everything in your life that you are passionate about, that makes you smile, and make it an obsession. You deserve it.

Jared Hopping
24 years old
Entrepreneur
Melbourne, Australia

197
Belief to Speak

I cannot remember a time in my life when I didn't have a speech impediment. No matter how many specialists I saw and no matter how hard I tried to speak simple sentences, my words were unrecognizable. I couldn't even say my own name.

I became so ashamed that I didn't want to talk at all. I lay awake in bed, praying my stutter would disintegrate overnight. I prayed to speak like a normal person. I lost count of the years of waking up, testing out my voice and then crying. I didn't want to speak, because I believed I couldn't. I didn't want anyone to acknowledge me, because I believed I wouldn't be valued. I became afraid of my own voice. Is there anything worse than being afraid of what makes you so special? Being frightened of your own power?

Belief is what made me find the strength to face myself. I could spend my life defeated... or I could achieve what I want, and be whoever I want to be. I didn't want to spend the rest of my life scared or victimized. The only thing worse than being afraid of something or someone is being afraid of your own power. The most shameful thing I could do was to not speak up.

Though speech pathologists would declare me 'cured' today, I still label myself as a stutterer. Why? Because I use it as ammunition. Channel your fears and use them as fuel. Let them drive you; let them push you; let them build you. Behind fear is the person you are to be. Know within yourself that you can do anything, as there is no excuse – zero – for not going after what you want in life. What would your life look like if you weren't always afraid?

Luisa Rivero
26 years old
Dermal Clinician
Melbourne, Australia

198
My Connection to Inspiration Saved My Life

J was crossing the street in a daze after my father passed away, when a thought within me shouted, "STOP!" I stopped. Then, I felt the wind from a bus whiz by, missing me by centimetres – a narrow escape!

I believe what we call 'intuition,' an 'inner voice or guide,' or a 'thought or idea,' are all 'connections' to inspired wisdom. Inspiration is not impulsive. It's removing paralysing clutter from your mind so you can hear wisdom, take action, do, be, and have more to contribute in a greater way to your world. When I bought my first Macintosh, I had an idea, "Buy Apple stocks." I had spare cash to buy 2,500 shares for $10,000; that would be worth $1,430,000 today. "It's too risky," reasoning muttered. I didn't know then how to hear and act on inspiration – and it cost me.

At another point later on in my life, I didn't listen, but this time the 'bus of life' flattened me. I felt I had failed myself and those around me. I used to beat myself up after big blunders or missed opportunities. Have you ever done this? But, I chose to take responsibility, seek solutions, and engage coaches to mentor me on mastering my inner and financial worlds. Since then, inspiration has empowered me to build inspiring and meaningful relationships, lose eighteen kilograms, and fearlessly trade the markets.

What is the 'clutter' inside your mind telling you? What is it stopping you from doing? Listen to 'wisdom' instead. What is it trying to help you achieve? What is it guiding you to do? STOP! Let the life-shattering buses whiz by. Take the actions you've wanted to take so you can be who you were meant to be.

Dale John William Peck
55 years old
Life Coach
Hong Kong, HKSAR

199
The Inspiration to Recover

I have a lifelong friend who has faced more challenges than most. Born into a rich heritage of debilitating addictions, her father, an alcoholic, was dead at forty-eight. Her mother, a perennial valium consumer, never recovered when at fifty-five, she suffered a stroke and died where she was institutionalised. Both were heavy smokers. Their behaviour, while destructive, was not as insidious as the diseases inside them. My friend calls it co-dependence. When we use people, places and things to replace what we perceive is missing.

When my friend tried to escape her heritage, there was no end to the challenges which manifested. Most devastating of these were the addictions that emerged in her children who fell prey to alcohol, heroin and marijuana. Low points were frequent. Phone calls to police, raging arguments with defiant kids under the influence, visits to rehab centres and prisons, anxious fears that the worst would befall them, ever present. After years of extraordinary duress, my friend crumpled. When admitted to the hospital's psychiatric ward, she begged the staff to let her die.

Throughout these trials, when there was silence, my friend and I would reflect quietly, envisioning something better — a life worth living. In those moments, she would talk expansively of her dreams of traveling, inspiring people, nourishing food, clothes, physical movement, and most importantly, educating and working with others to address their addictions. She would be paid magnificently for her service.

As I reflect now, I am proud of the friend I know so well. She often says I saved her life. That's true. My friend is me. I took steps, even when this seemed tortuous and impossible. Inspired, by what can only be done through me by the Universe, I now live the life envisioned in darkness.

Roslyn Saunders

58 years old

Co-dependence Coach

Brisbane, Australia

200
The Soul Ignites

A spiralling tornado of light pulls my soul out of my body. A star explodes in silent glory. Sparkling light fills a void of black sky and coalesces into the form of a glowing tree of light. There is a powerful essence that pulses from this light. Every particle of my being is infused with a wondrous sense of knowingness. One breath in. One breath out. I am filled with a remembering. Ancient and present. I am filled with peace. I am a breath of light in the dark of night. I am connected to all that is. The tree roots delve into the primal space inside my being and the branches expand to the outer reaches of the Universe. Instantaneously I know where I came from. Everything just is. No time, all is now. I consciously exist at the point of creation. In form and without form simultaneously. Exquisite unending joyous love. Close your eyes and experience you. Breathe. Feel. Allow this loving essence to shine through. Let it disintegrate the veil of illusion that is our human suffering and fill you with grace.

Call to the lost pieces of yourself:
Sparkling lights in the sky
The twinkling pieces of my broken heart
I am drifting aimlessly through the dark
Listening for the magnetic call of inspiration
To fuse me back to wholeness
Let me swell with the luminescent glow of joyful passionate creative exuberance
Ignite in me a spiralling tornado of unadulterated passion for life!

We are the creative essence of the Universe. Ignite your soul's power. Let it burn so brightly that the rest of humanity will be inspired to awaken to this joyous and enlightened being within themselves. Create your life magnificently, because that is the awesomeness of the Universe. To exist in the awesomeness of our own being-ness!

Megan Freeland
42 years old
Writer
Brisbane, Australia

201
Surrender the Marriage, Save the Love

"It takes great courage and commitment to stay connected in the midst of heartache and heartbreak."
Marianne Williamson

It was these very words of encouragement that held me in sacred space on the path of conscious uncoupling between myself and my husband of thirty years. At fifty, how do you end a relationship with someone you love and have spent the whole of your adult life with?

We had created a successful, happy, loving partnership – gifted with two amazing children, a lucrative business, a wonderful home, and treasured family memories. In this 'enough-ness,' though, there was an inner knowing that yearned to be fulfilled. The voice of the heart, louder than the voice of reason was screaming to that deeper more meaningful, connected part of me that 'knew' the truth. Our marriage was over. The goal was to surrender the marriage and save the love. The gift was to honour each other – our past, present and future. The outcome, it is possible.

Throughout this time, I've learned that love can be misapplied, misappropriated and conditional, but unconditional love cannot change. Real Love is a state of being, gratitude, reverence, honesty, trust, kindness, vulnerability and allowance. Our separation, coupled with grief, pain, aloneness, uncertainty and relief was worthy of respect and integrity. A compassionate heart and mindful head was imperative.

I learned it's important to align myself with people who honoured my choices, even if that meant being challenged to explore and reveal my deepest wounds. I learned my willingness to 'dive in' and embrace change with courage, confidence and commitment has led me to a place that includes more than just existing and evolving. It has led me to a space of thriving, prospering and living the joyful, creative, authentic expression of the greatness of who I truly be. For this I am forever grateful.

Angie Quinn

50 years old

Intuitive Life Coach & Parent Educator

Cairns, Australia

202
Oprah

*F*or most of my young life, I was lost in a haze. My childhood was a blur of bi-polar disorder, alcoholism and abuse, all defining how I played in the world. My parents separated when I was thirteen. I left home at fifteen and manifested an abundance of dysfunction. Somewhere very deep within me I knew that no matter what, I was going to be okay. But, I was still ashamed, confused and hurting. My teenage years were full of eating disorders and promiscuity. Despite my afflictions, I pretended nothing was wrong.

Hope came in the form of a woman who had been through far worse than me and was using her life to help others, Oprah Winfrey. She was my lighthouse. It may seem so cliché and waft-y, but when I was a young girl of fourteen, she shone bright through the haze. I saw a way out. I read some of the inspiring titles by authors she showcased, which became maps to my soul. I began to question why I was here and what life was all about.

I trudged through my pain. I finished university. I travelled. I opened up to life. Life opened up to me. I thought I had made it and yet deep down I knew I was still disconnected within. After having children, all other psychological wounds I'd suffered, opened wide. Exhausted from pain, I fell. Four years ago, I had a breakdown (breakthrough). In that moment I recommitted to me. I committed to learn how to love and be loved.

Since then, I have learned that all the dark was just a background to allow the light to shine brightly. It has all been purposeful so that I may wake up to who I really am. Oprah was right: "The whole purpose of life is to evolve into who you were meant to be."

Jen Lean
37 years old
Personal Growth Facilitator
Gold Coast, Australia

203
The Great Awakening

*H*ere we are: Born into a beautiful World of love, life, cultures, races, beliefs and differences. What a blessing and honour for us all to be here at these times; the most important times within man and woman kind: The Great Awakening.

What is this Great Awakening? It is the time, Brothers and Sisters, where we are faced with two choices: raise our vibrations and energies into the beauty and truth of who we are individually, and as a people, or become consumed by the energies and dramas of old that have held us all back for thousands of years.

People, young and old, are awakening at an alarming rate to the atrocities taking place across the World, to the lies and deception placed upon us by governments and world leaders, to the importance of energy and living at peace with all life, to the truth of who we really are and how we wish to live and behave in order to embrace the life we have all been blessed with.

As the survivor of a near-death experience, depression, anger and abandonment, suicidal tendencies, alcoholism and drug abuse, I experienced a radical life transformation and now give great thanks for my lessons and experiences, for without them all I would not see the beauty of my own awakening.

For those who are going through, or have been through, similar experiences, know that you are not alone. I firmly believe life is meant for living, and we have it within each of us to change and awaken to all the love and beauty with which we are blessed.

Breathe and awaken, Brothers and Sisters, to all that the Creator has blessed you with.

Life is yours. Almighty Blessings

Rameka Chin
35 years old
Psychic Medium, Guide & Healer
Gold Coast, Australia

204
Flow

*T*he old me was good at surface stuff. I lived to please others. I was excellent at putting what I thought others expected before my needs and wants. I would do things and go places because I thought I should: a word I was skilled at using! This was the guarded, self-conscious, weight on my shoulders me... until I met my son.

He taught me that life is too short to live someone else's life – to live any other way than the way I want it to be. It took a glimpse of death through my son to make me realise how quickly life can be taken away. It was in the moments of my son's health complications that everything changed. Each time it happened, a layer of me was stripped back, until one day I was so raw and bare that I hit rock bottom. I knew I needed strong self-worth from that day on. My life was full of "that will do," and living life saying "okay" and "should." I cleared out my emotions and belongings.

The flow of thoughts now passes through my body like the spectacular Murray River. As the water flows in and around obstacles, I allow things to flow through and around me. And as a river has days of varying stream, I allow myself to be in the moment with love, I trust that where I am in this moment is right where I need to be. My message to you is this: work back through your layers now before something comes along to do it for you; allow yourself the freedom of flow – let things come and go; be honest with yourself and embrace the life around you; you can have the life you want – it is all within you now. Flow.

Shanelle Cooper
33 years old
Mind & Body Strategist
Melbourne, Australia

205
Overcoming My Fear
of Drowning

*U*ntil my mid-fifties, I had a fear of water so debilitating that I refused to go into anything deeper than a bathtub. I knew that fears could be overcome. But this was no ordinary fear. I believed with certainty that in water I would drown. Scuba diving friends told me how wonderful the underwater world was. It sounded amazing, but in my mind I couldn't do it. I couldn't even swim, so how would I possibly ever have the nerve to dive? For me scuba diving would equate to drowning. Was it time to face my greatest fear?

I started swimming lessons and, months later, a scuba pool lesson. As I went underwater, I felt everything closing in on me. I panicked and clawed my way to the side of the pool. I sat there shaking and mortified. I couldn't do this! However, a small voice reminded me that if I never tried, how would I know if I could or couldn't? Could I believe in myself and learn to swim? And even dive?

A year later when I submerged, the fear was still there, but it was different. It didn't stop me. I believed I could dive and no longer wanted to be limited in what I could enjoy. While diving in Maui a week after my certification, I heard an eerie sound, only to discover it was a whale song — a rare and absolutely mind blowing experience. What a celebration to overcoming my fear and starting to experience a whole new world!

Facing my fears and dissolving 'limiting beliefs' extends far beyond the underwater world for me now. I truly believe that there are endless possibilities available to each and every one of us. All that is needed is belief in yourself!

Paulette Archer
65 years old
Women's Empowerment Leader
Brisbane, Australia

206
Life Starts at Sixty

"*Y*ou can if you want!" Those were the words my mother told me when I was twelve years old trying to do my homework. Or rather, she said, "Tu peux si tu veux," as this happened in a very small village near Dijon, France. Many decades later and on the other side of the world, these words still resonate clearly in my mind even though my mother had passed away. I keep challenging myself in many areas of my life; as in my mid-forties, when I started running on a regular basis and did a few small triathlons, fun runs and half marathons.

Five months after turning 60, I had the opportunity to start karate in the kyokushin style. I reached brown belt status before I turned 64. I am still training, hoping for black belt within the next two years. Twenty-two weeks before the 35th Melbourne marathon in 2012, I was challenged to run a full marathon at age 62.

As I had been regularly running shorter distances, I started a program twenty weeks prior to the marathon. At the start of my preparation, I set myself a goal of four hours and 45 minutes. At the conclusion of the program prior to the marathon, I reviewed my goal. I followed my plan, taking nutrients and using the drink stations, and finished the marathon in four hours, 11 minutes and 53 seconds.

In 2013, I ran in the 36th Melbourne marathon and beat my own record by eight minutes. In 2014, I am planning to run the 37th Melbourne marathon in under four hours. I did a half marathon in January 2014 in 1 hour, 54 minutes and 51 seconds: right on target! I believe we should keep challenging ourselves regardless of our age or ability. We can always do better. Remember: You can if you want!

Marc Frochot
64 years old
Chiropractor
Bendigo, Australia

207
My Calling

*A*s I sat with my daughter watching the love of her life suffer with the final stages of cancer, something unexplainable happened to me that changed the direction of my life.

I felt a calling from my late grandfather who passed away when I was a small child. He was telling me to work with the elderly. The calling was so strong that I could not block it out of my mind. It dominated my thoughts and plans for the future. Firstly, I resigned from my job as a waitress and enrolled in an an aged care course. I received a lot of negativity from family saying that I was too old to study, and how would I survive without a regular income. But I just kept going. I completed my Certificate III in Aged Care and volunteered at a local nursing home conducting a current affairs group. This nursing home offered me a position. I have gone on to complete a Certificate IV in Lifestyle and Leisure as well as two diplomas; but all of this is secondary to my purpose in life which is to look after the elderly.

I have had many challenges in my journey, but somehow things have always worked out. It is like my grandfather is guiding me as far as he can and providing me with what I need to fulfil my purpose in life. I have had many affirmations about my calling to work with the elderly: signs that I was meant to follow this path eight years ago, aged 46. My message to you is this: follow your intuition, be quiet and listen to the voice in your head, believe in yourself and never give up.

Tracey Frochot
54 years old
Diversional Therapist
Bendigo, Australia

208
Remember

*A*s the evening wore on, I became more relaxed despite the fact I was being bullied into a ludicrous argument. It was as though I was standing behind myself, watching myself. I laid down. I curled up into a tight ball, experiencing an un-nerving sensation. Nothing in my chest was functioning.

"Breathe girl, breathe!" I said to myself, but nothing: "Oh, this isn't good." I felt a horrible sensation as though I was being electrocuted – just under my skin. Every nerve was being fried. I thought that if I could figure out exactly where this sensation was, maybe I could change it. Suddenly, a huge, bright white tube encased me. Confused, I surveyed my surroundings and saw my body on the bed. Then – absolute peace. I was peace, love, and joy. No thinking, no judgements. I wanted to stay there. Telepathically, I heard: "Go back, you have work to do."

Immediately, I was thrown back into my body, but I couldn't fit. I wriggled until I was in. The tunnel and light were gone. It was morning, and I vividly remembered dying. The sensations, the tunnel, the white light and the peace, love and joy... and the message: "Go back, you have work to do."

We have been steeped in beliefs that no longer serve us well. Fear of death is one. Death of self, a loved one, losing something, separation, change, not understanding, are all deaths. Without deaths there would never be new beginnings, wisdoms, understandings, different perspectives – and those wonderful 'ah-ha' moments that bring newness, brightness, deeper awareness, and an amazing reconnection with our soul and spirit. The ability to change is the ability to heal... not just yourself, but all you encounter. You have the opportunity to change illusions of separateness and duality. Your soul knows you are a high vibrational being, connected to all. Remember.

Rosalie Alexander
67 years old
Body & Mind Healer
Brisbane, Australia

209
Twenty Years Later

I was fourteen years old when I stepped off the bus in the forest three hours from home. I had no idea that the week ahead was going to be so significant. In fact, I wouldn't join those dots together for almost twenty years. I thought I was just going to learn to ride a horse.

Our instructor, Jeff, was larger than life in his dry as a bone and Akubra hat. His knowledge of horsemanship was certain, and his knowledge of what made the Universe tick was even greater. A spark was ignited that let me know I could achieve anything. In that week, I learned what I would come to know as Universal Laws. I had light bulb moment after light bulb moment. When I arrived home, I was bursting with vitality. My family had never seen me so vibrant. I knew that this week was special. I never wanted it to fade; so for the first time ever I opened a journal and began to write everything I could remember about what I had learned.

Almost twenty years later, I was hunting for some photos when I found the journal. I sat on my bed and carefully opened the pages. As I began to read, tears started to fall down my face. I was stunned. Those Universal Laws Jeff had inspired me with all those years ago were now the foundation of my life and business. The spark really had been lit in me all those years ago, along with the belief in myself to make it happen. I was now the proof I needed for myself. I came away knowing with certainty that the difference people make in other's lives is seldom seen right away. It was worth waiting twenty years to understand this.

Donna Preedy

35 years old

Mind & Body Consultant

Perth, Australia

210
A New Purpose

*A*t age seventeen, I was months away from graduating high school and days away from starting my career in the Air Force. Then, I made the biggest mistake of my life. I was jumping off a bridge with friends and dove head first with a body-board. I hit the water, the board landed flat and my head smashed right into the board. It broke my neck, resulting in instant paralysis from the neck down. If it wasn't for one of my best friends I would have drowned. I was on life support and in an induced coma for two weeks. My first question was, "Will I walk again?" I had no movement from the neck down and the doctors weren't optimistic whether I'd regain any further movement. I chose to see the three biggest positives of my situation:

1) I'm not dead.
2) I had no brain damage.
3) I wasn't stuck on a ventilator to breathe.

I have been fortunate to regain partial movement of my arms, but I have no hand or finger movement. I rely on my mum for everything. She is my twenty-four hour carer.

Since the accident, I have found a new purpose in life. I do voluntary work for the Spinal Education Awareness Team Program run by Spinal Injuries Australia. I do awareness talks about my accident to school children to get them to stop and think before doing something risky. I can see they are deeply touched by my story. When they give me a hug and thank me, it drives me to continue doing what I do. If I get a message into at least one kid's head and stop them from ending up like me, I'm serving my purpose. No matter how bad things may seem or turn out, you can always make best out of a bad situation.

Kieron D'Netto

28 years old

Education & Motivational Speaker

Brisbane, Australia

211
Awakening the Beautiful Woman Within

I experienced low self-esteem from childhood. At seventeen, I was in an abusive marriage which made me feel like I was fat and ugly. After two years, I finally walked away from that relationship. My ten year-long eating disorder began. I used sex to feel in control and good about myself. For years, my life consisted of partying, smoking, drugs, sex, alcohol and bad relationships. To the outside world, it seemed I had a dream life hosting sexy parties and interviewing adult stars!

But, my happiness was associated with outside experiences. It wasn't real. Underneath, I felt empty and unlovable. I made myself so busy with all this 'stuff' so I wouldn't have to feel what was going on inside: pain, shame and fear.

This all changed when I met a man who I had an incredible connection with: a soul connection. After a short intense time together, he got scared and ran away, which brought up beliefs I had been burying: "I'm not good enough," "I'm not pretty enough," "There is something wrong with me," and the biggest one, "I am not worthy of love."

Instead of numbing the pain, I allowed myself to be vulnerable and feel my emotions. My healing journey began as I connected to my soul through facilitated healings, meditation, yoga, dance, honesty, forgiveness and making self-loving choices. Almost overnight, my eating disorder was cured and I let go of my false beliefs about myself. My whole life transformed. I awakened to my soul purpose as a healer. I now help others awaken and heal so they too can feel the love from within.

A woman's real beauty is the reflection of her inner happiness. I awakened the beautiful woman within by letting go of who I thought I was supposed to be and embraced who I am. And who I am is love.

Emmajane Love (EJ)

30 years old

Lovepreneur, Healer, Author & Speaker

Sunshine Coast, Australia

212
Letting Go of Beliefs, Guilt & Fear

J love *Eat Pray Love* where Elizabeth Gilbert immerses herself in new perspectives and finally tosses guilt and her last limiting belief and fear. You see, I've experienced that beliefs, fear and guilt are close relations. In my years in a religious community we were immersed in feel-good, idealistic beliefs about God's unconditional love and utopian plans, which were interlaced with fear-based beliefs about the eternal ramifications of disunity and temptations by the 'outside, fallen world'.

Questioning my beliefs and failing to live 'the ideal' brought anxiety, depression and sickness. Failure to 'save' my arranged 'eternal marriage' brought fear and guilt. I had night terrors of an angry ocean chasing me and 'saw' spiders on the wall. I now know fear doesn't prove a belief's validity, just that its neural pathways in the brain are strong. Guilt is a sign you are challenging a belief — that's all. Release the belief and you release the guilt.

Are you scared to try a new perspective? What if the 'truth' you cling to is merely a perception? Take a step sideways and your view will change. Try relaxing your grip on your 'belief-safety-chain' and let go. I did, and a loving Creator had my back. My feet touched firm, fertile ground. I stepped into new territories, tossing away old beliefs and guilt and making new neural pathways as I tried different ideas on for size.

Be curious. Test new waters. Pray for discernment then try on a new 'jacket' of ideas. If it's not comfortable, try another — or make your own! You don't need anyone's approval. Mine is a kaleidoscope of 'truths' I call 'eclecticism'. Whatever you choose, just make sure it resonates with the voice of YOUR soul and makes your heart sing 'FREEDOM'.

Wendy Millgate
50 years old
Editor & Writer
Brisbane, Australia

213
I Don't Understand Myself

*M*any would be shaking their heads right now, thinking, "I never understand him. I like him, in small doses, but, I just know he is weird." Many head shakers can recall moments of sheer joy at being around him, yet many would quite cheerfully strangle him. He says inappropriate things at wrong times; often only he understanding why he said them. He is loud, best watched from a distance, like fireworks.

He has few male influences in his life, yet he moves skilfully from circle-to-circle, from beer hall to boardroom. He has a stage face; kids are eager to form a line behind him; noise is his constant companion. If you make him care, he will always care. He is poor as a church mouse, with a wealth of creative ideas. He is quick to join in fun, but just as quick to leave a party for his own company. Daughters love him, yet is he lazy in all things. He sees beauty in life and is willing to share what he finds. He is worth loving, yet lives with no lover.

He brings erratic solutions to complex issues. Luck is on his side. He lets people see only the part of him they need to see. He's funny, with sharp wit. People either like or loathe him on first meeting. He has no achievements to point to; has lost in love, but won an audience. He's life-educated, university shy. Approaching his fiftieth year, he feels he should be better for the journey. He's lost a brother; never settled with a lost father. His self-worth is not dependent on others. He's owned a house; lost a home; misplaced a wife; walked in a foreign land; forgiven a debt; smiled under hardship; laughed with friends. He knows there's much more to go, but states openly, "I don't understand myself."

Michael Gray
49 years old
Undecided
Sunshine Coast, Australia

214
Mastering Your Life

*I*t was 1986, when I first became aware of my spiritual journey. I was reading Shirley MacLaine's book, *Out On A Limb*, when a friend passed away suddenly. I had a dream and became conscious of amazing events happening in my life. You might call these coincidences but I call them 'synchronicity.' With my mind open, I started to have great insights into life either in the shower, or driving the car.

Then, in 1989, I was diagnosed with a rare disease, Paget's disease. I was told it was a vigorous form of breast cancer. My doctor recommended a radical mastectomy of my right breast. I was shocked, but agreed to go ahead with the operation. However, a series of miracles happened that led me to change my mind. My doctor told me I was risking my life and informed me of other patients he had who refused operations and died. I walked out of his surgery shattered.

I had found another doctor who actually supported my new beliefs and actions and totally inspired me, so I cancelled the operation. I went to Crystal Lodge in Katoomba NSW (Healing Spa) for rest and recuperation, and I started thinking differently about my body and life. I returned home a new person. That was twenty-five years ago, and as you can see, I am still alive! I hardly go to the doctor. What I have learned and practiced throughout my sixty-five years is:

- You have the choice to be the victim or master of your own life.
- You are a co-creator with the Universe.
- What you focus on, you attract.
- What you think, you become.
- Keep company with people who inspire you.
- Read books that inspire you.
- Most of all, believe in yourself.

Mary Wiking
65 years old
Retired
Mount Evelyn, Australia

215
Make A New Decision

Throughout my life, I've had feelings of "I'm not good enough." No one would know because I never make it a feature in my decisions. In many situations, I've found myself in the 'underdog' position. It's like I had to achieve more in what I was doing to have equal recognition. In spite of that, I have achieved a reasonable level of success. I share this because one day I realised what determines success... my decisions. Since then, I've taken challenges head on. I'm determined and will never give up on something I'm committed to. I believe the only way I can fail is by giving up. Sometimes, I just need to change the decision.

Decisions have consequences, good or bad. There is always an outcome. Sometimes I've learned the hard way. At the core of our being, we know who we are. So I say, believe in a better you! You are not your behaviours or actions. You are your decisions. Decisions create behaviours and actions. Give yourself another opportunity: make a new decision.

Society teaches us that when we 'have' the happiness, money, relationship, then we can 'be' happy. It's not the 'having' that causes your happiness, it's your decisions. So, when you decide to 'be happy,' then you can make decisions to do what you need to do, so you can have what you want to have. Ask yourself, "Who do I need to be, to do what I need to do, to have what I want to have?"

Your reality is a result of your decisions; if you don't like your reality then change the decisions you are making. If nothing changes, nothing changes. You deserve to believe in a better you. So make a new decision! You are worth it!

Lisa Wiking
37 years old
Leadership Coach & Trainer
Melbourne, Australia

216
My Children

When I was a child, I had my whole life mapped out. I was going to do everything according to a well-defined plan – finish school, go to university, get a job, get married, have kids and live happily ever after. We all know that along with plans come choices, and we make choices that change our life path. So what happens when those choices are taken away from you?

Everything on my map was an exciting journey, travelling along to each point of my destination according to plan. That was, until it was time to start a family. What was supposed to have been a leisurely cruise to a beautiful tropical island became the roughest journey of my life.

At twenty-four, I was pregnant with my first child. Unfortunately, that soul was not to be. Miscarriage after miscarriage, it began to look like the ship was sinking. I felt I was paddling alone on a big ocean in a small canoe, rather than travelling on a cruise ship to my tropical paradise. Determined not to give up, I continued to paddle across stormy waters.

Each pregnancy was worse than the previous one: painful and life threatening. I was told to give up after the seventh loss. Could I put myself through any more disappointment and grief? Was this the time to give up? Not long after this internal struggle, I found myself pregnant again. And at ten weeks the telltale signs of a loss began.

Imagine my immense joy when I saw the ultrasound – a tiny baby with arms, legs, fingers, toes and a heartbeat! Tears of gratitude, relief and euphoria streamed down my cheeks. I was resolved that this one was to be. The journey was long. The journey was hard. But the journey was worth it. Today I have three beautiful, healthy children.

Eleni Szemeti
49 years old
Business Developer
Melbourne, Australia

217
Freedom Is Your Right

*I*magine two eggs, one black, one white. When you look at them closely they are different and yet the same. Go ahead, crack them open. What do you see? Inside they are both exactly the same. No matter who you are, we are all the same on the inside.

What really upsets me is that we do not have equality on this Earth. If I was a world leader I would stand for freedom for everyone. Everyone should have the right to freedom, freedom to laugh, freedom to smile, freedom to love and freedom to have peace.

Everyone should prosper; everyone should feel worthy; everyone is priceless no matter what you look like, where you come from, or who you are. There should be no more suffering, no more pain, no more grief or hatred. We should live in a world of prosperity.

I have been blessed to have seen and met many inspirational speakers. I was just eleven when I started attending seminars and worked with Jeff and Kane, Clinton Swaine, Rossco Paddison, Malissa Thorpe, Travis Bell, Lauren Reilly and many more wonderful coaches, mentors and speakers. I saw Emily the first time she was on stage; it was truly inspirational to me.

I know I'm only a fourteen-year-old, but I want to someday follow in their amazing footsteps. I want to help the third world countries and create equality between all races. Imagine a world where nobody has to face racism, face offences to their culture, be mistreated or belittled. It is time for our world to unite! There should be no racism, offensive language; everybody should be free to learn, free to love, free to do whatever they want in life. Freedom is your right!

Michael Szemeti

14 years old

Student

Melbourne, Australia

218
Ghosts

*D*o you believe in ghosts? My earliest memory was when I was five. I was playing with my dog, spinning him around in circles, while holding him in my arms. I suddenly heard a loud booming voice say, "Stop it!" Startled, I immediately stopped, looked around and there was no one there.

Coming home from fifth grade, I entered my house and heard what I thought was a business meeting of my dad's. I followed the muttering voices down the long hallway as they got louder and louder. I turned the corner and all the voices suddenly stopped. No one was there!

One day in junior high, a fellow classmate jumped me from behind and got me into a headlock. I was getting ready to punch him when someone or something grabbed both of my arms from behind. Once again there was no one there!

I experienced increasingly more phenomenon over the years. No one seemed to be able to relate to what I was going through. I was misunderstood by both friends and family. For a time, my ghostly friends disappeared. I was angry. I didn't want them to go away. I just wanted to understand what I was experiencing. As I tried to suppress my abilities and experiences to appease others, life seemed to stop flowing for me.

During my journey, I found I was being visited and assisted by spiritual guides and master teachers. There was nothing to fear or be concerned about after all. I was finally free to be myself. My journey of self-understanding and discovery began from within, and with the support of some wonderful people I've met along the way. When I chose to celebrate who I was and accepted my spiritual path, I could see my experiences as beautiful blessing full of wonderful rich life experiences.

Dr. Dan Fleishman
46 years old
Chiropractor, Spiritual Coach & Speaker
Dallas, United States

219
Fighting to Survive

*H*ow ironic! After years of wanting to die to escape the violence, instability and loneliness of my life, at eighteen, I was now fighting to survive. In a far-away land, I was experiencing what could be my last breath. I longed for home.

As the first wave hit, I was terrified. "Dive into it," my cousin yelled. In the split second I had to make a decision, I ignored her advice. That choice presented a new set of challenges. Under the water with half a breath in my lungs, I tumbled like a rag doll. Terror filled me as I tried to make sense of my position and how to extract myself from the powerful waves. My foot found sand; I pushed up firmly. I had barely taken a breath when the next wave hit, once again tumbling and dragging me across the coarse seabed.

Swallowing water, my lungs demanded oxygen. I fought to find footing and force my head above the water. I was exhausted. I just needed one more breath; one more chance at life. That breath, as I rose out of the water, was both bitter and sweet. Salt water choked my nose and throat as I gulped for air. In a split second, I was submerged again. I didn't have enough oxygen, let alone strength, to get me through another round.

I stopped fighting. I let go... My senses became alive in a way I hadn't experienced. Peace and calm filled me, and for a few seconds I was at one with everything. The ocean released me. I was free. That day I learned the power of letting go during times of greatest fear; of surrendering rather than fighting. When we allow this we have the opportunity to experience tremendous peace; being fully alive to experience oneness.

Nicole Donaldson

45 years old

Business & Life Enrichment Coach

Brisbane, Australia

220
Meditation is Medicine for The Mind and Syrup for The Soul

*J*always, in all ways, celebrate my life as a journey and not a destination. But the journey has presented some hurtful and disempowering situations, all of which I now see were an integral part of the divine design of my life, prompting me to stand in personal power and responsibility, outside of blame, judgement and the need to be anything less than my true self.

I spent the majority of my life exhausting reservoirs of energy by hiding my natural gifts and connection to the realms of spirit, fearful around the judgement of others. Four years ago this existence unravelled; I was 'on the carpet' – overnight, a single parent with a shattered heart, broke and zero purpose for anything.

In these dark hours, I made three decisions; to be of service, to trust (in the Universe and who I am) and to begin a meditation routine. I decided that five minutes meditation in the morning setting a positive intention for my day and five minutes in the evening feeling deep gratitude for every little thing was totally do-able – this commitment changed my entire life! Five minutes became twenty and I went from ragged to radiant in a short period of time.

Daily meditation quietened my mind, dissolved my fears and opened the doors to intuition and synchronicity. As my inner world expanded and embraced a deep love of self and the planet, my outer world naturally aligned with big flows of love, abundance and real magic. Today I let my smile change the world, not the world change my smile. I truly feel blessed beyond belief... Namaste.

Tanya Allison
47 years old
Meditation Facilitator & Editor
Gold Coast, Australia

221
A Suited Monk on the River

*T*he life journey looks like a river starting from the mountain, wandering around the forest, jumping from the rocks, crossing the dessert and finally reaching the sea. At the last moment, an individual life ends like a drop of water merging into the ocean. A life ends and a soul gets a home that is full of love, peace and brightness. I believe it. Yes, I do.

I was born in 1972 in a village in China, a very cold place with wild snow and wind. I had a bright childhood with mum's abundance of love. I had a successful education and career in the upstream of my life river. I became a business manager at age of thirty-three. I had a good title, income and reputation. While driving myself too hard for success, I experienced a relationship-crisis three years later. My marriage was cracking like glass. My world seemed to collapse in one night.

I reflected on my journey. I began to listen to my inner voice. My awareness lit up the darkness. Slowly after the crisis I discovered my core values: love, joy, and peace. We are living in a fast-paced and uncertain world. Like running a marathon, we are 'pushed' to run faster to keep a position, but forget our own rhythm and strength. It is so important to discover our authentic strength, values and purpose. We can live as a 'suited monk,' wearing a business suit in the business world but living from within as a 'monk' with clarity, peace and meaning.

Now I am living in Perth. Hearing the sounds of the waves, I feel myself like a drop of water merging into the ocean. Life is a journey, a journey of experience, learning and awareness; and it is awesome!

Larry Lee
41 years old
Life Coach, Trainer & Consultant
Perth, Australia

222
Creating Space for Inspiration

I firmly believe that inspiration is everywhere, and our attitude is the aperture that determines how much of it we see and recognize. These days I see a lot of inspiration. It is not something I take for granted though, as it is a skill forged through particularly challenging times; one of which was in January 2003 when the world's first recorded 'fire tornado' exploded through Australia's bush capital, Canberra.

Over ten hours, four people died and over 500 homes were destroyed: my parents' home included. We were forced to flee as the fire ripped through the forest across from their house. Like many others, we were thankful to have gotten out alive that day. But, at twenty-nine years old the landscape of my life had changed forever. Not only was the family home gone, even most of our beloved suburb was unrecognizable.

There is no doubt that such destruction, loss and shock is assaulting. However, looking back, even amidst this difficult time, there was inspiration all around. From the guy who drove around handing out bottled water to people like us sifting through the ashes, to the elderly lady who clambered over bricks and rubble to slip $20 into my mum's hand. The kindness and outpouring of love amidst strangers was palpable and inspiring.

The experience adjusted my attitude and enhanced my ability to see and appreciate inspiration in its many forms. You too can cultivate this skill – and you don't need tragedy in order to do so. Setting the intention to create space for more inspiration in your life is a great first step. This can be supported by physically and emotionally creating space through clutter clearing, simplifying your home, self-care and letting go of what weighs on your heart. This will adjust **your** inspiration aperture. May you always be inspired by the picture!

Emily J Rooney
39 years old
The Home Alchemist
Byron Bay, Australia

223
The Light of Inspiration within You

I believe inspiration is the light from deep inside that sparks a vision for new possibilities of wonder in life. It is the energy that moves you and others to bring that vision to life. This light of inspiration shines through darkness and allows you to overcome challenges and accomplish the seemingly impossible.

Mahatma Gandhi created a vision for an independent India that inspired a nation of 350 million people to stand up to and overcome British rule through peaceful protest. Steve Jobs created a vision for computers to be in the hands of everyday people. He inspired new ways for using computers and other devices now enjoyed by millions of people around the world.

I believe the light of inspiration shines inside everyone. When I reached my late thirties, I had never been in a relationship. I was shy and afraid to the extent of feeling paralysed about even trying to find a partner. Many times I thought to myself, "I'm not going to find anyone." I felt hopeless and lonely.

Then one day, I saw the light of inspiration shining through. I thought to myself, "I want a partner to share my life with." I conjured up the courage and motivation to search for the woman of my dreams. After two years, I still hadn't found her. Suddenly the miracle of my life occurred. I met the beautiful, loving, and attractive woman I was looking for. The connection we now share is magical. Every thought of her warms my heart and brings a smile to my face.

The light of inspiration has the power to produce a miracle and make a difference in your life and for people across the world. You have this power within you.

Rasik Rama

38 years old

Life Direction Coach

Melbourne, Australia

224
Let Your Past Refine You, Not Deny You

*G*rowing up in a strict religious family in QLD, the world seemed small and innocent for the first seventeen years of my life. Unsure of my 'path,' I did what my mum suggested and went into hospitality. Little did I know, four years later my mum would be dead. For the next nine years, I went off the rails, left my girlfriend and daughter, abused drugs and alcohol and avoided responsibility.

At thirty, I was invited to a course by a friend. I knew I was at a turning point and that if I did not transform my place in the world that I could be in prison, dead or on track for major health issues. A catalyst was required. The course turned out to be it. Undertaking an amazing weekend with 200 other people committed to furthering themselves enabled me to completely change my life and circumstances. During the follow-up course, I committed to giving up drug dealing, and on the final day of the course I upheld my word and walked away from that profession.

Fourteen years down the track, I have accomplished many amazing outcomes. I created a kid's charity that inspires young people. I radically transformed my career from drug-dealer to business owner. The thing that strikes me about looking back over my life is that every step contributed something new to my experiences. There is nothing I regret. However, if you let your past refine you by owning it and embracing the lessons learned then it will not deny you living a great life. I trust you embrace your past for the rich tapestry this represents of you.

Tim Lassig
44 years old
Hospitality Shopfitter
Sydney, Australia

225
My World's Richer for My Struggles

*B*efore my accident, I was independent and career focused. I swam in the Masters Games, helped my parents with their spaetzle maker business, travelled widely, spent a lot of time with friends and family and enjoyed my career as a leader of education. I had spent a year with my daughter in the Middle East, traveling and consulting with teachers, while teaming up with others to rewrite the national curriculum for Qatar.

My life changed when I returned home. I had a car accident. Through a poor rehabilitation program and a problem with me accepting my injuries, I ended up in a wheelchair. It was months before I could walk again and nearly two years before I could walk without the aid of a walking stick. Life was over for me. I was in a very dark place, lost most of my friends and grew further apart from my family. They didn't know what to do or how to help. I literally gave up on living a normal life.

Finally, I found an amazing specialist who was a no nonsense doctor. He worked with me tirelessly for over two years. I still see him now for pain relief (as the pain's still ongoing), but I now accept where I am in life and accept each day for what it is, whether it's a good day or bad day.

My world is tough. I deal with self-doubt and pain in my body every day. But my world is richer for my struggles. At the time, if anyone had said, "You're going to be better off for going through this...." I would have told them where to go. Now I have to agree and answer back, "If I can get through this, then I can get through anything in life."

Tan-Ja

49 years old

Writer & Blogging Trainer

Queensland, Australia

226
The Last Goodbye

*S*tanding at the pulpit with my brother at my side, my mind flashed to our last 'goodbye.'

"Dear, I want to die in God's house." It had been a big weekend and my father looked tired. "Dad, don't talk like that! You're not going anywhere, and when you do wouldn't you rather pass quietly in your sleep like everyone else? Think about the fuss, what that would mean firemen, ambulance, TV and even the news in Samoa."

"Dear, I want to die in God's house." We had had this conversation before. It was time to go. I rose and hugged my father. With tears in his eyes, dad held my hand like he always did saying, "I love you so much, dear." "I love you too, Dad. Everything will be alright. I'm back in seven days."

The next day, Monday 19 April 2005, my sister called. "Lia, what's wrong? Are the kids ok?"... Gulp. "It's dad..." I couldn't breathe. Dad's shift as verger of the Christchurch Catholic Cathedral had finished when an Australian couple arrived requesting a tour. The late afternoon sun flooded the magnificent glass panelled dome. Resting on the top landing, dad clasped his heart as he fell gently into the arms of strangers.

Strong firemen lowered our beautiful father amidst streams of brilliant light to the ambulance below. Blessed by the bishop and mourned throughout the country, dad's passing was broadcast on New Zealand National TV and the radio in Samoa. Such was my father's faith in God, it was difficult to grieve. Our tears were tears of sorrow for ourselves, for dad was with his God at last.

It's my turn to talk. The Cathedral was full. People were waiting. I spoke: "My father had incredible faith..."

Otila Osborne
52 years old
Company Director
Wellington, New Zealand

227
Moving with Love

*J*am simply a martial artist, travelling the path of physical training, combat and movement sciences. I have been exploring for many years, and today I feel truly blessed, for I have never been stronger, fitter, or healthier than I am right now. I remain in awe of the physical wealth possessed by all. It drives my exploration to uncover the mysteries of the human condition.

Three decades in the body-mind sciences has blessed me with a profound understanding of the magnificence of the human body, and of the powerful abilities we have locked within. We hold amazing gifts just beneath our sicknesses, inside our ailments. Gifts expressed as diseases and pains. Gifts that are waiting to be unbound, to be discovered with incredible potential to be realised and expressed. Our dreams made manifest.

The truth I have realised; is that we can release ourselves from despair or depression, from pain or suffering, from any prison or circumstance, regardless of the challenges we face, at any point in our lives. For freedom is enclosed within our physical constraints and is liberated through movement. Freedom of movement brings abundance of love. It is this love, that we all have the intrinsic ability to realize, through the gift of movement.

My odyssey into movement, into what it means to be human, has led me to this: Love is what we already and always are. The deep realization is that movement heals! Movement is life affirming. To move is to express the love of the Universe. You are exactly what you need right now. You are the change you need! Whatever you do, dare greatly! Start moving in any way that makes your heart sing. You have nothing to lose, except mediocrity and the pretensions that keep you from your magnificent truth and living an extraordinary life.

Dean Jones
46 years old
Peak Performance Coach
Johannesburg, South Africa

228
Honor Me

*L*iving in fear is a horrible way to endure life. I was one of those women who thought that it would never happen to me. I blamed myself constantly every time I got a beating. But I know now that it was not my fault. It had nothing to do with me. I thought that if I loved him more that he would change. Not only was I naïve, but with that mindset I was doomed from the start.

It was the isolation that kept me quiet for so long. Not being able to see my family or friends for any length of time took its toll on me. I sought help many times over the years but there was no use. Nothing changed. When he died, I lived with so much guilt and shame. In effect, I wanted to punish myself forever. That was easier than asking for help. I know now that we all need help. We can't do it alone, so you shouldn't have to.

My survival was a blessing not a curse, and I have gained strength in the knowledge that I am not a victim of circumstance. I have the inner strength to live life on purpose and to make a difference in the world. I want to empower people so that they won't feel alone.

I made it through the toughest of times with prayer and unconditional love from my family. I did not go to counselling because I didn't want to live in my story forever. True power comes from within. It's the choices we make and the love we give. I know that my experiences were to teach me resilience and compassion toward others. I have the ability to overcome any obstacles in life and I am very grateful for that.

Honor Turner
41 years old
Inspired Author
Brisbane, Australia

229
Soar Above Your Limitations

*W*hen you are living with illness, small things become big achievements: walking, catching the bus, eating a meal out, or driving for a few minutes. You become grateful for everything that others take for granted. Your body is supposed to walk, run, work, move, without you consciously thinking about it. But when it stops working, you pause to think about how your body and mind interacts with the world, and your place in it. This leads to new revelations, learning, appreciation, and meeting beautiful, like-minded souls.

I searched for my truth. Who was I? I had been hiding behind other people's perceptions. I allowed myself to be emotionally and verbally abused from a very young age until fairly recently, out of a sense of loyalty and fear. Yes, this was a choice I made, because once I became an adult, I should have chosen me.

I struggled with feeling helpless, useless, and worthless. I felt my body had betrayed me. But in hindsight, I had spent years beating myself up and allowing others to beat me with their words. Therefore, how could I expect my body to function optimally? The brain can't differentiate between what you tell it and someone else tells you. You become what you think. I became what I was told by the people who were supposed to love me and keep me safe. I gave up my power and became a victim.

I am slowly emerging from my cocoon and becoming a vibrant, lovable butterfly who chases their dreams and makes them a reality. I believe we can all soar above our limitations and experience the freedom of connecting with self. You can help heal the wounded child inside yourself: respect yourself, believe in yourself, and treat yourself with kindness. Everyday we're alive can be a miracle.

Maria Solano

41 years old

Life Learner

Newcastle, Australia

230
Birth Rites are Human Rights

*C*hildbirth is the most natural, normal and yet intense, powerful and rewarding rite of passage any woman will experience in her lifetime. As a society, we need to create more opportunities for women to have the option to birth in an empowered, ecstatic state than what is being accepted in our current medical model.

The most important approach to achieving a natural birth is to not engage your 'thinking mind.' If your neocortex is active, it will block the delicious cocktail of hormones and endorphins that keep labour going and provide you with pain relief greater than any pharmaceutical. Go within yourself to access your ancient limbic brain through quieting your mind. This is where your ecstatically blissful birth experience can be accessed.

Many know the 'love' hormone, oxytocin that is released during intimacy, lovemaking and orgasm is the same hormone that initiates and maintains labour. No wonder there has been an increase in labour dystocia, especially when birthing within the medical system. Not many women can have an orgasm with complete strangers in the room watching and assessing her. So, why do we think she will be able to labour in a room of bright lights, cold floors, and noise with different people coming and going?

Women need to feel safe for their inner sensual juiciness to flow in life and especially during pregnancy and birth. Sound, movement and touch can access her pleasure. When she is alive in her own body she will birth well. Birthing in this way, we become empowered mothers, who raise empowered children, who become empowered adults and make empowered choices and changes in our world. Women globally need more support to birth independently of a system that does not support them. I hope this inspires you to give birth naturally.

Rachel Di Ré
37 years old
Midwife & Natural Therapist
Brisbane, Australia

231
The Divine Woman

*B*orn into conservative, Irish-Catholic, middle-class environment set me up to break the mould. How did I go from violence and barely surviving on a government homeless allowance at sixteen with an attempt to end my life, to being a thirty-five year-old female living my dreams?

The conditioning of my earlier life trained me to be a conformist without a voice, who didn't question social norms. Yet I was relatively untamed, with an insightful introspection that had me willing to feel deeper into things than permitted by those around me. With that rebellious spirit, I learned to trust my instincts. And whatever age you may be reading this book in your hands right now, you are never too young or too old to listen to the wisdom within you.

So, what happens when a girl can no longer be controlled or defined by religion, media, society's expectations, family obligations, or anyone telling her how she should behave? I became a woman connected to her own divinity, with the strength to follow her own way in life and her own wealth, who doesn't need to compromise her quality of life with an uninspiring relationship or job just for financial security. I mined deep inside the world within me until I struck gold. That radiance is awakening women everywhere around me.

I believe you have a gift. You were born with it. Follow your wisdom wherever it takes you – even when it doesn't make sense at times. We are here to create love and beauty in this world, so it's our responsibility to polish these diamonds of our soul, to let them shine. Trust the mystery, may it light your way through the darkness, leaving a trail so others may also see. You are worth it.

Devashi Shakti

35 years old

Creatress of Tigress Yoga

Digital Gypsy

232
Stand in Your Light

*"Success is when you overcome the years of self-doubt and do
what it is you have been longing to do your whole life!"*

*J*f you have the burning desire to do something, no matter how big or
difficult it may appear, the very fact that you desire it means that you
have the ability to achieve it. I have wanted to sing and record music my
whole life but was always afraid to do it. I was led to believe that I had a bad
voice, nothing to offer and would only embarrass myself.

The catalyst for me to start my recording career was Christmas Day 2013 – I
received a voucher for a recording session and singing lessons in my Christmas
stocking. I was speechless and could not decide whether to kiss my wife or be
upset because of the pressure.

I procrastinated, delayed, looked for excuses to not do it, and even tried to
sabotage it. However, on 2 April 2014, I recorded my first song, not a cover of
someone else's music but a song I wrote, composed and sang: all within five
weeks. Once the decision had been made, once I got out of my own way, there
was no stopping me. I started singing, wrote my song in a single sitting and
recorded it.

It was not all plain sailing. I had doubts; when I first wrote my song I hated it. I
hated my voice and had technical difficulties in the recording studio. But, I kept
on going. It was an amazing journey. Sharing my gift with the world as we are
destined to do is inspiring. I took what was mine and stood in my light. You can
do this too. Take what is yours and stand in your light!

Tiny van Niekerk

45 years old

Entrepreneur

London, United Kingdom

233
Mel's Manifesto for World Change

I believe in a world where...

Women have all the rights that men do, and that men receive the healing that they need so that 'rape' and 'violence' are no longer a tolerated form of treatment of women or children in any nation on this planet.

Where love between women and men return, in its most divine essence.

The masculine energy is to give, the feminine is to receive and we all have both energies within us. One is no more or less than the other, but rather two sides of the same coin.

I believe in a world where...

A career or job's remuneration is not dependent on the sex of the employee and instead that the remuneration is the same whether that role is filled by a man or a woman.

Where a women who is assertive is known as a leader not as a bitch.

Where the emotional connection and sensitivity of women is seen as an asset to a company, not a liability!

Where women are recognized for their success positively, and where power is based on love and service not fear and control.

Where the people in power are focused on how they can make the world better for everyone, not just accumulate more for themselves.

Where we provide an environment that allows all people on the planet access to clean water, enough food to eat, the ability to grow up in a safe environment, quality education, and the belief that their dreams can and deserve to come true.

This is a world that I would die fighting for.

And just imagine if this was the world in which we lived, what as a global species we could create together...

Mel Houghton

28 years old

Business Coach

Dublin, Ireland

234
When You Think You Can't

*W*e all have goals, aspirations and dreams; things we want out of life. But how many times have you stopped yourself from going for those dreams? You see, you will always be able to find countless reasons why you can't achieve your goals: I am too stupid, too old, too young; I'm not pretty enough, smart enough; I don't have the right education; I've failed before! And the list goes on. Before you convince yourself you can't, consider the following:

- Harland Sanders started KFC at age 65. It is now the world's second largest restaurant chain (based on sales) after McDonald's.
- JK Rowling, author of the successful *Harry Potter* series, was told there was no money to be made in writing children's books. In 2004, Forbes named Rowling as the first person to become a billionaire ($US) by writing books.
- Palmer Luckey, a twenty-year-old college dropout, sold his company Oculus Virtual Reality to Facebook for $2 billion.
- Bill Gates' first business venture Traf-O-Data failed; while Henry Ford went bankrupt twice before finding success.
- Michael Jordan was cut from his high school basketball team, yet went on to become one of the greatest basketball players of all times.
- Ludwig van Beethoven composed many of his best loved symphonies while he was almost completely deaf.
- Richard Branson found business success despite dropping out of school, dyslexia, poor reading and maths skills.

The very reasons why you think you can't may well be the fuel needed to drive you to success. It's your uniqueness, your limitations that will force you to work harder, find a different path and do it your way. Only then will you create something extraordinary...something unique. And that's a true gift to the world.

Christele Canard

49 years old

Leadership Development & Training

Brisbane, Australia

235
No Other Option

I found myself homeless with my son in Sydney. We were sitting on a step on a street with nowhere to go, no one to help us, not knowing what to do next. I thought this was rock bottom for us, but I was wrong. I experienced a stress related breakdown and was separated from my son. I had a medical condition as well as mental and emotional issues. I went to hospital and healed whilst my son went to my mother's care in Adelaide.

As I healed, I pieced backed together what happened that led me to be in hospital and separated from my son. I was told by a social worker that I was being taken to court for a custody battle in Adelaide. The feeling in the pit of my stomach would not go away. I could not work out what to do, except to do all I could for my son to be returned home to me, and for me to deal with the things that led me to this experience.

People would ask me why I was doing all these things when I could have another kid and start over. I would look at them incredulously and full of disbelief at what I was hearing. It was then that I realised that there was no other option than to have my son home with me, and my family back together.

After nearly two years in the court process and being homeless during that time, I finally received my government house and my son came home. One of my mantra's during this process was that when I get a house my son will be home, and he was and is now, because there was no other option for me than having my son back home with me and us back on track with our lives.

Nicole Torrens
38 years old
5 Things BODY Coach
Adelaide, Australia

236
You

*T*his was written for you, the 'you' who has experienced deep pain, and the same you who has been a catalyst for the painful growth in others. So far on your journey, you have realized how incredibly strong you are, and that strength has come from all you have endured. You have learned to shield your heart, sparing you the pain of past wounds received. Perhaps shielding so masterfully, that nothing enters, not even real love.

You will seek out specific teachers; of these there will be many. You will learn that real strength lies in vulnerability, in being open-hearted, that everything happens for a reason whether you have acceptance over it or not. When at your lowest, you will take in the learnings and know that you will pass through this; you are never given anything you are unable to handle. These moments will define you. You know deep in your core knowledge that nothing can really hurt you in the end. You will be tested on the things you have learned repeatedly and in multiple ways. All of who you meet in life will help you... it just may take you many years before you realise that some of them actually, were helping you.

Your heart, once open, will lead you to a rich and fulfilling life; its language is subtle and will invoke courage. Listen and act on its advice for it is wise. It is during these heart opening times that you can be overwhelmed by the profound love and beauty you see in the world. Savour these breathtaking moments, these too will define you. Above all, know that you are very loved, know your value and know how much love you have to give.

You have so much to share inside of you: show us.

Toni Neill
40 years old
Events and Crew Director
Sydney, Australia

237
Give Yourself the Gift
Of Acceptance

*J*know a liar when I see one, because I am a liar. Most of us are. I am not talking about little fibs, I am talking about the lies you tell yourself: about who you are, your relationships, your vision, your accomplishments.

The truth is, creating an image of yourself, positive thinking and affirmations only get you so far. In the end we are always being pulled back to truth. We all have a brilliant, beautiful light shining inside us, and I wish we could let this light shine even more brightly. But we also have deep, dark valleys inside of us, and we ignore them by filling them with food, money, sex, accomplishments.

I know, because I tried. For years, I only wanted to be a 'happy person.' To only show the bright and beautiful side of myself. But you know what? It's exhausting. And life always brought me back to truth.

So, today I challenge you to stop. Stop trying to change yourself. Stop lying to yourself. Acknowledge and accept that darkness. It is part of the roller coaster that is your life. There may be something for you to learn. But the least you will receive is liberation. Liberation from trying to change who you are.

Know that the Universe does not judge you. Your higher self does not judge you. God does not judge you. You are how you are. Once you allow yourself to truly see, without trying to change or judge yourself, miracles will start happening. Life will start happening.

Because when you stop struggling with yourself, life is a celebration.

So as today's inspiration I dare you to be inspired by yourself, by seeing your whole truth, by giving yourself the gift of acceptance.

Janna Jungclaus

30 years old

Pmemess Trainer

Hamburg, Germany

238
Miracles

*L*ife can unravel at lightning speed. Mine did. A series of nightmare events in family life left me homeless with three young boys. My only lifeline was a block of land on the outskirts of town that wasn't selling. Crippled by grief and loss, financial despair and with no other option, I moved us there. The plan was to camp for a few days while I planned our next move. Days turned into weeks and months. There was no electricity or running water, except the creek. It was harsh. Then, what I describe as my series of miracles began.

Miracle 1:
We eat breakfast daily watching a wallaby family. My son says to me "We are so lucky to live here, Mum." His face is pure love. As tears threaten me, he adds, "We will have a house soon." Our morning ritual now includes being grateful. We visualized living in a beautiful home. We share gratitude for each other and our beautiful surroundings.

Miracle 2:
Driving to town I decide to take an alternate route. I drive past the house from our visualization. A sign saying, "For Sale By Removal," is being erected. I agree to sign a contract of sale the following day with a $2000 deposit. I have $40.

Miracle 3:
I continue to the bank. I hold the ATM slip, the balance showing $2040! Money I had written off years prior has been returned to me.

Miracle 4:
My work phones offering me a variation in roles, which enhances my credibility to the bank.

A few months later, on the back of two trucks, the very home of our visualization comes up our driveway. No life lesson has ever been more powerful than the loving reminder my little boy gave me about being grateful. Miracles happen every day to all sorts of people in all sorts of ways.

Kerri Nicholls
49 years old
Counsellor
Yeppoon, Australia

239
The Ups and Downs of Life

*A*friend once said to me that life is like a staircase. "What do you mean?" I asked. "Life is a staircase," he said again. I asked him to explain. He said, "You have choices right?" "Right!" I said.

"And with choices we take action, and our actions have a reaction like Newton describing an object in motion in a certain direction. The object will stay that way unless another force acts on it to help change direction. A staircase takes you up or down, which is symbolic for the oscillations of life. Your choice sets a direction, action is the reaction, and hence, the motion is set once again in a certain direction. How many choices, how many actions, and how many reactions will take you up to ascension or down to dissension?

That's the symbolic staircase; that's the symbolic direction; that's the symbolic scenery I wanted you to see. The step you're on is a result of your actions. The choice you make will set your direction. The future is an unknown but endless possibility. The realm of possibility an empty canvas; draw on it the direction of your action. Past to be as it is, never to come back unless you keep looking at it. Present to be in the moment of moments, the only thing that is real for everything thing else is a projection of past memories or future perceptions. Future... it has not happened yet. But, what is it that you see? Do you see a realm of possibility or a past projection? Or, do you see something untrue because it's all made up in your own head? Anything is possible right? The choices are endless. So what do you choose? Up or down? Life is like a staircase, my friend."

"Oh I see," I said.

Jatinder Singh Palaha

33 years old

Digital Strategist

London, United Kingdom

240
"Live Life, Don't Let Life Live You!"

*Y*esterday, today and tomorrow all have one thing in common. You! How we think controls the path we follow. Our bodies are created to run on their own, from inhaling to exhaling, happy to sad, the one thing that controls them all is you. You have control. You can choose your path and change direction any time. In this lifetime, we make decisions that determine how we live. Life is only what you make it; no one else can do it for you.

We all choose to live until either our bodies are tired or we feel we hit the end of the road. When life changes and we're not happy, we become sorrowful. We seek comfort in those that can change how we feel. We discuss life with family and friends that will lend an ear. We have a story to tell. We share, we cry, we laugh, and at the end of the day, we still have a choice on what happens next.

Early on, I had a choice. I chose to live. I was determined to control what and who I was. I laid out the rules, and discussed them with those in my life. For me, I only had one option, one choice, and one path to follow. I chose to live life and not let the life live me.

We have a limited time to live on this Earth. Live it well. If you find yourself back in sorrow, step back and remember the decision you made to move forward in your life. You have choices, but only one will be right for you. Make that decision and look forward to living your life your way. Living life and not letting the life live you. It's quite simple really. Listen to your heart, not your mind.

Mark Wariner

48 years old

Entrepreneur

Frisco, United States of America

241
From Our Toughest Challenge Comes Our Greatest Strength

*I*n 2009, an accumulation of years of spiralling out of control through hedonistic escapism and self-loathing caught up with me in the form of a brutal wake up call. On the 10th of March, I decided I served no purpose in this world. I jumped off the fourth floor balcony of a building.

Clearly, the Universe had other plans for me. After six weeks of lying emotionally and physically broken in a coma on life support, I finally woke up. This seemingly tragic event forced me to look deeper into my perception of the world and my thoughts and behaviours that were dictating my reality. I became open to the possibility that there was a reason for my existence in the world. Little did I know, the tragedy was to become a victory that aligned with my purpose.

Driven by my hunger for inner peace, I embarked on my own journey of growth and healing, which has enabled me to discover who I really am and live my truth. After a lifetime of feeling misunderstood and ashamed of all my perceived defects, I made a vow to live a life of cause, rather than remain a victim to the effects of life's inevitable challenges.

I devoured every self-help book I could get my hands on and studied a plethora of different healing techniques, until one day it hit home. My perceived defects and weaknesses were exactly what I needed to drive me to embody my purpose. Overcoming my greatest challenge has become my greatest strength and has enabled me to follow my bliss and live from intention. This enables us to respond to life's inevitable challenges, to live an empowered life of cause, rather than reacting to them and remaining a victim of the effects of worldly disappointments.

Hollie Rolla

28 years old

Speaker, Presenter & Coach

London, United Kingdom

242
Healed By Gratitude

J live a wonderful life. Truly, awesomely wonderful. Every day of my life is a gift. Each day I wake knowing that this will be another day of my own design. I am free, independent, loved, and incredibly grateful. It is gratitude that fuels the fire of my awesome life, fills my heart with love, and helps me to find my strength when I feel challenged. Gratitude is a force that fills every part of me; it drives me to higher levels of joy, love and fulfilment. Gratitude can change your life and there was a time when gratitude even saved my life.

As a teenager, I was horrifically injured in a car crash. My body was broken seemingly beyond repair. I sustained multiple disfiguring fractures and spent time in a coma on life support. When I awoke from this coma, everything in my world changed. In my overwhelming gratitude for the gift of my life, I left an old life of darkness behind – I experienced the miraculous power of gratitude.

I endured many reconstructive surgeries and the years of pain and disability that followed by tapping into the power of gratitude. I learned to use my lungs again, go to the bathroom and to walk again. It's been a long road, but today my body is healed beyond recognition, no wheel chair required. I have used gratitude to heal every part of me – body, mind and soul.

I am a walking miracle and a testament to the power of gratitude. I choose to be grateful for my life, for my body and for my healing every single day, rather than feel like a victim or think about the things that I've lost. Gratitude has created the life of my dreams and it can do the same for you.

Angel Goodson-Adams

32 years old

Director & Spiritual Entrepreneur

Gold Coast, Australia

243
True Health, Happiness and Love

*M*y beliefs around what makes a person truly healthy have transformed over the past fifteen years of my life. I used to think it was all physical, tangible, measurable, and predictable. "You are what you eat." Calories in, calories out. Know your fats, proteins, and carbs. You are a machine. Input equals output.

I transformed my physical self from fat to fit. I loved it. I thought it was all that mattered. From being bullied, rejected and unattractive to adored, accepted and admired. I was obsessed with the numbers. I wanted only to see the scales go down. All day long I thought about food, fat, and calories. Then, I learned the long term damage I was doing to my body and brain.

I had to get better. I had to focus on healthy. It was a rocky road; a bumpy journey. So many fears and struggles to learn to love myself for who I am inside; to not fear being unloved, rejected, not good enough; to realise that I am love, that I am more than enough.

Today I stand before the world embodying these knowings.

My greatest place of peace and bliss is right here deep inside myself. My message to the world today is different from where I began. It's so simple, so beautiful, so full of hope. We are all infinite beings. We all walk as embodied souls. Our essence is immortal. Our potential is infinite. Our ability to heal, grow, change, and transform is unlimited. I know this with every cell of my being. And my message to you is this: Everything you want, everything you are looking for – health, happiness, love, acceptance, peace – is all there now, right inside of you. Whatever you seek outside, look within. There you will find true health, happiness and peace. I promise you this.

Bridget Jane Thompson

32 years old

Dietitian, Health & Happiness Coach

Sunshine Coast, Australia

244
Born Inspired

*L*ucy loved life. She was happy and playful. She would dream the most amazing dreams. She had a wonderful home that was so relaxing, it could only be described as being curled up on the silkiest sheets on the smoothest of water beds every day. Lucy would have food and drinks delivered to her when she needed; she would have songs sung to her daily from an angelic voice; and she would be hugged tenderly to comfort her if she became restless.

One day Lucy started to feel uncomfortable. Something wasn't right; something was different than before. It felt like her whole world was being turned upside down. "Why me?" she would ask herself, "I was comfortable here!" Her home started to become less relaxing, less supportive, as if the silk sheets had been swiped from underneath her, like the waterbed had burst and just left her to perish.

She felt like she was being dragged from her home. Lucy's home was very different now, but regardless it was still her home. She felt like she was being dragged but she didn't want to let go. She wanted to stay in her world even though it was falling apart; it felt so familiar and was a part of who she thought she was. Her heart was pounding but her body was still. She was losing her whole world; everything that she had ever known was leaving her, even her life support had been ripped from the home. She was suffocating; her world was caving in. "I am dying!"

She detached from what she knew. She surrendered in her biggest fear. She simply let go when she was most vulnerable. In that moment, she took her first inspiration for life with her very first independent breath. The day that Lucy thought her life had ended, was actually the day that Lucy was born.

Christopher Bates
32 years old
Doctor of Holistic Medicine
London, United Kingdom

245
ARRG!

*T*hrough life's trials I developed ARRG (a 'feeling inspired' formula)! It sounds easy because, well, it is. We wondrous humans tend to complicate things. This formula is based on quantitative studies and life experiences that show reduction in stress and anxiety, through breath and movement. Life for me started with trials, and I'm thankful because I began learning from a young age how impactful attitude can be. While I was in diapers, orthopaedic surgeons reported that I was never going to walk properly or run because my hip sockets and femurs were deformed. Wearing braces and manoeuvring awkwardly around taught me determination. This resulted in a 'never say die' attitude and a full scholarship to University of Oregon as their fastest 400 meter hurdler.

After challenging times, feeling inspired definitely doesn't come easily, but it's absolutely possible. The thing is, you have to choose to be uplifted, and you really have to freaking mean it. Ask yourself: What am I willing to do to be happy? There's no magic pill, but there is the ARRG formula – an experiential daily practice:

Acknowledge. Take a DEEP BREATH and observe the negative emotions without getting sucked in. Deeply breathing for 5, of the average 21,600 daily breaths we take, allows us to step back and watch.

Roll & Release. Let yourself experience negative emotions with an intention to let them roll through you. Physically roll your shoulders, and find movement. This can release us from the emotion.

Gratitude. Write daily gratitudes, this invokes a life led by appreciation, not by fear, or anger.

ARRG formula strengthens our ability to be positive through subtle, yet intentional breath, movement and focused thoughts. Challenges await us all. We choose how much stress we let trickle in and out.

Nicole Barrote

39 years old

Yoga Dance Therapist

San Diego, United States of America

246
The Realisation

*A*s a young child, I had my voice manipulated, bullied and abused into silence by a sexual abuser. In my early twenties, I lost my Dad when he chose to end his life at the age of forty-two. These two unrelated events have deeply impacted my life. The abuse left me unable to effectively express myself; and my dad's death left me reeling with the pain of rejection and unworthiness. I did the best I could to carry on regardless, but it was not enough to put a sticky plaster on it and carry on 'doing.' It was short-sighted and a temporary 'fix.' The wounds were still there, waiting for my attention.

In my early thirties, I had a breakdown that lead to my own suicidal points in time, as I struggled to come to terms with my grief. The abused and abandoned child was still crying out to be loved. I sought safety, security, acceptance and kindness. I craved the love that I believed was out there somewhere. I waited, sometimes not so patiently, sometimes not so quietly. I waited to be picked up, to be held close to another beating heart. And I waited, until one day I had the realisation that I am the only person who can heal the wounds with my own acceptance and kindness. I am the only one who can provide the safety and security. I am the only one who can be relied upon to supply the love I so desired; then, and only then, could true healing begin.

I have learned that for as long as I looked outside of myself for the solution to healing my heart, I was in trouble. My peace is held within my heart, and it is always there waiting for me.

Louise Brister
46 years old
Soul Alignment Practitioner & Healer
London, United Kingdom

247
The Power of Meditation

*I*t's not a pill, it's not an exotic food, it doesn't cost anything, or require specialised equipment, and you don't need anyone's permission. Regular meditation is the one thing you could start doing today to improve your life. You might be thinking: It was too hard; I didn't notice any improvements. These are all excuses borne of the fear of coming face to face with the innermost core of yourself, your soul.

The benefits of meditation have been well researched and documented, and include increased immune function, emotional balance, fertility, lower blood pressure and inflammation, relief from insomnia, addictions and pain. Beyond this, meditation provides a vital link between the physical and the eternal spirit you. I believe we all yearn for a deep and conscious connection with our souls; this is the hunger that we try to feed in our search for the 'more' that we believe will make us happy. We are searching for happiness in the wrong places. Looking outside of ourselves and accumulating more 'things' can be fun, but without a strong soul connection, we still feel empty. We are looking for the other aspect of our self, the non-physical original self that is part of the creative consciousness of the Universe.

Meditation practice requires commitment to meditating every day for a minimum of forty days. You will need courage and discipline. Simple meditation rules are:
- Sit with a straight spine
- Slow your breath
- Calmly become the observer of your thoughts
- Focus on the present moment
- Start with three minutes; eleven minutes is great!

Daily meditation will give you many benefits and make your life happier and healthier.

Enza Deluca

51 years old

Yoga & Meditation Teacher & Author

Sydney, Australia

248
The Day a Kangaroo Saved My Life

J was lost in the Australian bush, unsure of which way to turn. I had come to a remote cliff top to watch the sun set over the Warrumbungles National Park. For over an hour I had been transfixed by the sight of the red sun catching thousands of spider silks as they blew out of the forest below me. I was by myself with this timeless landscape, apart from a large male kangaroo feeding nearby. Now that the sun had set and darkness had descended, I realised I had forgotten my torch.

Australia was still a new country to me. I had only emigrated there a few years before from my European home. I was slightly disoriented and beginning to wonder if I should stay put and wait for dawn to deliver me from the dark forest all around me. Taking the decision to attempt a return to my car I stepped onto the path. Immediately the kangaroo stood up, hopped in front of me and beckoned to me to follow him. Sure enough, he guided me the mile or so back through the forest to the car park. Imagine my surprise when I discovered that all around my car were a dozen or so more kangaroos, as if they were protecting it. With the light of gratitude in my heart I thanked them all for delivering me safely. The kangaroos nonchalantly hopped away as if this were a daily occurrence.

The lesson I learned that day was that when we least expect it a solution will always present itself. The most powerful solutions are always found in nature. This is where the universal mind expresses itself. My vision of a planet living in harmony was solidified that day. I realised the power of tuning in to the collective mind.

Olivier Maxted
42 years old
Sound Healer
Callington, United Kingdom

249
Transformation is Ageless

*M*y mom is really cool and I love giving her massages. When it comes time for one, she'll push it away even though she loves getting them; until recently.

Picture this. She's still under the covers when I ask if she's ready, and she gives her predictable response. On this occasion I confronted her about this familiar dance. She sheepishly pulls the covers over her head and giggles, hiding in embarrassment. What a crack up! It was so special. This wizened sprite of eighty-three years, hiding under the covers like she'd been caught stealing from the cookie jar!

I then blurted out, "Mom, when you say it's too much trouble, it hurts my feelings." This struck a deep chord within her. The penny had dropped. She slowly uncovered her face and looked me straight in the eyes in shock. We had a good cry over this, a long hug and a laugh, followed by a great massage. My mother thought giving her massages was too hard, too much trouble for me. She now sees her point of view as somewhat ridiculous, albeit a habitual pattern repeated over the years.

My mom wanted me to add she is very grateful for this experience. The impact continues to make ripples in both our lives, and we have caught ourselves almost knocking back heartfelt gifts. When something is offered are we too humble (or feeling unworthy) to accept? Are we so arrogant as to decide for this person (or the Universe) what they can or can't offer us? Or is it simply a time to say no? Our capacity for waking up is endless. We are never too old to have deep moments of heart opening, transformational awareness, whether we are in our fifties, eighties or beyond!

Nancy Zevely

52 years old

Author, Coach, Healer & Musician

Denver, United States of America

250
Why Not Me?

*W*hen I was a young student I spent much of my time on the naughty chair. You see, I was one year behind my sister who was a high achiever in most fields. Feeling I would fail by comparison and largely due to the low belief I had in myself, I chose the path of 'being bad.' I consistently achieved poor grades with no reason for anyone to expect me to rise above. (That plus my quirky ideas like, I would add the letter 'z' to words like 'pur-z-ple' because I felt that 'z' did not get enough word exposure.)

Being the child that doesn't behave or excel was fun for a while. It got me the attention I wanted. But there was one special person that could see right through me – my grandmother – who was also the school principal. She took me aside one afternoon and asked me why I didn't try. She told me that I did not have to compare myself to anyone, because I had gifts of my own.

Her words got to me; no one else had realized that deep down inside all I needed was a little bit of extra belief in me. From that day, with Grandma's words in the back of my mind, I began to try. All those years of not trying left me behind so learning to work was a challenge, but it paid off. My peers and teachers voted me the primary school captain. I really began to shine.

I am now in senior school. I am a well above average student, having received awards for academics, service, and all-rounder. I was recently awarded the Future Leaders Award. I attribute all this to that one special conversation with my grandmother, when I was inspired to ask myself the question: "Why not me?"

Renee Bradley
16 years old
Student
Toowoomba, Australia

251
The Light at The End
of the Tunnel

I sometimes joke that I lost my 'mojo' that night. In truth, I did. I lost my fun and free spirit, but I also found a new certainty and understanding of life. I know who I am and what I value most now: it is priceless. That night changed our lives forever.

Five men came into our home, pushed guns at our heads, beat us, tied us up face down on the floor and 'shopped' in our home. They threatened to kill us. It was terrifying. Would we still be alive in the morning? How would we recover from this if we survived? A lot can go through your mind when you don't know the ending.

And then they left. We recovered. Life throws you a curve ball and you deal with it. It was tough, but we searched for the blessings and eventually saw that it was perfectly designed. Our lives transformed in so many ways due to that fateful night that I would not change for the world.

I still get a little scared and choked up when I think of it, but then I think of my life, and I am overwhelmed with gratitude. I started consulting with unwavering conviction. I embraced danger and spent the night on the rim of an active volcano, a life-changing and heart-opening adventure. We moved to a beautiful home. My relationship with my husband deepened, and I realized I was actually the perfect mother for our children. Some of these things I had prayed for my entire life. It's hard to comprehend but it was destined to be. There are blessings in every crisis. Take the time to look for them. It's never easy but there is light at the end of every tunnel, one which is perfectly and lovingly designed just for you.

Louise Diesel

38 years old

Businesswoman & Facilitator

Johannesburg, South Africa

252
Education Is the Key

*M*y father's words grated whilst I was growing up: "They can steal your car or your wallet, but they can't steal what's inside your brain." Every time he said it, I thought, "Oh no, not again!" Little did I know that these words would shape my life.

At nineteen, I was married. I had three children shortly afterwards. I was a housewife and mother. After a few years my marriage ended and I returned to London with three small children and our suitcases. Our house had been sold. We were homeless and living on benefits. I hated it. I had been brought up to not rely on government assistance and to contribute to society by working. How could I get a job when I didn't have much education and three small children? I felt trapped.

One day I saw an ad for free adult education classes. So, I enrolled and passed my first exam since leaving school. I felt on top of the world. I did course after course until one of my classmates said, "Karen, you should apply to go to university." What me, go to university? You must be joking! When I was given an 'unconditional offer' I was shaking like a leaf. Only intelligent people go to university!

I always felt that I didn't know enough. It was hard, but I was awarded Adult Learner of the Year in 1992 and had an interview on local television. I thrived, graduated with honours, and started to feel intelligent. I went on to achieve a master's degree and enjoyed a career as a university lecturer. Education has now given me the confidence to change my career. I absolutely love learning. Every day I'm learning something new. Switch the television off, pick up a book, enrol in a course. Education is the key.

Karen Thorne
55 years old
Eating Psychology Coach
London, United Kingdom

253
Beacon of Light

*I*f heaven is really on Earth, then it's time to enjoy yourself and create experiences you'd really love. Be bold. Honour your core values. Don't change who you are to fit in. Freedom starts with the mind. You have the freedom to think what you want. Examine what you accept as the truth. Identify and release limiting thoughts. There are no cannots or should nots in this world of unlimited possibilities. Do you have to live in a particular place, do a certain thing, act a specific way? What will it take to experience the desires you are drawn to? Keep asking until the answer reveals itself. New awareness can create instant shifts that align with your heart's desire.

Change is inevitable. All structures are unstable. You never know when something is going to be given to or taken away from you. This is forever occurring in life. When you experience loss, appreciation often comes afterwards. Be thankful now. Allow gratitude to attract new opportunities. Agreements and contracts keep the ego happy, but they're a temporary source of security; they help you to function in the world. You are growing, and so the world must be growing with you. A new 'form' is manifesting. A new you is emerging. A lot of things boil down to confidence. It's all about feeling good enough: "Am I good enough to take on this new opportunity that I desire?" "Do I have enough belief in my own abilities to solve this problem?" Take the leap before someone else creates a crisis for you. As you strive towards an inspiring challenge, the support will come.

When the sky is dark, people look at the beautiful stars. They pay attention to the light. Pay attention to your light. It's time to let your beacon of light shine.

Amber Thorne

32 years old

Well-being Coach

West Sussex, United Kingdom

254
Dad

*S*ince 30 November 2013, I am grateful for you when I find you:

Within others when they show discipline in their daily lives no matter what happens outside, which is a trait of yours.

Within others when they complain about me because you used to show me anger in my childhood, which made what I loved clearer and bigger. Under the pressure of anger and complaints, I found my true unshakable voice within. That is my true voice from my heart. I could give myself permission to express it no matter what happened outside.

Within my ten-year-old daughter when she works hard on mathematics because you used to be a dedicated math teacher.

Within my mother when she tells us the importance of fair exchange, which is one of the foundations of mathematics, and when she shows unconditional love to my brother and me no matter what we have or haven't done.

Within me when I teach my students, when I read books, when I drive a car taking my family to nice places, when I help people in need, when I help my daughter do what she loves, when I help people beyond my local community, because all of them are your traits.

Dad, with gratitude and tears, you have been bigger and bigger, deeper and deeper within me and around me. That is because I found your love incredibly massive and unconditional, which gave me courage to go for my love and genius beyond my comfort zone.

I know you did not pass away but passed your torch onto us. I am looking forward to seeing you again in many different forms in my life. I live with you as long as I am a teacher. Thank you and I love you, Dad.

Tsunehiro Nonaka
47 years old
Teacher
Brisbane, Australia

255
What Do You Want to Create In Life?

*W*e only regret in life the things we didn't do and wish we had the courage to pursue. At the end of your life, what do you want to be proud of? What do you want people to remember you for? A person who added value, love and inspiration to people's lives, someone who made the world a better and nicer place? What do you want to create with your life that would bring lasting fulfilment and joy to your life and others?

It is time to bring forth our God-given gifts and talents and create an extraordinary and spirit-filled life. I believe we either create or disintegrate. I feel the pain from not achieving the life we are called for is worse than actually stepping out in faith and achieving our dreams! Are you ready to step out in faith and create an extraordinary life? Proverbs 29:18 states, "Where there is no vision, the people perish." It's time to dream again and create a vision for your life. Here are five simple steps to get you started:

Step 1: Write down in a journal what you want to create, including your life's purpose, and anything else that you want to create in any area of your life.

Step 2: Why do you want to achieve this? List 50+ reasons.

Step 3: Create a vision board of all the pictures associated with what you want to create and achieve in each area of your life including your life's purpose. "If you can see it, you can achieve it."

Step 4: Take action daily towards creating your dreams. Small and consistent efforts stack up to big results!

Step 5: Never give up! Winners never quit and quitters never win! Always focus on what you want and not what you don't want, as energy flows where attention goes.

Julia Huzziff
30 years old
Life Coach & Entrepreneur
Auckland, New Zealand

256
Healing From Within

*A*fter the birth of my first child, I developed Glandular Fever but it didn't get picked up until years later. The Doctor kept saying it's normal to be tired after having a child. After the birth of my second child two years later, I would cry when my children would wake up. I was trying to be a great mum but it was very hard when I was exhausted from just having a shower. The Doctor wanted me to go on anti-depressants but I knew I was not depressed and this would not solve the cause of my tiredness.

Finally, after four years, I was diagnosed with Chronic Fatigue Syndrome – there was no cure for it. So, I started looking at alternative health. Why had I created this dis-ease in my life? What changes did I need to make for me to be happy and healthy? I changed my attitude to being positive and grateful for all the blessings in my life, seeing the gift in every situation, being conscious of my thoughts, letting go of the hurt and pain from the past. Doing all this released me from being a victim and allowed me to be the best I could be. To love myself unconditionally. It is my responsibility, no-one else. I used to be an Accountant and now I am doing a job that fills my heart with joy.

Having chronic fatigue gave me the greatest gift of life. I know that everything I need is already inside me and I am now very blessed, happy and healthy. My growth has also allowed my husband and children to follow their dreams too. I wish this for you too.

Connie Helbig
49 years old
Master Healer & Aromatherapist
Melbourne, Australia

257
Just Take the Next Step

*J*t was August 2007, I had so much to be grateful for. I had a wonderful life, two great children, a gorgeous partner and a thriving business. Then came the phone call that changed my life. "I'm so sorry. Ryan passed away this morning." In those words my oldest son was reefed from my life, my baby, my beautiful gregarious young man. This wasn't meant to happen! Parents don't outlive their children!

Despite my grief, one day followed the next. I had a younger son and employees. Somehow I needed to go on. I tried to make sense of my deep well of sadness. I wanted to curl up and drift away from the pain. The day came though, when I knew I needed to make peace with my loss. I couldn't face living the rest of my life in despair. No matter how sad I felt, I could not bring Ryan back.

I started to notice good moments when I was absorbed in something else, then came the first time I laughed without feeling guilty, and the first day there'd been no tears. There were also the days when I wanted to scream: "It's not fair!" I chose to just keep taking steps, acknowledging my progress, sharing what I was learning with others who needed support and looking forward. Each step brought me closer to living as Ryan had, with excited anticipation.

How wonderfully resilient we are! I have rebuilt my life. It's not the same as it was before. How could it be? But I have a new normal. I have faced the worst and I am here, strong, healthy and happy, making my contribution to the world. I believe there is nothing the human spirit cannot overcome – we just need to choose to take the next step.

Lenore Miller

50 years old

Speaker, Author & Mentor

Newcastle, Australia

258
Perfection

When I look in the mirror
I see perfection
Perfectly created
Even when I do not agree some days
There is still perfection
In the imperfection I see

I am hard to please when I am imperfect
I am ungrateful when I am imperfect
I am angry when I am imperfect
Within all that though
There is perfection

Just like the flow of life
There is high, there is low
There is light, there is dark
There is want, there is un-want
So am I, so I am

We are born in perfection
We grow in perfection
We die in perfection
Always in perfection
Every moment of our lives.

Catharine Boon
46 years old
Intuitive Guide
Sydney, Australia

259
A Meaningful Life

What is the meaning of life? That's a question that many of us ponder. After years of asking this myself and searching for an answer, I eventually stumbled upon it. The answer is simple, and it was right under my nose: the meaning of life is determined by the meaning you give it.

Simple – but not necessarily easy. So, how do you give your life meaning? You do it by doing things that have meaning for you, things you find fulfilling, things you find yourself drawn to, things that make time disappear, things that warm your heart, things that nurture your spirit, and things that feed your soul.

This is different for each and every one of us. No one is exactly the same. Just like the artist's canvas where every brush stroke is unique, where every brush stroke is as important as every other, where every brush stroke contributes fully to the richness and composition of the overall piece. So too do you add equally to the richness of life, your own life and our collective lives.

You add fully to the canvas of life when you live your life with meaning, with purpose...whatever that is for you. Stop looking at and following others. Let go of the conditioning we all grow up with that says we should be something we are not. Learn to trust yourself. Follow your heart. Do what you love. Start slowly if you like...or take a big leap. It doesn't matter how you get there. But enrich your life and give it meaning by being yourself. Allow yourself and the world the honour of living your life with meaning and purpose. You have a unique contribution to add to the canvas...please make it. We will all be grateful that you have.

Danny Swanson

56 years old

Purposeful Transformation Alchemist

Gold Coast, Australia

260
Deep and Lasting Healing

*T*he shame and guilt, the anger, despair and grief have risen up and raged through me like a storm that never clears. I have lashed out, cried in the night, trembled, shouted, sworn, ranted and raved; I have banged my head against walls, threatened to jump out of windows, to throw myself out of moving cars; I have reached out, got burned, wallowed in inadequacy, smashed things, bashed things, smoked hundreds of cigarettes, got absolutely hammered times without number; I've stuffed my face, starved myself, hidden under the duvet, chickened out, caved in, cancelled, let people down. I have bitched and whinged, gossiped and cringed; I have been emotionally unavailable, worn my heart on my sleeve, obsessed and yearned and struggled and given up and fought a losing battle with all the passion in me I thought was lost.

And now.

Now, I awake from this crazy dream and find myself in a small boat with provisions in a wicker basket, floating gently on calm water. The sun is bright and cheerful overhead, yet I notice I still scan the horizon for storm clouds. I have a small, white sail. It puffs itself out, testing the breeze, and catches it. I set out across the water, confident but apprehensive, like a child in a school play. Of course, it goes without saying, it's a musical – and I've been given the starring role.

Through a conscious experience with my higher self on 16 February, 2005, the chronic depression I'd been living with for nearly twenty-five years disappeared overnight. I know from personal experience that life can turn on a dime and deep and lasting healing is possible. All that's required is to open a small window in your mind and allow the thought to waft in:

Life has more imagination than you do.

Hilary Cave
44 years old
Writer
Oxford, United Kingdom

261
What's In a Name?

J was named after my father's mother – Chiara, and went through life known as "Kerri." Why? Because a few hours after I was born, my mother had everyone call me "Kerri." I guess it was the closest thing to "Chiara" she could think of. She preferred that and believed I'd be happier and more comfortable known as "Kerri." So for the first thirty years of my life I was known as Kerri Louise Tino.

Years later, I lived in Sydney, and a few days before my thirtieth birthday my family came up for the celebration. I was ill at the time, but despite that I soldiered on. One morning mum and I got into a taxi; the driver's name was Zorhab, he was Russian. As I sat in the back seat, he looked at me through the rear view mirror and said, "You are not well!" To which I responded, "No, I'm not." He then proceeded to tell me he felt strongly compelled to doing my numerology.

Minutes later, we were in my home, and Zorhab wrote my name on a piece of paper – Kerri Louise Tino. He said, "This isn't your name! What name were you born with?" I said, "My birth name is Chiara but I'm Kerri." He said, "This explains things! You are Chiara, and you are living as Kerri. This is why you're not well." I sat there looking at him blankly, and yet something in what he said made sense to me. He repeated those words to my mother explaining that I wasn't living my soul name. "Her name is Chiara," he said firmly.

As a result, I changed my name by deed poll. Within a year of this experience, I felt my passion arise, and I developed a strong urge to study alternative therapies. Life as Chiara would never be the same!

Chiara Tino
49 years old
Young Living Global Consultant
Melbourne, Australia

262
My Unexpected Lesson in Practical Spirituality

*J*n 2013, I travelled to India for a sixteen-day silent meditation retreat. My goal was simple – go deeper into my meditation practice. I had no other expectations. On the very first day, I had many chances to go deeper – four to be exact. The first three meditation sessions were two hours long, and the final one was three hours long. That three-hour session was the most painful physical and mental experience I have ever encountered.

The following day, I followed the same meditation schedule. When it was time for the final three-hour session, I had the expectation of another painful experience. At that moment, I had an inner calling to reach for my Mala/Prayer beads that I brought but – for some reason – had not yet used. I quietly chose affirmation after affirmation, saying each 108 times. Using my prayer beads, the three hours passed with ease, and I was in a state of deep bliss. I continued this practice for the duration of the retreat.

What I had unconsciously discovered was how I can use prayer beads and affirmations to change the mental atmosphere of my subconscious mind. This tool is one I now use every day, choosing between fifteen and thirty affirmations each day.

Every great teacher says our thoughts create. But I feel it is not just about individual thoughts. It's really about the collective atmosphere of all our thoughts. Through the use of prayer beads and affirmations, I had discovered a practical way to change my thoughts and my mental atmosphere. Others who have also embraced and used this practice have seen tremendous results in their lives.

Lee Wolak
63 years old
Master Teacher of Conscious Living
Highland Village, Texas

263
To Infinity and Beyond

*W*e are all perfect beings. Not one of us is sullied, fallen or evil. These conditions are simply incompatible with the human hard-drive. Recognition of this is like an atomic expansion to our consciousness. On truly knowing this, your energy field begins to absorb and radiate the true sense of wonderment that is 'being.'

Many years ago, I began to spontaneously leave my body. While sleeping, a light or vibration would visit me, wake me up, and take my consciousness to another reality or dimension. Now this was pretty confusing, as you could imagine. I began to question my sanity as I was shown things from past lives, to guides, to extra-terrestrial intelligence. As a natural sceptic and prankster, I pushed the envelope of this uncommon experience. I even experienced my own death!

The sticking point to it all was that these realms I visited were ultra-real when compared to 3-D reality. In this luminous state, my senses were vastly expanded, and I lost any sense of fear or annihilation. I would return with tears of ecstasy, deeply mysterious and moving. I began to recognize that we were infinitely more than the confines of our physical form and its limited, shackled thinking. I came in touch with an inner power that was detached from any form of judgment, and content beyond imagining.

All the twists and turns of my life, all the apparent dead-ends that had stumped and frustrated me so, suddenly made sense. Everything was as it was; everything had happened as it should have. There was no failure or fall. This was a tremendous release to my spirit, and an end to the victim that had defined me. It was the beginning of genuine self-acceptance – of self-love – and the dawning of a new and enticing reality.

Greg Doyle
52 years old
Auhtor, Healer, Astral Traveller
Brisbane, Australia

264
The Trunk

*I*t was 11th April 1990 and I was at Fiumicino Airport in Rome. With my four children ranging from nearly two to fourteen years of age, I was emigrating from Italy to join my family in Perth. It was not a festive occasion, as there had been a marriage breakdown and the children were leaving their father, their country, their culture, their language and friends behind. I was thirty-nine and thought that my life was pretty much over.

We had one large trunk with us that carried most of our worldly goods. The pressure cooker took pride of place in the centre, stuffed with other bits and pieces. It was bursting at the seams and we had used rope and packing tape to secure it as best we could. Being oversized, we were sent off with the trunk to the commercial weighing scale. If the trunk weighed over ninety kilos we would have to send it by sea.

With baited breath we watched the arrow... 86... 87... 88... 89... 89.9! There was a moment of hushed awe and then "Wow! How amazing is that!" Till today I can almost see an angel underneath the scale holding it up with a smile on his face!

That was the start of our journey, and there were to be many other miracles. We are not always aware of the gracious hand of God in our lives, but I believe that making gratitude an integral part of our daily lives helps us to be aware of our blessings and helps to sustain us through the trials of life that are common to us all. Today I am happily married with grown up children and my first grandchild. At the entrance to our home is a hall table and underneath the table is... yes... you guessed it! The trunk! Lest I should ever forget!

Francesca Posney
65 years old
Retired
Perth, Australia

265
Strength, Courage and Determination

*L*ooking back at the last three years, where does one start with a story like mine? I took my eighty-day-old baby boy Jayce's life in an unsafe bed-sharing accident. My nanna died. I fell pregnant with twins and lost one. I found out Dad had liver cancer. I got married. My pop died. At seven months pregnant, I had a breakdown and my husband left me during my breakdown. I became suicidal. My dad died. Ten days later I gave birth to Chance.

Chance cried six hours a day with colic. Surviving off three hours of broken sleep a night with no support. Then I contracted glandular fever and had to crawl on my hands and knees to tend to my boys. Thinking Chance was going to die, I developed anxiety. I saw Chance as my deceased baby when he was asleep. The doctor diagnosed me with postnatal depression, PTSD, and anxiety. I couldn't escape the nightmare inside of my own mind. I became suicidal so I admitted myself into a mental hospital, and got wrongly diagnosed with postpartum psychosis. Four days later, I was released.

Although all of the above has taken place, and I have been judged and abandoned by many, including my sisters and best friend, I feel blessed to be alive. I owe my survival to my fourteen-year-old son Jaiden who stepped up when others walked away. I am the proudest and luckiest mother. Mental illness can kill and should not be taken lightly.

I know my life purpose now – to help people through hard times – and I work on it every day. I live to be an example to others and to show what is possible for them, even with a mental illness. I hope my strength, courage and determination will inspire others to never give up hope no matter what life throws at you. **I will never give up.**

Bec McMillan

35 years old

Mother & Future Counsellor

Buderim, Australia

Desperate Dad, Inspired Son

J was born in a remote location in the North Island of Fiji. Our home was surrounded with rainforest, fresh-water streams and coconut trees. With no school nearby, my Dad was desperate to educate me. At six years old, I was sent a long way from home to live with elderly relatives. It was the worst feeling: alone with no one to provide comfort. It was an overnight change from happy-go-lucky to having major responsibilities such as cooking, cleaning, washing and farming before and after school. I endured physical punishments for seven years and studied under a small kerosene lamp late into the night. Years later when I finished high school and joined the workforce it became apparent that all the suffering and hardship had finally paid off. I now live in Australia with my family.

When I was young, my dad always reminded me about the importance of education for a better lifestyle. His advice led me to several degrees and employment as a tax auditor for twenty-five years, followed by pursuits as a business owner. My dad had no education, but his foresight years ago were one hundred percent correct. Education has given me a comfortable lifestyle. I've had hardships, but each time the resilience of my childhood experience allowed me to rise from every fall, time and time again.

Looking back to where I was born and how difficult life was for me in my childhood, and remembering back to my parent's sacrifices, all I want to say is: "Dad, you inspired me to be a better person today. Your teachings will live forever through generations to come. You taught me respect, honesty, persistence and resilience."

It is not how hard life is but what you make out of it in the most difficult of circumstances.

Mohan Singh
60 years old
Business Owner
Lynbrook, Australia

267
Trials, Trauma and Triumphs

My son Jeremiah was in a horrific bike accident on 4 May 2009. Jeremiah was flown from the Pakenham Bypass to the Alfred Hospital Emergency Unit with life-threatening injuries. I was on the phone when someone knocked at the door. Police officers stood there, bringing news that changed our lives forever: "Jeremiah has been involved in an accident." Ruth, my friend, drove me to Alfred Hospital. I walked outside to cry out to God: "Father, please don't take him; he's not ready!" I saw two visions:

1) A sparrow was in an oak tree amidst a hurricane. I was protected in God's arms in the storm.
2) A cross with coloured stones was moving up and down Jeremiah's operating table. Jesus's blood was healing Jeremiah.

Grief overwhelmed the family when we were told of Jeremiah's diagnosis. He was to look at four walls and never rise again. I began to walk in faith, declaring: "Jeremiah will walk, talk and eat again." Day and night, I sat by his bed and read the word of God, impacting his spirit whilst renewing his mind during his recovery. What man saw as impossible, God began to make possible. After sixteen operations and six major moves through the hospital and rehabilitation systems, Jeremiah now talks, eats and has started walking again. God does his best work from seemingly impossible situations. Suffering builds character and purifies our faith.

Jeremiah wrote this poem recently:

I sit and wait, watch and wonder when God's going to fix me that I wonder
He's picked up the pieces and put them together
through rain and shine and every weather
His love though strong he's never wrong, my heart
keeps beating with every meeting
He is my Father and I am his son; that I treasure without measure.

Donna De'bo

61 years old

AHC

Melbourne, Australia

268
Authenticity Is the Path

*A*s the sun rises and illuminates the Earth, imparting its brilliance and warmth to the darkness, I watch in awe the beauty unfold and experience the joy and authenticity that the moment brings to each and every day. I choose to start my day being present in the now and being grateful for all that surrounds me. My life is full of love, joy, passion and energy; there is a calmness, a sense of being at peace – a real contentment.

My life wasn't always like this. I was too consumed by the busyness around me to even notice a sunrise. I worked long hours chasing the corporate dream, beating a path as I went, filling up mornings and evenings with networking, squeezing family time in if I could. I enjoyed life; still something was missing. I was making a difference, no question people's lives changed as a result of my work. I was also achieving income goals and collecting 'things' as I went, except I was concerned with what people thought and what I thought they would want me to be. I wasn't being true and doing what mattered to me?

One day, someone intuitively picked up on this. They sought to enlighten me as to who I was being and shared a poem about authenticity with me. It wasn't until nearly a decade later that the poem had meaning. Three years ago as I wrote this, I gave birth to my third child. He has been such a blessing, giving me so much joy. By taking time to just 'be' with him, he has taught me so much about myself and life, most importantly who I am. This has led me to connect with my purpose, reinforcing the message in the poem: be authentic. Authenticity is the path.

Alison Rogers
41 years old
Leadership Mentor
Hobart, Tasmania

269
Dream Big Dreams

*D*ream big dreams because there is no magic in little ones.

As a young girl, my mother presented me with an outfit: a hand-me-down all-in-one shiny silver jumpsuit with a bonnet. It was tight-fitting, and I looked like a Martian from out of space. It was my favourite. I danced, twirled and pranced enthusiastically, alive, free and entertaining. I wanted to delight others, encourage them and make them smile. Life happened, these precious moments, forgotten until recently. I moved from South Africa to Australia after a traumatic event with my family to a place of safety and opportunity; a place of restoration and new beginnings; a place to find my lost self.

There's a saying: "A journey of a 1000 miles starts with a single step." Eighteen thousand miles and three years later, I remembered the silver jumpsuit. I recalled my dream to encourage and inspire. Today I help individuals create businesses and lives they love that are congruent with their values and in alignment with their strengths.

Hold on to your dreams. If you have buried or forgotten them, please take out your shiny silver jumpsuit, whatever that is for you. The first thing God does to build your faith is give you a dream. When God wants to work in your life, he gives you a dream — about yourself, about how he's going to use your life to impact the world.

The Bible tells us that God "by his mighty power at work within us is able to do far more than we would ever dare to ask or even dream of — infinitely beyond our highest prayers, desires, thoughts, or hopes" (Ephesians 3:20 LB). It's never too late. I want to encourage you to start dreaming again. A dream so big only God can fulfil it.

Brenda Tsiaousis

45 years old

Potentialist, Business Coach & Speaker

Hobart, Tasmania

The Best Version of You

$\mathcal{M}$any teenagers face the challenge of fitting in whilst growing up, including me. I lacked self-esteem, self-confidence, self-acceptance, and self-worth. I feared being rejected if people found out what I hid. Although I knew many people at school I felt alone and isolated, I didn't talk to friends, family, or doctors about it. In high school I went through depression whilst seeking acceptance from people who couldn't give it to me. The one person who could give me valuable acceptance ignored me for years: me.

I grew up with a rare medical condition called Kallmann Syndrome (KS), which caused me to not go through puberty like everyone else, have no sense of smell, and was born deaf in one ear amongst other symptoms. I struggled through teenage years with the added challenge of being bullied. I didn't accept or understand it or why I had it. I kept wondering how good life would be without it. I wanted to be 'normal.' The more I thought negatively about it, the worse I felt. Something had to change. I made the decision to change how I saw myself.

I have always played sport whilst growing up, however, when I started lifting weights at seventeen, my self confidence increased. My nutrition and mindset improved. I created habits that supported me including writing down things to be grateful for, my strengths, and positive traits I possessed, including KS. I am now twenty-three, and it is not a burden like it used to be. I have found a way to accept myself. I use it as a source to push myself to be the best that I can be. I strive for excellence whilst helping others become the best versions of themselves.

"Compliments from other people can make you feel loved and accepted, however self-love and self-acceptance comes from within."

Jason Russell
23 years old
I.C.A.N. Vitality Coach & Author
Bunninyong, Australia

271
Universal Structure

*T*he Universe has a structure that we can follow to find the essence, the sense of life and of our self, the grail: in the fifth element. The elements, life forces, are available to everyone everywhere. With those, we develop our own tree of life and heal deeply. This is my approach; my truth for everything.

1. Fire: It is the father energy. Life is perfectly orchestrated. All is designed for us specifically. Experiences are here to push us out of the comfort zone. Our own physical father shows us our beliefs of life and self when we were born. The gap between him and the unlimited view of the Universe is your own gap in frequency, showing us what we have to heal. Impulses, hard lessons, difficulties, diseases are the flames to wake us up and show us the way.

2. Water: Surrendering: it is the woman energy. Our life shows us our mirrors. We are these others, good or bad, that we interact with. Surrender means facing, seeing, understanding what life shows us about ourselves, welcoming the truth to make peace. This awakens the flow: life energy.

3. Air: It is the masculine energy. We are transforming our inner self by facing our shadows, fears, denied parts. We release, let go of our old 'self,' to build the new self in tune with our hearts.

4. Earth: It is the mother energy. It gives birth to us exactly how we are inside. It is where we grow, protected, having exactly all we need for our path. Our physical mother shows us our relationship to survival, money, support and care until our consciousness evolves and remembers its right to abundance.

5. Ether: Quintessence, our true self is revealed with a balanced relationship to the four elements.

Julie Lobel

34 years old

Sophrologue-Magnétiseuse

France

272
Life Is What You Make It

*T*hroughout my life I have come across some wonderful words of wisdom and life mottos that have shaped my personal outlook and continue to guide and inspire me. When I was a teenager travelling in Italy I read, "Live everyday as if it were your last but never doubt there will be a tomorrow." This stayed with me, as it seemed like a great way to approach life: to live each day fully and to remain ever hopeful.

Years later, I discovered written on a wall in Kathmandu: "You cannot change the past, but you can ruin a perfectly good present, by worrying about the future." This inspired me to live in the now: to simply let go of things you cannot change or control, to trust greatly and to worry less.

In India, I learned the best approach to life is to believe and fully understand, "There is no problem unless you make a problem." There is only 'reality'; the bottom line of all circumstances and situations that just is what it is! Good or bad you have the power to choose how you react to life. This is the key and it makes such a difference. Try to keep a large-scale view of your life and choose to see any problems as small.

Simply, fear not your future or your past for they are no more or no less than you decide to make them. You can't change the past but you can change the effect it has on your future. If it is a problem, you can decide that it will no longer be a problem. Choose to see your life bathed in golden light and it shall be so. May these wise words guide you in the wonderful adventure that is your life.

Claire Johnson
51 years old
Artist & Author
Brighton, England

273
The Flame of Potential

Whether or not you know it, you have a divine purpose to fulfil during your lifetime on Spaceship Earth. Deep within, if you give yourself permission to look, a flame glimmers in the shadows – a light your society has convinced you may not even exist. Smothered by day-to-day responsibility, the ember glows softly, eternally shimmering in the recesses of your mind.

It may begin only as a pinhole – a sharp glare in your mind's eye. It is in our nature to look away and to shield our eyes from such an intense and piercing illumination. Our intuition knows that once the light has pierced fully into the space of our conscious mind that we can never go back. What has been seen cannot be unseen.

Awakening genius and stepping into leadership by activating one's potential is our highest calling. To be loved for whom we are, we must first give ourselves permission to look into the light and gracefully nurture the gently burning ember into a voracious fire of inspiration and gratitude. But how?

Our daily actions define who we are. In this moment, breathe deeply and become present. Take this opportunity now to look upon the days and the weeks and months just passed, and look for those daily activities which define who you are. From this day forward, make the commitment to take one action daily towards the accomplishment of your most meaningful and inspiring goals. Record your gratitude each evening for the actions you have completed and the results you have achieved.

As you begin, you may not be willing or even capable to look directly into the light. Breathe deeply. Your eyes will eventually become accustomed to the brilliance that lives deep within. As days turn into weeks, you will be surprised at who you've become.

Alexander Ford

26 years old

International Speaker

Calgary, Canada

274
Your Life is a Testimony

*J*n December 2013, the cross-cultural business exchange in South Africa changed my life. This experience expanded my heart beyond imagination. Even now, I can still distinctly recall the powerful voices sing the words "Your life is a testimony." The way each word was sung; held so much emotion, depth and meaning. It was sung as though it was the last moment, last breath... last opportunity.

I had never experienced anything like this before; it moved me to tears with an overwhelming sense of gratitude. Behind the people, history, struggles, love, culture, and new generation thinking of this country, is a kaleidoscope of lessons to be learned, shared and embraced by the world. As a refugee immigrant to Australia, having the opportunity to live and work in Australia made me realize my life was full of hope in comparison to those living in South Africa.

The luxury of safety, education, work and having choices hit me like a ton of bricks. I had taken these privileges for granted. Being invited to work with these entrepreneurs left a lifelong inspirational footprint. I was so inspired by how driven, positive, funny, courageous and 'normal' they were.

I came back to Australia full of drive and passion. Having to move out of home at the age of fifteen due to alcoholism and violence, I know the impact of having the right attitude, belief and support systems. I practice every day setting and executing goals, which has over time become a life-changing habit. I now focus only on delivering my intent and purpose with love in everything I do. In turn, I hope to inspire and support others to do the same because your life is a testimony. Make every moment count. It could be your last.

Annie Luu

33 years old

International Business Consultant

Sydney, Australia

275
Responsibility is Power

*R*esponsibility, not blame, has given me a sense of power and massive control over how I think, the actions I take, and the words that I choose to use. I reached a point at forty-eight years old where I was heading for a second divorce. I had a strained relationship with my kids and massive financial debt. I was caught in playing the 'blame game': a victim mentality.

In 2004, I was invited to attend a self-improvement course. That course became a turning point in my life. I now have an amazing relationship with my wife and my kids are like my friends. My daily activities allow me to assist others in their journey, and empower them to lead a life that they love. I flipped my switch around money and now invest. I studied many different ideologies, philosophies and practices until I found a set of ideas that worked for me.

Find routines and daily habits that work. Have a mentor for all areas of life where you want to excel. Surround yourself with people who will encourage you. Keep your word and stay focused on your 'why,' and trust that the 'how' will happen. People enter your life to teach you a lesson; anything you recognise in them, you have in yourself to some degree. Drop the comparisons and celebrate the differences. Be present to your own power, the world will show up as you create it. Recognise that you already make a difference, and raise your awareness so your influence can leave a positive impact.

Choose your thoughts wisely, and learn to let go of past fears and future worries, and get that you only ever have now. So, what will you do now that your future self will thank you for?

Phil Pollard
58 years old
Career Coach & Master Trainer
Melbourne, Australia

276
I Thought I Saw You

Listen closely my dear friend...
Your heart...sweetly, it melodically beats.
Your breath...comforting hums of a lifelong companion.
The one true friendship you never had to seek.
The essence of simply 'being' leaves little to do.
Listen closely my dear friend...hear that?
The magic of life has been given to you.
Come closer dear friend...
The outside world is a kaleidoscope of colours,
Inconsistent...a chattering, merry-go-round of constant change.
Don't pin your happiness on moving objects my dear friend.
The concept of reality is far beyond your visual range.
Trust your intuition my dear friend.
Listen...that's right, to that little voice within.
Don't pin your happiness on external objects my dear friend.
Inner happiness is where the truth begins.
Look closely my dear, dear friend...
Your dreams...bound, only within the chrysalis of your mind.
Freedom...Mother Nature's gift to embody,
Should you choose to live with purpose, the way life should be defined.
Grateful...to be fully present in this body, in this time.
Balance...to be in perfect harmony, the quintessential paradigm.
Hold compassion close to your heart and your wings will be set free.
That's right...fly high my dear, dear friend.
Live your life deliberately.

Kelly Nichols
32 years old
Wellness Coach & Yoga Teacher
Perth, Australia

277
Valued

*T*ormented, lonely, and inauthentic, I was unlovable, plagued by the tyranny of inauthenticity. Being Inauthentic isn't necessarily being untruthful. It is about not sharing that you feel lost, unappreciated or unloved. It's about burying those feelings and trading the pure you for a hollow shell. The damage this caused me was relentless and unmeasurable. I was living in my weaknesses, constantly lacking self-love with no foresight, and in a consistent cycle of reaction. I was paying the price for this unconsciousness.

After my second marriage failed, I was emotionally destitute and had lost myself. I embarked on a deep inner journey to uncover my truth. I needed rapid and wholesale change in order to prevent me from becoming an end to myself. The inner journey this triggered was confronting, torturous and exhausting. To acknowledge that I had been responsible for every event in my life was a challenge I was unready for. I realised that no matter 'who' had done 'what' to me during my life, it was a result of my choices. The blind spots I had created in my psyche rendered me powerless. By making an agreement with myself and allowing this healing, I not only emancipated myself but freed those around me.

Every relationship I have, functional or not, is a result of my choices. Things in me that I tried to suppress, not feel or make wrong are pieces that are in everybody. The angry reactionary, the inconsiderate arsehole, the loving father, the jealous guy, the insecure boy, the scared man, the generous lover, the protective warrior, the compassionate saint, all need to be owned and embraced. Through this journey, I have learned to trust, love and accept myself as I am, while empowering myself to give so much more to others, knowing that all these bits of me are not only valid but valued.

Mike Rogers
43 years old
General Manager
Adelaide, Australia

278
An Inspiring Journey

How confusing can it be – when looking out for what seems 'free'
We as beings on this Earth – take on much when given birth
The journey of the soul can be – a full one, filled with fun and glee
When you open up to free – the inner child to feel and be
What does this mean you may ask – stuck behind the human mask
When I did that I was hurt – caught up in the mud and dirt
Next time I'll react, avoid – I'll hide or fight or fill the void
With food or drugs or run and hide – or find another on my side
I'll give more, looking to allay – the feelings that can cause dismay
Within the body pockets form – protected, nurtured, safe and warm
Hiding what is real and true – and what your soul is meant to do
Go forth now, find what's right for you – for only you can shift the glue
That binds your pathway to the past – allow what's new, what can stick fast
Now ride the wave of truth and trust – your heart to help you clear the rust
Create a new life, filled with more – of what can serve you to ensure
That you now find connections pure
And keep those who are there for you – who share your journey and can view
Your changes with support and love – and feel like friends sent from above
Inspiration is the key – and when you find your sync you see
All that you are meant to be
It matters not your sex or age – or what has happened at what stage
For when we can ignite the fire – our only aim is to inspire

Linda MacDonald
59 years old
Life Transitions Mentor & Healer
Melbourne, Australia

279
The Power of the Next Step

J am obsessed with 'the power of the next step.' You can achieve your wildest dreams just by taking the next step. I talk about it, read about it, think about it, do it and help everyone I can every chance I get. I learned the power of the next step when I trained for my first marathon. For a hack runner like me it was a big hairy goal, but it turned out to be the most incredible journey that shaped and changed the direction of my life and work.

When you start pursuing your goal, like training for a marathon, you usually don't have a clue how you are going to get there. That's ok. The power of the next step is, "What do I have to do today to move towards my goal?" For a marathon it may be join a running club, researching the Internet, and talking to someone who has already done it. The important thing is not to look too far ahead, or get overwhelmed and give up. Just find the next step. And then do it... and keep doing it. Before you know it, you will have achieved your dream.

So many things stop us from doing things we know will fulfil us: fear of failure, lack of knowledge, lack of belief in ourselves, business, indecision, knowing what you want but not knowing where to start. What would happen to those fears if you just took the next step? You are capable of more than you believe. It's true – fun really does happen outside your comfort zone. Pick something simple that will make you happy. Take the next step and see where it leads you. The next step in the right direction may be the step that changes your life.

Fiona Cossill

47 years old

Business Strategist & Personal Coach

Gold Coast, Australia

280
Change Your Tag Line

*J*t was one of my lowest moments as I started my journey in the training arena years ago. I had called one of the training colleges for work. The lady (I use that term loosely) on the other end of the line asked whether I was on the teachers' register. I happily confirmed that I was: "Well, there are over three hundred teachers on that register, when your turn comes up, we'll call you!"

When I explained the incident to my ever-positive friend at the time, he just shrugged his shoulders and said: "Beggars can't be choosers, I guess." From that day, I decided to flip that saying on its head: "Choosers can't be beggars." Yes! That's better. You are not a beggar. You should not tolerate any hint of being treated as such. Not only that, but the saying suggests something worse: putting up with being treated as less than what you deserve.

We have sayings, tag lines, and beliefs that need tweaking – or total eradication. During a presentation at an educational forum. I remember saying: "When we have changed government policy regarding education, when we have given teachers better tools for teaching literacy, after we have guaranteed funding for technology in classrooms and we have chosen better teaching methodologies. What if after having done all that, students don't want to learn?"

There is something fundamentally wrong when we ask students to sit through the protracted process called schooling and insist there are no jobs at the end of it. So, I suggested, we need to change the tag line. Instead of telling students that there are no jobs, show them in which industries there are jobs and how to pursue them. Sometimes all we need to do is to change the tag line. What is your tag line? Do you need to change it?

Mario Cortés
37 years old
Corporate Trainer
Brisbane, Australia

281
Recovery

*F*eeling lost in my head, an empty shell of who I once was, I literally function to get through the day and enter into night where I would send up my prayers and cry silent tears. I would pray that I would not wake up in the morning to endure another day of what seemed useless and limiting, of being a failure in every moment.

You see, I was not certain that I could permanently end my life, so I would pray that God would put me out of my misery. No one knew this part of my world; I would not let them see it. I would hide it, as I felt ashamed. It was hard enough to see the failure in myself without someone seeing the failure in me. Keeping self-hatred within was important during the day. The time of freedom was at night when I could pray that I would be taken and my family freed.

The days were long and the nights short. It felt like it was never going to end. I would call out for help, but no one was listening. I felt like I was screaming and very obvious in my needs and there was no one there. My baby girl had her immunisations at nine weeks old, and then was unable to digest breast milk or prescription formula. The need to syringe milk into my baby's mouth to keep her alive seemed to be missed by the doctors. Three major hospitals, two of which were children's hospitals told me that she still had wet nappies so she was fine. The stress of this situation had me spiral into post-natal depression and my feelings of worthlessness were massive.

Today, seven years on, I am grateful my prayers were not answered. I am grateful for the experience so I can now go forth with the rest of my life. I feel that I have finally made it home. I am at peace with the resourceful and the not-so-resourceful me.

Sarah O'Reilly

42 years old

Coach & Healer

St Ives, Australia

282
Become Your Own Master

*S*everal years ago, I attended a talk by a spiritual master. That night, one sentence became etched into my mind: become your own master. It resonated deeply because I knew it was true.

Growing up in a middle-class family, it seemed I had everything to an outsider: good home, fun friends, private schooling and university education. But one crucial element was missing: emotional nurturing. Whilst physical needs were met, emotional needs were unintentionally ignored, and despite external bravado, I was crumbling inside. In my late twenties, I experienced a mental breakdown, which was really a 'breakdown' of old patterns and beliefs and a 'breakthrough' to a new consciousness.

However, my unconscious need for approval led me to overwork to exhaustion, and then I spent ten years seeking solutions for chronic fatigue. Through healing the past and becoming emotionally masterful, I peeled back the layers of false self. Through the childhood traumas of parental divorce, abusive care-giving, school bullying, loss of loved ones, being torn away from one's homeland, people with chronic fatigue often come to falsely believe: "I'm not good enough." Underneath this is the largest fear of all: not being unconditionally loved.

Childhood disempowerment leads people to become the 'victim' of their circumstances: a desperate need for acceptance, combined with a false belief of being unworthy to receive it, translates into unhealthy habits and behaviours, which in turn lead to sickness... because authentic health can only be built upon a bedrock of robust self-confidence, self-esteem and healthy self-image. With the numbers of chronically ill people in epidemic proportion, it seems emotional disempowerment is the pandemic of our age. It's time for us to rebuild our crumpled self-concepts and return to our natural state of self-mastery: to become our own master.

Kim Knight
52 years old
Health & Personal Development Coach
Auckland, New Zealand

283
Coming 'Home'

*T*he year 2007 began with me caring for a relative with cancer. Then my wife fell pregnant. Soon after, I became acutely ill. After various misdiagnoses, I became extremely anxious. The anxiety began to perpetuate a cycle of sickness. I spent months in hospital. My wife and I separated. Our son was born without me present. My world collapsed. It was hell. Strangely, though, I am grateful for what happened.

In the midst of the chaos, I learned a valuable lesson. I connected with my well-being. For years, I had looked for it by trying to control circumstances. Then I began to see that I wasn't living in the experience of my circumstances, I was living in the feeling of my thinking and my ideas about how life 'should' look. I thought controlling life would help me find my well-being, but that was just my noisy, unfulfilling mind. So I surrendered.

An amazing thing happened. I started to recover! I came 'home' to a sense of well-being. I connected back to my wisdom and saw insights about life, which I realized that I had always fought against. It left me feeling separate, unclear, and disconnected. What if I didn't need to fight? What if my well-being was always available, like the sun behind the clouds, but for my thinking that it wasn't?

However bad things seem, there is hope. 'Home' is not a set of circumstances. It is just one thought away. There is an intelligence to life. You are not separate from it. It is beating your heart and growing trees. It is waiting to bring you wisdom to navigate you through your challenges. But wisdom doesn't lie in your noisy thoughts. It exists in the unknown - in the voice of your heart. Just listen to the part of you that 'knows.' You will be guided.

John El-Mokadem

38 years old

Hope & Inner Wisdom Catalyst

London, United Kingdom

284
Inspiration for Peace and Harmony

The body, mind and spirit are one
Cherish them all and learn to have fun
Love, laugh, cry, create, take time out to meditate
Have a vision, have a purpose in life
Let go of all your troubles and strife
Get to know the 'you' deep inside
Be a friend to yourself, there's no need to hide
Pay it forward with random acts of kindness
Accept one another, let go of your blindness
For we are one people who share the same air
Let's learn to live in peace not despair
God gave each one of us a gift to share
So share it and let your light shine through
And you will be an inspiration too
For others are a reflection of you
So feed your soul with creativity
Be the gift that God meant you to be
For you will be inspired, just wait and see
The ripple effect on humanity.

Julie Knight
56 years old
Counsellor/Complementary Therapist
Gladstone, Australia

285
Finding Wealth

I've found the key to happiness, purpose and a meaningful life. It's not a lucrative job, a perfect romance or designer shoes. To find happiness, I've broken the success rules. Now, I lead with my heart and live what's true for me. Living this way, I've never felt so energized, alive and free! But it wasn't always like this. Just months ago my life looked very different...

Since childhood, I remember feeling pressured into the 'perfect life.' I fell into the superwoman syndrome. This perfect life cost me my health and relationships. Yes, I played by the 'rules' and earned a spot at the biggest trauma hospital in the southern hemisphere as a radiographer. But, that was having it all – and having nothing!

One day, as I wheeled a patient to be x-rayed, I had a flash, a signal from my soul and a childhood memory. I wanted to do something big and meaningful! Suddenly, my golden surroundings looked like golden handcuffs. I had forgotten my mission to be extraordinary! I hated physics and machines yet they surrounded me. Everything I worked for years to achieve suddenly looked empty and meaningless. It was like a hamster wheel slowing down just long enough for me to question where my life was headed. And, when you question one thing, you question everything.

The truth was that I built a castle that felt more like a prison, and my big achievements had nothing to do with why I'm on the planet. I had blindly followed the path to the 'perfect life' and couldn't have been more miserable. During New Years, I hit rock bottom and had to make a decision – change my life or continue feeling unfulfilled and miserable. It was time to find the real me, stripped of all the academic achievements and job titles. Because I made that decision, a series of miraculous things happened.

Stella Ungphongphan

27 years old

Holistic Practitioner

Mosman, Australia

286
From Abusive Relationship Victim to Happily Ever After

I believe everyone deserves the best relationship no matter what has happened in the past. I am grateful for what happened because it shaped me into who I am today. I came from a background of an emotionally and physically abusive relationship for six years. My ex-partner was very violent, never hesitating to express anger and aggression. One day, as I looked at myself in the mirror, I felt a sense of hopelessness and desperation. I knew something had to change. So I made a decision to leave him.

After I left, I decided to focus on myself, and started my journey of self-development. I realized everything I looked for outside was a reflection of what was missing inside me. I realized that in order for me to have an amazing relationship with someone, it had to start with the relationship I have with myself. As I started to say yes to myself and treat myself with the love and respect I deserve, everything around me started to change. I met an amazing guy who was everything I dreamed of. We have been happily together ever since. One day out of the blue, he asked me to be his wife and I said yes to our 'happily ever after' dream.

I believe the dream does come true if you have the courage to aim for it. I am on a mission to inspire the world to create their relationship dreams. Never let what happened in the past define your future. If you are going to spend the rest of your life with someone, you may as well make it the most loving and exciting relationship of your life.

Jane Nguyen
27 years old
Author, Speaker & Relationship Expert
Melbourne, Australia

287
You Are Worthy of Great Love

One of the greatest challenges in life is being ourselves in a world where everyone wants to change us. We feel unlovable because of the condemnation or displeasure of others. When we feel disapproved of, we behave in a manner where we believe we are not worthy of love. We minimise ourselves and attract below average and sometimes cruel treatment in our intimate relationships.

Pain is often our greatest teacher. It teaches us to set clearly defined boundaries as to what is acceptable in love, and what it should look like. At some point we will claim our right to be accepted for being who we are, our authentic selves. The first step to being treated in the way you want and deserve is to be clear about what you like about yourself. What uniqueness do you bring to the world? What do you want in life? What you would like to accomplish and experience? What makes you feel good? A healthy sense of self and self-love is paramount to this journey.

Many years ago when I was experiencing a very painful loss, I was comforted by the words of a close friend who gave me something that, at that point in time, I lacked: clarity. She said the time would come when my 'self-love jar' would be full again, and when that happened, I would be open to a new love experience.

When we have love, understanding and acceptance of who we are and what our wants, needs and requirements are, we are open to loving and receiving love. When our 'self-love jar' is full, we give from abundance, not lack. Exactly who you are now, with every mannerism, trait, skill, strength and talent is enough. You are worthy of great love.

Shelley J Whitehead
49 years old
Relationship Coach
London, United Kingdom

288
A Letter to My Child

*I*t may seem strange that I've written this letter to you here, so exposed, but I want to share this letter with the world, Niamh, so it may give other mummies and daddies the courage to listen to their children.

Being incredible parents isn't about how many toys our children have; it's about understanding how healing the act of listening can be. When you were three years old and your sister just a baby, we had to leave everything behind. Removed from preschool, your cosy yellow bedroom and the first playmates you had; it was heart-breaking. Acts of cruel strangers forced us out of the place we thought was our 'forever home'; it was no longer safe. The media called it 'neighbours from hell.' We called it a living hell. We lost everything.

The law helped us 'win' on paper, and we began rebuilding our lives, but the pain didn't go away. The memories were vivid. Mummy and daddy were hurting inside for a long time. I didn't want you to see me afraid, or sad. I felt I had let you down. I convinced myself you were too young to understand, but you did. You just didn't yet have the words, and I didn't have the ability to listen.

One day we met a doctor who helped you find words, and I finally found the courage to listen. I heard you like I had never heard you before, and it was then that I realised it didn't matter how much we owned. Slowly, we learned to listen to each other and as a family began to heal.

I hope this letter inspires you, Niamh, to keep using words. To everyone else, ours ears are our greatest tool. I hope our story inspires you to go and listen wholeheartedly to someone you love.

Lucy Doyle
32 years old
Nutritionist, Motivator & Speaker
London, United Kingdom

289
Dear Mummy and the World

J am happy that you have written in this book with me because it might help other children find words to say how they feel. Reading your letter, it was the first time that I cried about what happened. I knew you loved me, but I didn't know how much. Now I do.

Mummy, toys aren't that important to me. Having you and daddy is amazing and I am very lucky, as some people do not even have that. I don't mind if we live in a big or small house, all that matters is we are together. I do remember what happened to us, and although you were smiling, I could see the sadness in your heart, and that made me feel afraid. I never wanted to ask questions in case I made things worse.

The day you took me to meet Dr. Kim Jobst ("The Wizard") I suddenly found the words to explain how I felt. I was so happy because all I wanted was for you to listen to me properly and to understand me. He helped you to hear me in a different way than you had before, and now I don't feel poorly anymore; I feel safe and happy.

My message that I would like to share with the world is that having a family is the most important thing, and you can end up with nothing but actually have everything you really need! I believe that children know more about feelings than adults realise, and I hope that parents are inspired to stop sometimes and take the time to sit and listen to their children. I like using words now and this is my favourite saying: "It doesn't matter how you look, it matters how you feel."

Niamh Doyle

9 years old

Adventurer

London, United Kingdom

290
The Journey

L eaving the comfort of my home and family, I came to Australia when I was twenty two-years-young to pursue my masters in environmental management. My epic journey from getting off that plane with no more than two bags of clothes, knowing nobody, starting from nil to working my way up in a profession I love, has taught me some very valuable and inspirational wisdom that I would like to share with you today.

- Your current conditions are the echoes of your past choices. Realize that in the moments of your decision, and your destiny is shaped.

- As you live your day, you craft your life. You only get this day once in your entire life. Give this day your absolute best.

- One day you will just be a memory to the people you know. Do your best to be a good one.

- Instead of wondering when your next vacation is, you ought to set up a life you do not need to escape from.

- In this age of dramatic distraction, stop managing your time, start managing your focus. Start small, stay focused, and grow stronger.

- Daily ripples of superior performance add up over time to a tidal wave of outrageous success.

- Practice does not make perfect. Perfect practice makes perfect.

- When passion becomes purpose, magic becomes reality!

- Finally, I would like to highlight what Carl Jung once said: "Your vision becomes clear when you look inside your heart. Who looks outside, dreams. Who looks inside, awakens."

Infinite love, peace and gratitude – until we meet again!

Willbur Glenn Colaco

32 years old

Scientist, Author & Speaker

Adelaide, Australia

291
Harald

*T*here was once a young man named Harald, who had great talents and skills. He put these abilities to work on Brommapjorna's longboat and received what he needed to live in return. This was a satisfying situation for Harald until he realized that Brommapjorna was watching every move he made, gradually introducing KPI's and installing security cameras on the longboat. Harald was even being watched as he slept, for his 'own good,' as explained by Brommapjorna. Harald's enjoyment of exploring other lands was now gone. He felt beaten and even noticed that he was being watched when he was home after a voyage. Thorsen, the master blacksmith in the village, asked Harald for his birthdate so that he could send him a birthday card, again, the reason given was 'for his own good.' Harald was sick of it all, so he organized his own voyage with a hand-picked crew.

On the journey, Harald discovered that his crew did things differently, as they were all dissatisfied with the constant pushing, surveillance and profiteering. Harald noticed that the crew had arranged themselves according to their abilities, where those who were good at certain things, did them. The other tasks were then divided according to necessity by the crew themselves. They cooked, ate, and slowed down together, and began philosophizing and enjoying each other's company. There was no need to check with surveillance cameras and bully the crew. They had organized themselves according to skills and need and were motivated to work for each other. Together, they had created an abundance without setting foot on dry land – for the crew, life had become about the journey – the journey now had meaning, and they could stop plundering other lands because the journey had become their paradise.

This is what I do, and what I believe that everybody could do to build a better world – together.

Robert Muller

53 years old

Creative Agitator

Adelaide, Australia

292
Doodles

*P*lease take out a blank sheet of paper and a pencil. What I am now going to ask you to do requires no words. Let's use simple pictures instead. We'll call these pictures doodles.

I would like you to doodle on this page all the emotional hurts you have had over a lifetime. This might include mistakes you've made, regrets you have, failures and hardships you have gone through, and anything else that brings you pain. Just let everything out on that single sheet of paper. Be completely vulnerable, honest and open about your pain. No filters allowed.

It's of course perfectly okay if this stirs up some intense feelings. This is part of the healing process — it's part of letting go and moving on. Just be in the moment and experience every emotion through your doodles. Looking at your paper canvas as a whole, see all the pain contained within each and every one of those doodles and acknowledge how this pain is holding you back from the life you desire to live.

Now, take out an eraser and scrub out everything you have just doodled. Yes, keep scrubbing until you wipe the canvas clean... and then, exhale. It's time now to doodle again over that same canvas, but this time doodle not how life was, but rather how you would prefer it to be. Create some new memories that will no longer hold you back from the life you desire to live.

Every time you awaken in the morning, you are reborn with a blank canvas. You can start over and begin again. You can create a new set of memories that will empower you to create a better, bigger and more inspiring future. In fact, every minute is just another chance to doodle something anew.

Adam Sicinski

37 years old

Visual Thinking Coach & Doodler

Melbourne, Australia

293
The Voice

When is it in youth,
That we absorb the words of another?
They become our dark voice,
That we suffer with others.
Why is this the voice
That we continue to hear?
The voice from within,
We allow to bring us to tear.
What if instead,
We spoke to ourselves with love?
From our own heart and,
Embraced that which is and all of.
Everything you are
Is perfect right now.
I wish you knew this.
I wish I could show you how.
One day, this,
You will understand.
You are as you are,
It's time to take a stand.
Love yourself exactly as you are.
You are everything you need.
Please hear this, instead.
Plant a new voice to seed.

Elise Hutley
27 years old
Author, Trainer & Start-Up Developer
Adelaide, Australia

294
Jack

*J*am proud of the fact that I have been on a personal development journey for over twenty years. I thought I had it all together. I had come through a challenging childhood, divorce, become a business owner, and migrated alone from the USA to Australia. I finally had the life I wanted; a business gaining momentum, a love for Australia, and the man of my dreams. After ten years together, Jack and I married. He left his job and became the IT administrator for my company. Four months of marital bliss and it seemed like life was our oyster. We worked together, invested in real estate and continued growing a business that changed lives.

On 21 April, 2010 Jack and I went jogging. We were focusing on fitness and planning our future: it was going to be huge! At 8:30am on 22 April, 2010, Jack had a freak heart attack and died in my arms. He was forty-nine. My birthday was the next day.

For the first time, I experienced thoughts I never believed myself capable of having. I contemplated taking my life. I couldn't imagine how I could find happiness without Jack. Mixed with feelings of despair, I was confronted with a choice. I could let it destroy me – or I could build the future Jack and I had designed. I chose to create the future. Here's what I did to get through:

- Every day I asked myself: "What would Jack expect of me? What would he want for me?"

- Every day I looked for ten positive things – and wrote a list.

- Every day I reminded myself of what I stand for – and what I am here to accomplish.

Every day I got stronger. Today I carry on the legacy we were both connected to. I now have another wonderful man in my life, and love is once again blooming.

Frances Berry
48 years old
Company Director
Perth, Australia

295
From Tragic to Magic!

*W*e think what we accumulate and what title we wear is what matters most in life. I discovered at age forty-six that none of that mattered a bit. In 2007, I lost absolutely everything after thirty years of working. Within a six month period, my marriage failed, my business collapsed, my car was repossessed and I lost my home and all my money. I had no source of income and no vision for my future. Everything that was once important to me had totally evaporated. I was left with nothing but precious memories and a few cents in my wallet. The depression I fell into was horrific.

Little did I realise, the inferno engulfing my life back then was actually one of my greatest blessings. I had no inkling that I was actually being prepared for the next exciting chapter of my life. Like the Australian Banksia wildflower that needs a bushfire to release its seed so its life cycle can continue, my own inferno discarded everything around me to reveal what my true life purpose was... to bring joy, laughter and inspiration to others!

We're each like artists. Every one of us has the opportunity to paint a brand new 'life canvas' every single day with the words we use and the thoughts we think. Our life canvas can be a bright, colourful work of art that attracts all the happiness and success we desire, or it can be a dark and colourless piece that repels all the good that we truly deserve in our lives! So, I urge you to become a great master like Picasso... and paint your life like it's a living masterpiece!

David Laws
53 years old
Spiritual Advisor
Gold Coast, Australia

296
The Puppet

*F*or most of my life, I lived as a puppet version of who I thought I should be. Like a chameleon changing colours depending on its environment, I would change depending on what I perceived was necessary to belong. I never did exceedingly well or particularly poor: standing out would create attention. Life felt like a struggle, dangerous and judgmental. My strategy for survival was to blend in and be like everyone else.

The first twenty-three years of my life consisted of blood, sweat and tears. With countless hours in the gym, partying up a storm, and constantly looking to be validated in my finance career, I realized I was missing something: Me! Instead of spending my time out in the big wide world, I began to find me. The catalyst of change occurred when I cancelled my New Year's Eve plans to sit at home and draw a circle, which I divided into four quadrants: physical, emotional, mental and spiritual. I realized all my attention was on the physical, and I had almost no relationship to the other segments. The penny dropped: to live a fulfilled and happy life I was to embrace, accept and know all parts of myself, and to start an epic quest of 'knowing and experiencing me as me.'

This decision changed my life forever. The only way the outside world would accept me was if I accepted me. Through building a strong relationship with my heart, following my intuition, and creating an expanded mindset, I now am an inspirational speaker, coach and facilitator. As Gandhi said "Be the change you wish to see in the world." We are all a unique expression of creation experiencing itself through its unique perspective. Find your piece of the humanity puzzle, and find your joy and inspiration.

Nicolas Perrin
31 years old
Transformational Coach
Sydney, Australia

297
Choices

*I*n my childhood, I found inspiration in normal role models and superheroes. I've always dared to dream. I quickly learned that I would only come unstuck if my outlandish sense of possibilities impacted others negatively. Through experience though, I learned that not everyone plays by these rules. One of the bizarre things about victimization is that the sane person, the victim, still wonders what they could have done differently. It doesn't speak of stupidity or naivety. It is hope and optimism that can't be stamped out by anything. Stalked, drugged, threatened and frightened are my yesterday, not my today. So, what is today?

Choices; in absolutely everything.

I choose to see the light in my children's eyes and reflect love back, not fear. I choose to open to the love of a beautiful man, and give without condition. I choose to contribute to society with a hope and optimism that means engaging in my work is magic. I choose to empower, educate and share. I wake up each day to the new and exciting. The majority of my life experiences make me laugh so hard that my sides ache, for not one experience was in vain. And I know why: I am sensitive and an empath.

What gives my incredible and zany life meaning, is that my experiences give me a sense of reality. They write on the slate of who I am. I cherish the experiences because of what they bring to my work. And this is my purpose, my path, untainted and absolutely real. And, in turn, this helps me to support others to heal and move forwards every day. There's no monopoly here – you can do this, too.

Nicole McHenry
48 years old
Psychic Medium
Melbourne, Australia

298
Guided Back by the Divine

*S*everal childhood experiences made me feel like I was constantly being punished, not allowed to enjoy life, and worthless. I resisted through escapism (drugs, comfort eating, thrill-seeking and self-endangerment). Ultimately, I was creating physical pain to cover up emotional pain. I was depressed and oftentimes suicidal. And, one day, I was about to attempt final escape; to jump from a sixteen-story building.

But the divine had other plans – sending an angel to cross my path. He came from nowhere – a dead end – and said to me, "How are you?" My honest answer to him was, "I'm good." That positive affirmation woke me up. He showed me that, no matter how bad I 'feel'... I am fine. Nothing can harm me unless I allow it. What I learned that day was part of a universal truth: without self-love, we cannot be aligned with our true purpose.

After that day, I changed my entire life. I learned how my thoughts sabotaged me, and how I could change my mindset to acceptance of my situation instead of resistance, about seeing challenges as gifts instead of punishment, and about having positive self-talk. On a spiritual level, I have learned methods of transmuting my pent-up emotions: meditation, breathing exercises, yoga, visiting spiritual healers and – most importantly – accepting who I am while both letting go of and learning from my past.

Having worked through pent up emotional and spiritual baggage, I have awakened my consciousness and brought light to my darkness. Challenges still present themselves, and it doesn't get easier; but I have become stronger. And with that strength I connect to the divine. My journey has brought me to study numerology; and I now know my purpose is to spread this light to others that are still in a self-imposed darkness. I accept my purpose; I am the light.

Mark Murphy
28 years old
Management
Brisbane, Australia

299
Surviving Danger

*W*hat do you do when three large men are shouting death-threats at you, attempting to steal your passport and kidnap you, until a large sum of money is paid, because they changed the deal, and you're overseas, on your own, not speaking the language?

Shouting back wouldn't help. I remained calm and sought a way to make myself safer. Fortunately, the police were called, which meant I was able to negotiate 'voluntarily' staying at a hotel while funds were raised. Police agreed I'd broken no law, but couldn't guarantee my safety if I left. Once in the hotel, all I could do was lock myself in the room and wait for head office to pay the ransom.

I could easily sink into despair: why was this happening to me? Instead, I remained as calm as possible and decided, rather than ask 'why,' to ask the more powerful question of 'what.' If there was a lesson in all of this, something powerful for me to learn, what was it? I may not have caused the situation, but I was responsible for how I reacted. By thinking in this way, I was able to turn a horrible situation into a source of growth. It wasn't easy, but it made me stronger.

I knew harbouring ill will toward my would-be captors was pointless. It would only harm me, not them. Their actions were a result of their upbringing, culture, and situation. To paraphrase Nelson Mandela, "As I walked out the door toward the taxi that would lead to my freedom, I knew if I didn't leave my bitterness and hatred behind, I'd still be in prison." So as hard as it was in the moment, I forgave them, which actually brought me immense relief. No matter the situation, we can either despair, or we can seek to learn and grow from it.

Keith Blackmore-Noble

48 years old

The Confidence Alchemist

London, United Kingdom

300
How Do We Inspire?

*T*he most common way we inspire is by drawing air in through the mouth and nose to fill the chest and belly. The oxygen dissolves through the capillaries in our lungs and sends life through every cell. The breath continues as we exhale carbon dioxide to support all of the plants that live on Earth.

A similar process occurs through the food we eat, the emotions we feel and the actions we take. We become more and more alive when we expand our sense of 'self' to include all that is around us, and following the burning whispers of our heart.

Perceived barriers lock you in prison walls
Because an action for one is an action for all

Your choice is the key in learning to see
That the world is free if you let yourself be

Breathe in from 0-6
Breathing out will complete the mix

Adam Oldmeadow
25 years old
Health Coach & Energy Therapist
Melbourne, Australia

301
What Is It?

*W*hat is it? That we want, that we need, that we chase, searching for, so convinced, so conditioned that we are not whole, that we have a void that has to be filled, so desperately, childishly driven to "get it."

"I don't get it..."

"I don't have it..."

"I want it..."

"I'm going to make it..."

What is it...? So many tired, asleep, drugged, dimmed stars of people marching to the same frequency!

What is happiness? Right now, are you happy? Do you know a happy person? Why is it so rare? Why is it the minority, the weird, the outlier, the deviant, when did simple happiness become such a perverted, negative, frown induced, head shaking, unknown? We fear the unknown; we hear this in every humanistic, fantastical scripted version of celluloid, digital reality! We fear the unknown, the weird, the different, the outlier, the divergent.

I say embrace this fear. Stand in front of it, slowly reach out to it, touch it, rub away the dust, the dirt, feel the beautiful smooth surface underneath, slowly begin to recognise the reflection underneath the layers of dirty conditioning, slowly see the light being revealed, slowly see the star shining, slowly see with your real eyes that star is you, and wash away the fear!

What is it...?

What it's always been...

Robert Kavanagh

34 years old

Physiotherapy Clinic Owner

London, United Kingdom

302
Say Yes to Your Good

*M*y marriage was coming apart. I was out to dinner with my husband, and he was describing his dream to visit Tibet. As I listened, I became intuitively aware of an image of a clock around me: 12:00 was directly in front and 6:00 was behind my back. I saw his dream at 12:00, and my dream was at 4:30, heading behind my back, out of view. I knew instantly that if I put my energy into his dream, I would lose my own. So I said, "No."

The next morning before work, he calmly said, "We're not dreaming together anymore. It's time for us to part." Yes, it was time.

I pulled out a map of the United States and a pendulum for dowsing answers. "OK, God, you've got me. Where do you want me?" I had no fear and was rather spiritually smug in that moment, as I was sure I would be guided to the western US. I moved my left hand westward across the southern states while dowsing with my right hand. I slowed down when I reached the states where I was going to be guided to live, but the pendulum continued swinging 'no,' How strange!

As I moved my hand north and eastward, I wondered why it wasn't working. Suddenly, in my mind, tiny East Coast Cape Cod jumped off the map and my pendulum started wildly swinging yes. I yelled out loud, "NO! West Coast!" For three days I fought with spirit. "NO!" Then I heard the clear words that I will never forget: "My Good waits for me in Cape Cod." I let go of my plans. "Yes." Seven weeks later I moved cross-country. Fifteen years later, my life continues to overflow with good! Say yes to your good.

Nancy Canning
64 years old
Hypnotherapist, Author, Lecturer
Cape Cod, MA United States

303
Smart Phone or Smart Ear?

"*N*obody listens as you do." How often have I heard that? Indeed as very enthusiastic artist and teacher desperately longing for time to work, I paradoxically used to always find myself listening for hours to others' frustrations, comforting friends and strangers, old and young, educated and not — for decades. People felt so relieved that I had welcomed it as a calling.

One day after a loud party, my ears started to ache tremendously. Harmless sounds became intolerable — which is still the case. Hospital, patronizing doctors (helplessly) and all sorts of alternative therapists – desperately paying much to not even get at least that authentic listening I had been giving for free all my life. Loneliness. The absurdity of it nearly destroyed me.

It has been four years. Just whipping eggs still causes me extreme discomfort, even wearing my ear defender. Nobody knows whether this is reversible. But, now I feel blessed. Life has been wisely teaching me what I never dared teach others. Let me share it now.

Harmony is not to be found by repeatedly tipping out your ego-self-made inner movie into some-body, 'some-ear,' real or phone, in whose response you will only listen to what makes you feel good about yourself. Nor will it be found in Facebook-ly reshaping an uninteresting outer you.

REAL answers are to be found IN SILENCE.

Inside.

Tuning in with the DIVINE you.

Interestingly, no spiritual tradition does without some silence. How do we hope to grow when we let ourselves and our younger ones be polluted by compulsive public and private noise interference? Dive into this unlimited cosmic love inside your heart to clean your words before giving them to the world. Your voice will sound more beautiful, centred, mirroring your life. Words and sounds are far too sacred to be debased.

Marie Malherbe

39 years old

Artist

Vienna, Austria

304
The Girl in the Photo

The young girl in the photo radiates joy. Safe. Her whole life ahead.
One day, her world changes. A new baby brother arrives.
He is sick, won't survive. Wrap him in cotton wool; take him home.
But he is strong and fighting. Determined to not let this beast slay him.
The road is rough, with many setbacks. But he perseveres.
No hospital stay brings him down. No barrier holds him back.
Six months of Year Twelve in hospital.
An honorary pass is refused. He achieves it on his own.
He never uses his illness to get anything he hasn't worked for.
He wins career awards. He's respected by all who know him.
He is funny, popular, insightful. He loves life. He inspires all around him.
This girl spent her whole childhood in fear.
When will he leave us? Why is he so sick and not her? What did she do wrong?
But knowing him, learning from him, his amazing attitude to life,
Blessed her with the tenacity her father so admired.
For twenty-three years, this Earth was blessed with his light.
And his memory continues to inspire
young family members he never even met.
His light is so strong it burned in his father's heart till the day he also left this Earth.
A father who could never accept his illness,
who spent the rest of his days in mourning.
And they are united once more.
This world is blessed with many beautiful souls.
Some here for only a short while.
Life is a blessing.
Let your light shine from your heart, for yourself and for those all around you.
A vibrant energy leaves a vibrant memory. Never to be forgotten.
The girl is me.

Deanna Hewett

48 years old

Energy Practitioner & Trainer

Melbourne, Australia

305
And I Sing

*A*t kindergarten, there would always be that one kid who hid behind the teacher and didn't fit in. Well, that was me. I was tall, shy and lonely. I was easily embarrassed and I cried a lot. It made me sad. I longed to be liked by the other kids, but I was so scared of being seen. At home, I sang – a lot. It was my thing. It made me feel good about myself. In 2008 I found myself in front of over 200 people. I still have no idea how I did it but I did. I sang *Somewhere Over the Rainbow* and they loved it. They loved me! Was that a dream? No. I did it.

Little by little, my confidence has grown. Each time it gets easier. I have had lessons, joined choirs and sung at soirees. Now I am in year eight. It has been six years since then, and in the performing arts department, I am going steady. I have had many successful auditions, performed in children's productions, and I sing at events whenever I can.

I sing because I feel like someone when I sing – like I am special. I want to connect to people. I want people to connect to me. I want them to see who I am. The support of my family, friends, teachers, and my audiences keeps me going. But though my confidence grows, I am still the same girl underneath. I am shy. I read; I draw; I write. And I sing.

I want to encourage anyone who believes that they can't do something. Just like a flower, if you can learn to grow and nurture it, it will bloom beautifully. You are amazing. You just need to believe it.

Belief does amazing things to people.

Nishika Hewett

13 years old

Student

Melbourne, Australia

306
Wisdom and Intelligence

*E*very word we think, utter or write is an expression of our soul – a communication conduit to help us understand our own intelligence. I liken the soul to an antenna, transmitting and receiving information to help us reflect on the different chapters in our lives so we can redirect our energy to convey the essence of who we are.

I lost direction in my life during my teens. Other people's words distorted my ability to hear the signal from my soul. Six attempts to attain my English exams resulted in my being told I was illiterate and that I'd never amount to anything. My failure to achieve at school was the start of a battle to believe I capable of accomplishing anything. I was in a violent relationship. I suffered a miscarriage, had two failed marriages, my house was repossessed and I was constantly broke. It was as if I was living the same chapter of my life over and over again. I felt I had nothing of value to offer. I was not worthy of either receiving or holding on to anything of value, nor was I worthy of having a relationship with anyone who valued me.

Having children changed my world. I wanted them to be confident in themselves – to do whatever they wanted without pressure of living up to any expectations. It was an echo of what I wanted for myself! The adversities I'd experienced were messages for me to retune the signal to my soul so I could listen to my wisdom and create my own measure of success. I finally understood why the great philosopher Ralph Waldo Emerson wrote: "To be yourself in a world that is constantly trying to make you something else is the greatest accomplishment."

Philippa Ross
53 years old
Energy Health Consultant
Whangarei, New Zealand

307
First World Problems

*E*very experience is an opportunity. Four weeks in India and Nepal opened my eyes and had me evaluating my life. Imagine: people living in ramshackle dwellings on the footpath; bathing in a bucket; the kitchen, lounge, bedrooms are one room shared by the family; no toilet, you share the community facility; lining up daily to join the job queue hoping to work; animals searching through rubbish heaps for food; people digging through rubbish for plastic water bottles to recycle; children begging for food or money; fresh running water available only every four days. This is daily life for some people.

There were many wonderful experiences, beautiful sights and people as well. A Sikh temple fed thousands of people daily – regardless of caste, race, or religion – for free. Volunteers helped make food – our guide said some people couldn't give money so they gave their time. There are communities with their own commerce; communities that support and look out for each other. These communities are filled with happy, grateful, welcoming and helpful people.

It hit home how ridiculous my first world problems are: getting worked up over something I can't control; letting trivial things upset me; wishing I had this or that; feeling sorry for myself. How many times have I focused on these 'problems,' which aren't real problems? I was wasting time and energy when I could be enjoying my life now. Traveling to India and Nepal was an amazing experience. I have a greater appreciation for my life and my opportunities.

At Buddha's birthplace in Lumbini, one sign says, "All that we are is the result of what we have thought. Mind is everything. What we think, we become." I can choose to be happy, to love and enjoy life, to be present, to pursue my goals. It's on me.

Shannan Knight

34 years old

Project Manager & Property Investor

Brisbane, Australia

308
Forgiveness

*T*he ability to truly forgive another who has wounded us is the way to peace and the only way to happiness after the pain of insult to our heart and soul. Intellectually, we may know this, but how do we forgive that which seems unforgivable?

After the death of my baby son in 2003, the result of medical intervention during childbirth, I spent years lost in a wilderness of grief and despair before finding the way to forgive those responsible. Or rather, forgiveness found me... because I wasn't even looking for it. The ability to truly and utterly forgive is one of the greatest blessings we can receive, and it cannot be forced.

It is not something we do with our brain, rather it can only be found in our heart. In opening our heart and sending forgiveness to those who have hurt us, we heal ourselves. Sometimes, the key is forgiveness of self first. Forgiveness does not mean turning a blind eye or condoning harmful, hurtful actions. Nor does it mean that we allow others to ride roughshod over our boundaries of acceptable behaviour.

No, the forgiveness of which I speak is on a spiritual level. In forgiving, my own spirit was released from the tyranny of bitterness, resentment and victimhood. Love is love, and it is eternal. Often, those we love are the ones who hurt us the most, but true love for our family, partners and friends never dies. We may not be able to see them or speak with them but love remains, always, in our hearts; and the human heart has the capacity to love many, many others. I am humbly and eternally grateful for the gift of forgiveness. It frees me to walk lightly and joyously, unencumbered by the past, and fully present to live in the moment... and so it is.

Kari Tonkin
49 years old
Author, Writer & Speaker
Melbourne, Australia

309
Laughter Is the Best Medicine

*J*n Feb 2009, I found a lump in my breast. I began the roller-coaster ride of my life: experiencing what many would say was a time of loss, loss and more loss. I lost my home base, part of my breast, my previous good health, my hair, a friend from cancer, and also my job, which I was passionate about.

Though the cancer diagnosis was big and overwhelming, I also realised that I did have choices. I could do the treatment or explore alternative treatments. I could play the victim (which everyone would completely understand) or be the maker of my own destiny. I *knew* the way to survive was to focus on what I *did* want. I planned a reward for the end of treatment – a trip to Bali, which I chose to believe I would be alive for.

Over twenty months I had: two surgeries, four doses of heavy duty chemo, twelve doses of 'regular' chemo, twenty-five doses of radiation, seventeen treatments of IV drugs every three weeks, and the side effects of pericarditis and pneumonia. I became like a building supervisor on site: I kept records of appointments, organized family and friends to accompany me to chemo so I wasn't alone, learned to ask for help – with cooking, driving, etc. I knew that 'laughter is the best medicine,' so I asked friends to send me funny emails. When I couldn't get out of bed, I would read them and feel my spirits soar as the laughter came from me.

I had my last treatment on the morning of 10th Sept 2010, and that afternoon I flew to Bali. I gained so much more than I'd lost – new friends, release from stress, a new career, a new home and importantly, a better version of me!

Sonja Preston
58 years old
Senior Parenting Consultant
Hobart, Tasmania

310
Love Harder, Live With Passion

*L*ife is so crazy and short that it would make absolutely no sense to not follow your highest dream. The Universe is so vast and large, and our existence in it is such a miracle that it astounds me beyond understanding. Scientists have been able to observe up to ninety two billion light years away from Earth. A light year is around about one thousand times the length of our solar system. Wow. The clarity that I get from this notion is that we need to make the most of the time.

All human beings are blessed to be such a conscious species and live on this beautiful planet. The Earth has been around for four and a half billion years, which equates to approximately fifty-six million times the average cycle of human life (eighty years). The scary thing is that it is going to continue to drift on by for another fifty six million cycles of life into the future. We get so caught up in a box that we put our mental potential into worrying about what people think and comparing ourselves with everyone else, instead of looking at the truth of life, which is that we can literally do whatever we want, whenever we want, however we want, with whomever we want.

Every single person on this Earth has no more than a one percent difference in genetic ability, which leads me to the heartbreakingly obvious truth that we all have the same potential. Every single person on this Earth is bound, purely by his or her mental strength. Next time that you find yourself getting stuck, use the perspective that comes with the craziness and shortness of life to shrink the fear that stops you. Love a little harder and live with total and utter passion.

Ryan Magdziarz
21 years old
Dream Dealer
Melbourne, Australia

311
Trust In the Process

A few years ago, I was a modern day Bridget Jones living a ground hog day existence and in desperate need for a fresh perspective on life, love and my purpose. So, what was stopping me? Fear! We all need something powerful to break us out of the rut. I needed courage to arrive in the mail so I could at least take the first steps towards my dreams. And just when I needed it, life threw me a big dose of perspective to help me get moving. Needless to say, a fortuitous event was about to occur.

My friend invited me to a women's networking event. I was seated next to a cardiologist who was also a quadriplegic. She was an inspirational woman, full of life, purpose and focus. She was sharing her new passion for creative writing. I asked her: "It must be good to forget about the process of science and enjoy your creativity?"

Her answer changed my life. She said, "It doesn't matter if I'm in surgery, cooking or writing, there is always a process to follow in order to get a result. As long as you follow and trust the process, you can do anything." After a few minutes, I realised she shared the key to breaking through any fear; because everything has a process and once you learn to trust the process, all you need to do is follow it.

1. Find something you like
2. Believe in Yourself
3. Follow the process
4. Trust in the process

I look back at that time and think of all I have achieved by finding and following its hidden process. This concept can be applied to your career, writing, cooking and love. Maybe this is your time to trust in the process.

Elizabeth Tyrell

39 years old

Empowering Women Entrepreneurs

Port Melbourne, Australia

312
Labels Do Not Define Us

*J*couldn't read until I was ten. I could recite stories written for school perfectly, but if there was a gap between writing and having to deliver my essay verbally I couldn't remember what I'd written. I simply couldn't read it. I was referred to as "lazy" and "unwilling to try." My Year Five teacher sent furious letters home to my parents, asking for meetings regarding my inability to read, and sent me home with a set of flashcards from the Reception class, which we had to work with every night.

I remember one incident clearly: one of my favourite movies had been *Dot and the Kangaroo*, which I could recite verbatim. As a reading project, I'd borrowed the book from the school library. While my mother prepared dinner, I 'read' the book to her – instead reciting the movie version word for word. When I closed the covers, feeling very smug, Mum came to sit beside me, opened the book and said, "Now, read it to me."

We worked with those flashcards. I don't remember when, but suddenly, unexpectedly, something clicked. In the space of one year I went from being unable to read basic words to devouring 1000-page books. In the last year of primary school, with encouragement, I began writing: short stories, poems, song lyrics. In Year Twelve, I won an award for a story on domestic violence and went on later to start work on writing a five-book fantasy series.

I am also the owner of over 3,000 books, which have all been read, and some re-read several times. Now, the lazy kid who couldn't read a word is asked to proof-read for other people. Makes me wonder: how much about ourselves do we discover when we refuse to let others' labels define us?

Amber Averay
31 years old
Author
Adelaide, Australia

313
Relationship Wisdom

*A*fter ending a long-term traditional marriage, I began exploring what I really wanted in a relationship. Whilst connecting with various partners and working with clients, I discovered that there are a few powerful things that, when embraced, become the secrets to forming extraordinary romantic relationships. Relationships that provide personal fulfilment and depth of connection for as long as the individuals' desire.

Authenticity: Realize that you are unique and absolutely deserve to have the romantic relationship you desire; join with partners that appreciate your gifts. Your individuality, when allowed to be free, enables you to live and love in a truly authentic way.

Vision: We all want different things so be clear in your wants, needs and desires. By creating a relationship vision you identify your 'true north' and a means to guide you to achieving it. Communicating it with partners allows them to contribute what they feel they can add to the overall experience of relating.

Integrity: My heart-felt thoughts on how to thrive in romance and love gravitate towards having 'Integrity.' This means having your actions match your words and fully living up to promises made to partners. When you choose to live, eat, sleep and breathe by it, romantic relationships flow easily, leaving time and energy for more exciting aspects about being in love!

Ethics: For the most part my world revolves around alternative, romantic relationships. Whenever a person is operating outside of societal norms, a strong set of morals and principles need to be applied. It is easy to take a hedonistic view, but remember that you are relating to real humans who have feelings and beliefs that need to be honoured as well as your own.

When these aspects are brought together they set a solid foundation, allowing romantic relationships to be all they can, including the one with yourself.

Darren Ramsey

51 years old

Alternative Relationship Guide

Coffs Harbour, Australia

314
All You Need is Love

No matter what life presents us, challenging times, challenging situations, challenging people; the answer will always be love. When we come from a place of love, we can find the good in any situation. Our actions as a result, can cause a ripple effect that others benefit from. With a simple change in attitude, love really can save the day.

We have all felt hurt, neglected, misunderstood, abandoned, betrayed and so on. These moments can leave you feeling like the world is conspiring against you and you are powerless to do anything about it. Nothing could be further from the truth.

I have felt this way many times in my life. Although some of these moments were painful, I knew I had a choice about how I dealt with these moments and how they affected me. I could look at these experiences through either love or hate, good or bad. Dark thoughts and feelings brought only destruction, but those originating from a place of love opened my heart to a freedom not available any other way. Reflection of my life experiences gradually changed my perception about how powerful I am, and that we can only grow through love. Most importantly, to me, I found the only way to bring healing to not only myself but also to others was to come from the heart. It has helped me create a positive experience for all concerned.

We all attempt to do our best in every situation. If our thoughts, and subsequently our actions, originate from a place where there is no hate or judgement towards others, including ourselves, a place where there is only love and light, we can live a life of truth and happiness. We can shine a light so bright that all can bask in its beauty.

Sarah Jane Lima
35 years old
Writer, Speaker & Consultant
Gold Coast, Australia

315
We are One, We are Family

J learn differently to most people, I always have. But I don't mind, because I know anything is possible, and we are all special in our own ways. And I want everyone else to know that they are special too.

No matter how different we all look, what colour our skin is, what we believe in, what we each do for work or fun, or even how we learn; we are all the same. We all have feelings and dreams; we all breathe the same air; and we all look at the same sun, moon and stars.

The world is our home and we are all family. We need to look after our home and our family just like we would look after our house and our mum, dad, brother and sister. We only have one home and we share it with many, including the animals. Animals have feelings just like humans, and we are making them sad by making a mess in our home by killing forests and killing them all for money and greed.

Humans need to stop being so angry and carrying so much hate. I would like people to not be so greedy - we all need to be more grateful for what we already have and look after it. Try to not be mean to another person or animal, and to not say or do horrible things. People also need to talk nicely and stop using horrible words that only carry more hate and will only hurt people.

I would love to see everyone practise compassion. We should do some lovely things to people and also animals and help someone every single day. I want all people to have peace and love in their hearts and be happy.

Phoenix Lima

11 years old

Student

Gold Coast, Australia

316
I Love You

*G*oogling "Where is my joy?" and finding Laughter Yoga saved my life in 2007. Its practise has given me an amazing life tool kit that is simple to do, no matter how I am feeling emotionally. I invite you to find a quiet space, away from technology, snuggle up and slowly read the words below to yourself, relaxing in the conscious intention of love.

As I am breathing easily and deeply... I am breathing out a long breath... Haaa...

And, I am relaxing... I am allowing any tension to go from my body.

I am bringing my mind into stillness... Focusing on my heart... I am breathing out a long breath... Haaa... And, I am relaxing... I am breathing inner peace into my heart........... easily and deeply... I am relaxing into my heart... It is opening to love... And, I am listening to myself saying three simple words ... I love you.

I am breathing in my love... I love you... I am allowing this love to go deeply within... Feeling the love that surrounds me ... I love you.

I am breathing in the energy of love... deeply and easily... into every cell of my body... I love you ... I am breathing in love in all its magnificence... I love you.

I am breathing in all the love I have ever wanted in my life... deeply and easily... I love you ... I am breathing in so much love that I am bursting to breathe out love... I love you ... I am full of love... I am love.

I am fully embracing myself in love... Healing love... I love you... I have never ending love within... For myself... Forever more... I love you.

Lynda Andrews
57 years old
Teacher
Paekakariki, New Zealand

317
Imagination and Gratitude

*J*remember staring into my mirror at the age of nineteen. I was crying, confused and scared about my life. I was living at home, with no job, no car, a relationship that failed. I basically felt hopeless. I had dedicated my life, my days and every second of my time to becoming the best tennis player in the world, and it was the day I decided enough was enough and ultimately, I had failed. I felt like I had sent my parents broke and let down the people that mattered most in my life.

I felt extremely lonely, and for the first time in my life I had to see myself in the mirror for what I was, and not the ambition, goals and identity that I preferred to discuss. In my reflection I knew it was time to design my ideal life all over again without tennis. I gave myself the power to imagine. I read every self-help book I could get my hands on. I sat in the dining room of my parent's house answering every question from these books for months on end until I had piles and piles of reflection and direction.

Today I am a reflection of the notes that I made almost five years ago. Today I am twenty-seven and have everything man can desire. I am thankful to have a gorgeous fiancé, two awesome puppies, a network of family, friends, coaches, and mentors that truly light up my life. All of the hardship I have experienced as an athlete is now my strength. Rather than igniting human potential and being an example of imagination and gratitude.

Tristan Enright

27 years old

Gym Owner & Crossfit Coach

Melbourne, Australia

318
The Recipe of Life

*S*ara is crying uncontrollably as she sits on a bench; her stomach feels like it's on a roller coaster. Her body is flooded with emotions of worry, despair and an aching heart. Sara's friend Megan sits quietly next to her. Megan has a radiant beauty about her, like a rainbow that magically appears on a miserable, rainy day. Sara looks up at Megan as she wipes away her tears and takes a long deep breath. The nourishing air fills Sara's body with relief.

Sara looks at Megan with a confused expression and says, "Why does this always happen to me?"

Megan smiles warmly and says, "Sara, would you like me to share my great grandma's favourite life's recipe?"

"Oh yes," says Sara, who is still feeling tender.

"When I was at grandma's, feeling upset, she used to say, 'Megan it's time to wake up to your natural whispers! Remember the natural ingredients to a happy and fulfilling life. If one ingredient is missing, then the cake won't rise, and neither will you, my dear.' She would sing playfully, 'Let's go bake a cake. Here are the natural cake ingredients:

Nurture yourself: add little moments that make you smile, laugh and heart sing.
Active compassionate communication: it's the glue of life.
Trust and believe in yourself: you are worthy right now.
Understand giving and receiving must be in balance: life is about ebbs and flows.
Receptive and open to feedback: listen with an open heart and flexible mind.
Ask quality questions: Leiden wisdom is all around you.
Listen to your body: your gut is more trustworthy than your brain.
Method: Add exactly one ounce of each ingredient. Whisk gently with love and gratitude. Serve cake straight away with a smile, and dance.'"

"Thank you, Megan," says Sara, with a beaming smile. "Let's go bake a natural cake."

Sue-Ellen Cordon
40 years old
Video Marketing Wizard
Adelaide, Australia

319
Things are Not Always as They Seem

*T*rue empowerment comes when we start to look deeply at our beliefs. I had to do just that when my health just wasn't giving me the vitality I desired. Every few months, I would have a three-week period where I could barely drag myself around. This became quite debilitating and made work almost impossible. After going to the doctors and putting up with it for too long, we discovered my iron levels were dangerously low, to the point that if I had an accident, it would be touch and go if I could be revived.

Being a woman of forty-four with young adult children at the time, the specialist suggested that a partial hysterectomy would solve all my problems since I had finished having a family. I thought, "Great," as this was really impinging on my quality of life. However, I kept getting this continual nudging that this wasn't the answer; look past the symptoms. Look for the cause and the source of the problem. Delving deeper, I discovered that these symptoms had emotions and beliefs attached that were not the truth, and were manifesting these symptoms. Amazingly, once cleared, the symptoms disappeared. I no longer needed surgery.

"Things do not change, we do."
Henry David Thoreau

If you are struggling with your health, career, finances, or relationships, check your beliefs. Do you believe you are not worthy of success in all areas of your life? You can change them! You are not a tree planted in the one spot or carved in stone; you can move and change. Decide to change and your life will transform. Beliefs shape your reality more than reality shapes your beliefs. Become the true you, the one the world is waiting for.

Kirstyn Marriott
46 years old
Mind Transformation Specialist
Brisbane, Australia

320
Choices From Love

"No one will listen to you until YOU start to listen to yourself."

Debbie Ford

We have all had defining moments in life. My biggest one was October 2012 when I became seriously ill with Psittacosis, a lung disease caused from wild parrots. It was one of those freak events that came out of nowhere. At the time I felt like I was going through a rebirth, where everything that needed to shift was burnt to the ground, and out of the ashes a new courageous path was forged.

This was the most difficult journey of all. I had never felt so fragile in my health before. I couldn't muscle my way through anything. Relationships broke down, sadly some beyond repair, and my daughter ended up with severe anxiety. At times I thought there was no end to the challenges that kept slamming me down. Each day, I kept fighting the battles. What was different this time than the other times in my life was that I was listening to what I needed to do for myself and my young daughter who was going against most people's opinions, expectations and judgments.

The words above from Debbie Ford, my teacher, became my power statement. I finally understood what true courage was. It wasn't the choices made in fear and resignation, it was the choices based in faith, trust and a bucket load of self-love. For the first time in my life, I truly felt liberated and free to be myself.

There is a courageous warrior inside each one of us. Mine carries me forward when I struggle to do it for myself. She keeps me connected to the present moment, listening to my heart and committing to living a life being unrecognizable to myself, each day and every day.

Heather Passant
50 years old
Courage & Relationships Expert
Mt Beauty, Australia

321
Healing With Horses

My heart is beating so fast it feels like it is going to burst. My hands start to shake, and I feel like I am going to be sick. I am scared, and I start to cry. This is what happens when I have a panic attack, which was almost every day for a long time. From the time I wake up until I fall asleep I feel like I am going to be sick. That is not a life I want to live!

My name is Elina, and in June 2013 I was diagnosed with severe anxiety. There were a lot of things that created it – family problems, getting sick with an unknown virus, and when Mum was taken to hospital. The doctors told Mum that she had to put me on drugs but she refused, telling them she has something else she wanted to try first.

I always had a love for horses thanks to my godmother Anita. When I was at my worst our friend Linda told us about Daisy, from a local horse riding company teaching natural horsemanship with kids. As I progressed in class, I started to feel better. When I am around the horses, I feel happy and loved, everything is perfect, and no one can hurt me or my feelings. I felt so connected to one special horse named Mica, a beautiful golden palomino. Even though she was Daisy's horse she felt like she was mine for a short time.

The one person who has always been there for me is my mum. She taught me how to meditate, how to blow all my fears into a balloon and watch it float away, and she has given me lots of great experiences so I have something to good to think about when I am upset. Even though I am not fully over my anxiety, I still feel that my life has completely changed thanks to the horses and everyone who helped.

Elina Passant

11 years old

Student

Mt Beauty, Australia

322
An Encouraging Voice

*H*ave you ever had moments when you wondered who you really were and why you were put on this earth? Experiences you know have existed for the sole purpose of shaping your character for a bigger destiny? What do you do with a life filled with adversity? One experiencing school bullying, domestic violence, panic attacks, single motherhood, burnout, suicidal thoughts, bipolar type two, declining small business? Do you have a pity-party, or rise above it to become inspirational and change the world?

Imagine the rising of Atlantis, the secret city, which reveals a hidden beauty locked away for far too long. That's how I see my life, when at the age of 45 I envisioned a concept that would change my life and incorporate every experience I'd ever had. I stopped conforming to others' expectations and released the true me.

The defining moment came in 2013 when I responded to looming business failure not with defeat but positivity. I had energy, determination, a desire to help – and I saw people who wanted what I could offer them. Sometimes all anybody needs is an encouraging voice and support in their beliefs, and I've thrown myself into being that supportive voice, whether it be helping sufferers and survivors of domestic violence, providing the driving force behind young businesses, or building up confidence in those unsure of themselves and their abilities.

I don't know what word best describes me, but I do know that I am making an impact and changing lives – thankfully, for the better. I believe that 'God works all things together for good for those who love Him' and I knew that when things got tough for me that I was capable of something greater. We're all greater than any adversity life throws at us. Rise above it, and you will fulfil your dreams: 'We are more than survivors; we are heroes.'

Lorelle Molde
46 years old
WIN - Inspire, Empower Transform Inc
Adelaide, Australia

323
Who Are We?

*W*ho am I? I am a woman; I am a mother; I am wife; I am a student of life; I am a coach. I am a commitment to actualizing 'a world that works for everyone with no one and nothing left out.' I am a determination that we use the advancements in technology to accelerate that commitment. But most importantly, I know now that it's not about the inquiry of "Who am I," but asking, "Who are we?"

Remember how energizing it was when we first fell in love with someone? Remember opening up our hearts to someone? Remember holding our babies in our arms for the first time? The experience of love is not an individual act; the experience of love occurs in a dance with someone or something. Let's not get trapped in the endless cycle of finding self- love (even though self-love is where to start), as you are more likely to fall in love with yourself when falling in love with another. Let's accelerate the journey together and love each other deeply. Let's not be choosy, include everyone. What are we waiting for?

It is proven that when we reduce ourselves down to the smallest particle, we are energy and light. This knowledge relates to everything. We affect it all; we affect each moment. At the very core of our cells, we are affecting every other cell we come into contact with through our thoughts, feelings, and interactions and with our energy and light. Why not affect each other through love?

Who are we? We are the space and the potential for love and creating deep contact with others. Maybe love and deep contact can truly catalyse 'a world that works for everyone with no one and nothing left out.' Let's love each other like never before!

Alexandra Joy-Smith
48 years old
Intuitive Results Coach
San Francisco, United States of America

324
We are What We are Looking For!

*L*ike the majority of fortunate human beings, I was born into love. I received love with ease from the moment I was born. I can't remember when I learned to fear instead of love, but I sure did become a master at feeling afraid of being me. When anything 'bad' happened to me I would decide it was because of me. I was too useless, too fat, too spotty, or too poor. I was never quite enough compared to others.

I distracted from feelings of angst with binge eating, yo-yo dieting, and addictive spending. I was becoming my fears, slipping further away from the love filled being that I was born to be. Ten years passed and the anxiety, depression and sickness grew. Nothing was changing. Would I always be this way?

No! I would not. I suddenly became filled with a fire, a passion for change. I had been on the 'dark side' for long enough, and now I needed to fill myself with light. I gave up trying to be perfect, find perfect self-love, and buy my way into happiness through diets, clothes and material objects. There was one thing I hadn't yet tried...

I looked within. Looking inside, I felt emotions that I had run from, faced fears I had pushed down, re-visited past pain that held me prisoner, and I learned to let it go. I let go of trying to control and of being afraid of being hurt. I gave in without giving up hope. I found a girl full of love lurking there, I threw loving food, thoughts and care at her, and I found me — perfect — just as I was, and had always been, waiting for love. I found my purpose, which is to inspire everyone I meet to find themselves again. Self-love is as vital as the air we breathe.

Leanne Marie Ball

29 years old

Inspirational Blogger & Author

Sydney, Australia

325
A Life Motto

Start each day with a grateful heart and each day you will have more to be grateful for.

Heidi Sayers
33 years old
Advertising Professional
Bondi Beach, Australia

326
A Message to My Grandchildren

*T*here is a small carved rosewood box that belonged to my mother, a repository for some of her favourite poems. Today, I open it and put inside a message to my grandchildren and to the children of the world.

"Precious ones, take your magnificence, your lightness of spirit and inner beauty and share it abundantly with the Universe. In you lie the hopes, dreams and wisdom for the future of mankind. Cherish your gifts, use them well, and above all, love always with an open heart."

I have been blessed to live a long, exciting and rewarding life as a wife, mother, grandmother and filmmaker. I have also known hell, bereavement, serious illness, injury, despair, depression and even suicidal thoughts. This is all of me, my story. It was in those deepest, darkest moments that I learned my most valuable lessons from the best possible teachers. Some would call them angels. I would call them messengers from God.

One especially dark day, these words appeared before me, "I have looked into your eyes with my eyes, I have placed my heart near your heart." They are the words of Pope John XXIII, and as I read them I was filled with an inexpressible peace combined with an unshakeable certainty that I would become healed, and live. That was twelve years ago.

I wish I had known then what I know now; that each of us has within us the wisdom and knowledge to heal ourselves. If we take care to observe our thoughts and make them kindly, all manner of wonderful things will begin to materialise. By living joyfully and treasuring each day as if it were our last, we become one with the Universe. What greater joy can there be?

Annie Paul

75 years old

Documentary Filmmaker & Retired

Worcester Park, United Kingdom

327
Speak Up

*H*ere I am: readying myself to present to an audience of 100 people. Here I am, a person who stutters whose working life relies on the spoken word and clear communication. But how can it be? How can a person with such an overt communication disorder effectively inspire and succeed in a fast-talking world?

My stuttering fluctuates and it can be very unpredictable. So how can I be a confident speaker? How can a person who strains, grimaces and struggles to utter a word at times be a good communicator? What is the secret? Really, there is no secret to be taught or told. It all comes down to owning your life. When I was younger, I learned some key lessons about life and my stuttering:

- The world does not owe you. If you want anything, you have to earn it along with respect. You are nothing special, in fact you have to make yourself special. You are a unique individual. Forge your loves, interests and achievements. Become someone special to yourself, society and the global community.

- My "disability" is not a negative. It is what I perceive it to be. I choose the labels I wear. The world is not against me. In fact, the world is trying to support me. Face the world with a positive attitude.

- Do not listen to those who say, "You cannot" without evaluating the situation realistically yourself. Some of these people will try to influence your decisions to justify their own failures and insecurities. Not listening may also include the little voice in your head that may at times try to influence you. That internal voice sometimes tells lies. Be true to yourself and inspirations. Most of the time your initial instincts are correct.

Grant Meredith

42 years old

Academic

Ballarat, Australia

328
Living Your Passion

J struggled as a teenager to realise my greatness because I couldn't find a career path that I could 'fit into.' I had slight nerve damage to my left hand that restricted my ability to type fast enough to reach the industry standard. This affected many areas of my life including some sports, playing a musical instrument and anything that required the finer skills of using my hands. Computers did not exist then and typing fast was almost a necessity. The competition was too high, and I watched many of my friends take their place in the workforce while I lost my way and my self-esteem.

After decades of searching and observing people I admired being able to do what they love every day, I started to ask 'how' I could too. This led me on a journey of discovering personal development programs I never new existed at school, which I continue to be inspired by daily. I finally discovered I never needed my hands to inspire others, as my passion to share my knowledge was enough. It's amusing that my friends used to say to me: "Dianne, if you got paid for talking you would be a millionaire!"

If you ask someone you aspire to how they got where they are, in my experience, they will usually tell you. This may sound too simple to be true, however, I have learned this is the biggest secret to living your passion. I also believe that when 'our mission' is bigger than ourselves, we find fulfilment through serving others. There is a joy that comes from helping someone in need that touches your heart often at unexpected moments.

My wish for everyone is to do what they love so they never have to work another day of their life.

Dianne Caldwell
57 years old
'Flow' Consultant
Victoria, Australia

329
What Do You Really, Really Want?

*W*hat do you think will solve all your problems – if only you can get enough of? For different people it will be different things, but I know you want whatever you think you lack. So, if you don't have a lot of money, you think money will solve your problems. If you don't have love and relationship, or have bad health, you want that. All of these are a part of life and are all good, but these are all surface things and cannot satisfy what you really want. Things on the outside of you can only satisfy and fulfil the outside. What you are yearning for is your innermost being, and only the inner can satisfy that.

This is where we get everything confused. We see the easily recognizable needs on the outside and go for their fulfilment. Eventually we realize that the inner is still left empty, so we try harder, thinking it must be because we haven't got enough, done enough. We then work even harder and waste our lives chasing more money, sex, things, achievements, health, and approval – without looking to the other side of ourselves.

You also have an inner being, the part of you that came into this world whole and perfect – your innermost soul. Right now it is covered with your beliefs, thoughts and experiences from the past. As you carry that past into the future, you miss the present and cannot come into contact with reality. That is what you are searching for, and nothing from the outside can ever fulfil it.

In all that mad rush of the world to get more, remember silence – the inner. Search for your truth and being because that is the only thing that will satisfy and last forever. What are you rushing towards?

Blazenka Krasey

42 years old

Foundation & Life Skills Trainer

Seaford, Australia

330
Time

*T*his poem was inspired by a conversation I had on a dreary winter's day while sitting on a hospital bed, in London, with my friend Hannah who had just been diagnosed with cancer for the third time. This time it was serious. We talked about love, life and death. These words tumbled out of me as I lay in bed that evening, aligning me to the deep universal truth that love is eternal.

I held her in my arms today, as we looked death squarely in the eyes.

"I'm scared," she whispered.

Pale faced. Body trembling.

"I searched for him all my life.

My love.

He's here now.

I don't want to leave him.

So soon."

Time, distorted and elastic.

Minutes last an eternity.

Days merge into minutes.

Grief and love.

One temporary.

The other eternal.

Danielle Marchant
37 years old
Coach, Writer & Speaker
Cornwall, United Kingdom

331
Hannah's Legacy

*T*his piece has been written by me, Emily Gowor. Hannah passed away, surrendering to a battle with cancer, before she was able to submit her contribution. A woman of many words, Hannah was devoted to bringing her messages to the page so others could be part of something greater. With a blog that inspired a following of over 50,000, Hannah touched people's lives in deep and meaningful ways — and her presence remains in the hearts of people who knew her. I chose to dedicate this page to her, to assist her on her mission to bring her writing to the world. From one writer to another, Hannah, you have brought so much to this world. Although you are gone, I feel your presence now and then when I touch pen to page.

The following piece has been selected from Hannah's blog in honour of her memory.

"If I hadn't abused my body the way that I have done, I would never have had this gift of profound insight of understanding that life is always in perfect balance. I would never have put down my shield and just surrendered to people, allowing them into my life and to help me. I have allowed the therapists to look after me, to feed me and bath/shower me. My old shield and ego would never have allowed me to do this. In fact if I had tried to fight this with a warrior spirit, I would probably have gone to the other side by now, as I simply didn't have the reserves. Since I have lost the warrior attitude and since my 2011/12 bouts of cancer, I have changed immeasurably and as a result have manifested some of the most wonderful people into my life."

Hannah Foxley
Forever 36 years old
Passed Away
London, United Kingdom

332
The Butterfly Effect

*H*ow does a mother shift her mindset after a breast cancer diagnosis the moment her son asks: "Is this going to kill you Mum? Are you going to die?"

My life and my beautiful family flashed before me. The confronting realisation of this possibility exploded at my core. What did I need to do, and who did I need to be to survive this? A period of deep reflection on my purpose in life followed as I considered Anthony Robbins' enlightening statement, "Life is a gift, and it offers us the privilege, opportunity and responsibility to give something back by becoming more."

Some days, I was enveloped in the darkness of a cocoon trying to find the strength and courage to emerge and embrace the same delicate, fragile and beautiful life of a butterfly. It has been proven the slightest movement by a butterfly's wings can be felt on the other side of the world. I wanted the wings of my 'butterfly effect' to encourage others to live their life believing that "the essence of life's beauty is not just the ability to dream, but the courage to embrace those dreams and take action to achieve them."

My illness became a catalyst for change, the gift of a second chance. I was in control of my choices. It was up to me to reignite my life with a clear purpose and the belief that I had the power within me to become more, make a difference, and touch the hearts and souls of others. The butterfly became a symbol of my hope for renewal and rebirth as a new professional journey unfolded. Just as a flame lights the fuse on a stick of dynamite, so too can we experience the power of making a difference with the most essential flame within us for an empowered life: choice.

Lynn Lapham
53 years old
Independent Consultant & Advisor
Tannum Sands, Australia

333
Inspiration Is

*W*riting this was most challenging for me; hours were spent searching for the inspiration which I hope to pass on to you. Then, as I sat to write, I set up my space; candle, coffee, water, notebook, pen and music, hoping to feel inspired. At that moment, a random music selection played: Prince's song, *The Most Beautiful Girl*. I have this crazy 'knowing' whereby I trust I will hear the right song at the right time. This is no exception. I've heard this song hundreds of times, but in this moment, I appreciate the beauty behind the lyrics and I am inspired.

Inspiration is beauty born from the heart. When you feel inspired, it is a moment of clarity and represents all that is beautiful to you. Moments of inspiration are pure magic. All that's possible in the world aligns at the perfect time to gift you with the perfect inspiration.

For months, I have been questioning anyone who would answer, "What is inspiration to you?" No two answers were the same. For some, its conquering mountains and crossing oceans; for others it's those who overcome insurmountable challenges and in doing so, find cures and a cause to devote their lives to. What I found to be common to each story, was courage; courage to see yourself as perfection, as an inspiration to others, and to act. Whether some or all are inspired by your work, does not matter. What matters is how you feel inside and whether you choose to courageously follow your heart, so that others may feel inspired and courageously follow their own truth.

Take those moments to breathe and be open to receive your inspiration. It's a gift from the Gods. Use this gift to guide you to courageously live the very essence of who you were born to be.

Latiecha Henman
39 years old
Aspiring Yoga Teacher
Sydney, Australia

334
Wisdom about Life

I often ask myself, "What is happiness?" and I've found a few answers: Be patient. If you think carefully, most good things come over time.

Let go of regret. It's okay to say no and not feel bad about it. Never regret anything that put you in a better mood.

Ignorance is bliss. There will be people who dislike you; but in the end, hoarding feelings of hate for someone does nothing except hurt you. The other person may not even care about you or what you think, so it is best to just let them leave your life.

Become your own best friend. Learn about yourself; what truly makes you happy, what makes you uncomfortable, what makes you feel great, what music makes you dance, what makes you cry with laughter. Spend time with yourself because only you can make yourself truly happy.

Explore new places. Humans were originally hunters and roamed the Earth freely. Don't let any excuse keep you from getting out and enjoying time with nature.

Practice a smile and sunny attitude. Everything is seen better through smiling eyes. Give the world laughter and optimism, and it will come back to you.

Laugh hard and often. It's good for you, your health, your mood, your friends, your environment, and your abs.

Be grateful. Appreciate every moment in your life. You may not have the chance to experience those moments again.

People are like sculptures. Every kink, dent, corner, line, curve, and detail was created intentionally. Sculptures look amazing with these details, so why would you think differently about yourself?

Life is like a bull. It's going to toss you around, and you're going to get hurt, but love it anyway. Create a life you'll have no regret living.

Ariel Tjeuw
14 years old
Student
Sydney, Australia

335
A Place of Love

*B*efore we are born we come from a place of love. When we revive, we return to that place of love. We all do. I constantly ask why we can't live a life filled with love and respect, a life of love and honour for all that is and all that we are.

I've been hurt and let down so many times. I needed to understand what was it about me that I keep allowing this to happen. I decided to look within to really find out what I has holding on to, holding back from. Who was I really? It's simple; I am a being of love and light. I got that when I stripped off every part of my being, my rawest darkest moment. Within, there is a light, an internal switch that at my darkest point I turned on to embrace all that I am, a woman filled with love, passion, and joy – just as any other man or woman. This wasn't enough for me. I had to go deeper within; on an internal retreat to find me – my real truth.

It was in this search that I really discovered the truth; I already had all the love I needed within. It hasn't been an easy journey, but through the tears and wanting to give up I gained the greatest gifts: love for myself, love for life, love for all that there is, living with humble honour. When we get this, we get that we can overcome anything. It is in this realisation that life completely changes; we realise we have it all within us! Be true to you and all that you are.

It is a humble honour to be here in this moment. Enjoy, with love, all that you are. Live with love and honour for all that you truly are.

Kylie deMole

38 years old

Spiritual Love Coach

Melbourne, Australia

336
The Gift of Cancer

J have learned that with our challenges in life we can either be defined by our circumstances or be liberated despite them. I believe 'It is what it is. What I am about it is what matters most.'

At the age of fifty-four, I received a shocking diagnosis of cancer. It seemed like everything screeched to a halt and the world as we knew it crumbled. Over the next few months my husband and I experienced life as if we were on a giant roller coaster ride that we couldn't get off. I lost my hair during chemo. It was a huge defining moment in the cancer journey. I realized how much my identity was associated with my long red hair – and I was losing it – and couldn't do anything about it. I was devastated!

Eventually I came to a decision. I decided to totally change how I dealt with the whole experience. I decided that I needed to own my baldness! I couldn't control losing my hair but I could own my new look! And I did. I refused to hide it. This was the most liberating thing I had done since my diagnosis. From then on, I owned how I dealt with my ongoing situation. I became more understanding and compassionate with both my own emotions and those of my family and friends. I relaxed more and accepted that I had the choice to own how I looked at my experience.

Two years on and in recovery, I accept a lot more of what is. I go with the flow. I choose to believe now that cancer was the gift that helped me reconnect to my truth – and discover the depth of courage that all of us have inside when dealing with adversity.

Kate Welk

56 years old

Public Speaker, Facilitator & Mentor

Melbourne, Australia

337
Love

*M*y innate essence in this lifetime: To Love

Your innate essence in this lifetime: To Love

My mission: To show you and remind you - that you are Divine Love

It is interesting to me that love is talked about, written about, and discussed so often by so many people, and yet... it is still is not 'used' by everyone.

Love is a doing word, a verb – not a noun. Love is best experienced, felt, given, and received; and it begins with self. Love embraces all aspects of who we are and can be, and all aspects of others, knowing everything is in Divine order.

It took me many years of blaming and judging the people around me and my external circumstances to realise that until I love myself, I will not see it on the outside- in my life. There came a point where I knew I had a choice. Stay in the 'seeking' of love or the 'becoming' of love, which may seem more difficult, but the pain of seeking is far greater than that of discovery. And once it begins, miracles occur.

I want you to know, that you too are capable of great miracles. You possess inside of you so much greatness, so much wisdom, so much joy and empowerment that you truly are a shining light, so brilliant, that every living thing can feel your energy. The world is changed in some way each and every day you are here. We are blessed with your being. You are love to the highest degree. I only need to look in your eyes to see your essence. Look in a mirror... closer. Can you see it too?

Imagine if we all loved who we were. What an amazing presence to live in. What an incredible energy that would be to coexist in. I Love you.

Trish Rock

50 years old

App Developer, Author & Speaker

Canberra, Australia

338
My Gut Feeling
Changed My Life

J like to say, if I can do it you can too. I came from a traumatic, abusive childhood and had to bring myself up own my own; my transformation has been fifteen years in the making. I suffered debilitating depression, was suicidal, and have been through the lowest of lows. Somewhere in the chaos that was my life, I always felt I had a higher calling and was destined to do something with my life. That feeling got me through; it was my glimmer of hope amongst the darkest time of my life. I held onto that feeling, not knowing how or when I would get through this. I used that feeling, that spark of hope, as my drive to begin to heal my life from the inside out.

Looking back fifteen years on, I arrived at a place where I live authentically, and love and accept myself. I know who I am, and I have inner peace. I am comfortable inside my own skin, and I love the life I have created. The journey began for me when I realised the first step to take was inwards and made the decision to heal my life.

I am not perfect and have human moments all the time; however, with practise and awareness I can navigate through the human moments. I know I don't have to be perfect, and it's ok to feel my emotions, so I honour them and express them with love. I made a decision fifteen years ago, a decision to take responsibility for my life and my happiness. While it's been a journey and the growth never stops, there are still tough days and moments. My decision was the best decision I ever made, and if I can do it you can too.

Melissa Gibbons
33 years old
Author, Well-being Mentor & Speaker
Hastings, Australia

339
Your Presence is Pivotal

*Y*our current discomfort is the seed for something valuable. Let me explain why.

I have experienced many losses. I lost my home and business twice, avoided bankruptcy and repaid $80,000 in two years, survived cancer, tolerated a violent relationship for three years, lost my first child, and had ten car accidents in an eighteen month period. At the height of all these losses, my second partner left with another woman. His parting words were, "No I don't love you, and I never loved you!" At the time I thought, "If that is the truth, then everything I know is not true." And so I disintegrated.

My general practitioner prescribed Prozac, but I refused it. Then during a 'chance' conversation with a magician, I had an epiphany! My higher self said: "Oh my God, we have radiology, pathology, haematology... but not joyology!"

This was the forerunner of personal evolution for me. At this point, I still harboured anger and resentment around my recent life events; however, I was intent on moving forward with integrity. From that point onwards, I committed to two things: one, whatever came up in my life I would take responsibility for; and two, that I would journal consistently. These two enduring commitments helped me stay focused and be present. I became sure of my life purpose, was self-monitoring, and learned to be more of an observer than a judger.

My life has been perfect in its paradox and synchronicity. I have been led to bring joy where it appears there is none. I have done that by harnessing my authentic, compassionate and creative self — irrespective of current circumstances. Your presence here this lifetime is pivotal and you are meant to experience it all.

Pat Armitstead

61 years old

Joyologist

Auckland, New Zealand

340
You Can Do Anything!

J was diagnosed with a severe mental illness when I was nineteen. My journey of recovery has had many highs and lows, setbacks and triumphs, and has been incredibly challenging but also rewarding.

At my lowest point, I attempted to commit suicide by jumping off a major bridge in Sydney. I was critically injured, breaking my spine in three places and suffering major internal injuries. I spent two weeks in intensive care, and it took twelve months and five operations to put me back together again physically. The emotional impact lasted years, and I really lost my way for a while. If it wasn't for my family and friends helping me to get back on my feet, I wouldn't be here today, and I am so grateful for their support.

I am really well and happy now but sometimes it's still a struggle. I work in mental health and have my own business empowering people on their journey. I live near the beach, and I have a great life. I have achieved things I once thought wouldn't be possible for me, like travelling extensively overseas. My journey has been a huge opportunity for learning and growth. Everybody has challenges in life; there are good times and difficult times for everyone. It's how you respond and what you focus on that really matters.

- Never give up, there is always a way!
- Always remember the people who support you and love you.
- Give as much as you receive.
- Trust your intuition.
- Learn how to believe in yourself, you're worth it!
- Look for the positives in every situation.
- Gratitude is the fastest way to feel better.

Life is a brilliant adventure. You can do it, just take one step at a time!

Kate Sanders

35 years old

Mental Health Facilitator & Life Coach

Cabarita Beach, Australia

341
Transforming a Situation

*G*rowing up, I worked hard to obtain "book smarts," but I did not have a lot of "people smarts."

My life took a dramatic turn almost a decade ago; I had a series of devastating external events happen to me and had a hard time coping with all these disasters occurring almost at once. I started to question many things and needed to find true and extraordinary wisdom. So, I got out there to learn more about life by studying numerous topics that could help. I also learned other new skills like dancing and volunteering. Doing these activities helped me to understand more about how society worked. What I didn't realise at the time is that these experiences woke me up from my false beliefs. I have learned to be much more resilient, and hopefully I am able to teach others what I've learned.

Life is not smooth sailing, as it is mostly transforming around us and things constantly change. There will always be challenges in life. Even though it can be very hard sometimes, there is a hidden support and meaning within it. It is there to remind you that you are a living being, and if you can recognise it, it is one of the many means of teaching you something and to help you to grow, be grateful, and bring out your true self.

Every situation, object, person, or crap you get handed in life can be considered a resource, a fountain of value, or a fuel that could be transformed and reapplied in another manner to achieve an alternative result. I've always liked the saying, "When life gives you lemons, make lemonade," but I would also like to add, "and turn it into gold!"

Thanh Lam
37 years old
Project Manager & Cultural Educator
Perth, Australia

342
One Truth

*T*here is one truth far greater than any other we could ever imagine. Its purity and resonance has the grace to soar even the darkest heart. It does not know comparison and judgment, for they are the misguided slaves of fear. They build fortresses around our hearts, convincing our bewildered minds that our peace has been disturbed and the untrue shadows of our illusions circle menacingly nearby. Alas, it is the will of fear that has us guarding nothing more than emptiness.

Truth, however, is always with us, for we are made from its fabric. Its thread connects us to each other, to all things, and to the stars and heavens beyond. It is ever present, not limited by our ignorance or illusions, for it exists regardless of our efforts.

And when we are still and silence our untamed thoughts, we hear its calling. Its voice whispers to us as clear and pure as a gentle mountain spring, bubbling words of sweetness that drip like honey from our hearts. It is the sanctuary of our peace, it stills the turmoil in our minds and humbles the lies we tell ourselves.

If we fail to know it, it is just a change of thought away, and in a state of gratitude we recognise its grace and generosity. Its essence melts away boundaries and its gentleness reaches across humanity, opening hearts to beauty and joy. It allows us to heal ourselves, if we so choose, by extending ourselves out to others. For we have been gifted to each other from the heavens above – guardians of each other's well-being.

This one truth that all hearts recognise, no matter where they are, is none-other than the tender blessings from above. It is the gift that heals as it is shared.

It is the gift of perfect **LOVE**.

Mary Patrinos
47 years old
Poet, Author & Clinical Hypnotist
Adelaide, Australia

343
Thank You

I love expressing myself through my poems, so please enjoy my words below. My wish for you is that my words of thanks will inspire you to express your own, because life is full of thankful moments!

Thank you for the skies I do see, thank you for the Earth beneath me.
Thank you for the flowers so bright, thank you for the sun that gives light.
Thank you for the plants and the trees, thank you for the rivers and seas.
Thank you for the rain on the roof, thank you for the words that are truth.
Thank you for the warmth that I feel, thank you for my every meal.
Thank you for the giggles and fun, thank you for daughters and sons!
Thank you for the man in my life, thank you for me, being his wife!
Thank you for my hair that is long, thank you for the words of a song.
Thank you for the children I know, thank you for my special grandma glow!
Thank you for the skin I can touch, thank you, I appreciate it so much.
Thank you for the way I can dance, thank you for tomorrow's big chance!
Thank you for the love that I feel, thank you for the need not to kneel
Thank you for the stars in the skies, thank you for the blue of my eyes.
Thank you for the books I have read, thank you for the crusts on my bread.
Thank you for the clothes I wear, thank you for the happiness I share.
Thank you for the poems in my head, thank you for the comfort of my bed.
Thank you for everything I see, thank you for letting me be me!
Thank you Thank you Thank you!

Claire Camden-Burch

55 years old

Intuitive Life Guide

Croydon, Australia

344
The Decision

*H*ave you ever asked yourself, "Why does this keep happening to me?" I think almost everyone on the planet has said that, or something to that effect, at least once in their life. To be completely authentic and transparent, this used to be my escape clause. This very simple and very inaccurate question was part of my addiction to drama. Life was happening to me, not for me. I was at the mercy of the Universe, or so my victim 'self' thought.

I could tell you every painful moment of my experience with breast cancer. Add to that the demoralizing dance with homelessness. Then top that off with the gruesome details about the suffering I experienced at the hands of a man. But that's not half as exciting as how my life changed as a result of me making The Decision. "What decision?" you may ask.

The decision was to never, ever, not in a million years, let the stupid, ridiculous, obscene, disgusting, pathetic, revolting, absolutely putrid, self-limiting belief that I was not enough rule my life again. After I made that decision, I was able to find the appreciation for everything and everyone who was already in my life or who had been in my life. This change of focus was my 'ah ha' moment. In finding the ability to change my focus from what I didn't want, to what I was already blessed with and what I did want, I was finally able to access the phenomenal and unlimited opportunities, and an abundance of health, physical and spiritual wealth that is our true birth right.

The Decision was to remember my innate magnificence, to honour the divinity within me. Is it time to remember yours?

Constance Fairleight
50 years old
The Magnificence Magnifier
Grays Point, Australia

345
The Young Girl

I want to share a story about a young girl who never felt good enough. No matter how much her parents loved her or how well she did at school, she felt unloved. As a girl, you don't know that the way you are feeling is completely flawed; you just go about entertaining whatever comes into your mind, unsuspicious of the ingrained belief systems you are unwillingly creating for your future self.

This beautiful young girl lived life with anxiety, too embarrassed to go to the bathroom in public and anxiously thinking she had done something wrong. As this young girl began to grow up and entered her early teenage years the lure of alcohol, drugs and attention from boys proved to be the perfect escape from her growing self-hatred, low self-worth and lack of meaning in life. For the next ten years she wandered through life in a haze of addiction, sleeping at salvation army hostels, stealing food from supermarkets, trying rehabs, and isolating herself from her family because she was so ashamed of who she had become.

That little girl is now a thirty three-year-old woman who has been living a clean, happy, spirit rich and constructive life now for over nine years. She is the mother of a beautiful three-year-old daughter: a gift from God. That little girl is me. The one glorious thing I know in my heart today is that the only thing that truly matters is to be able to love and accept yourself and where you are in life. Even when life seems to be falling apart it is usually falling together in ways you haven't seen yet. Enjoy developing and seeking out a connection with yourself and our creator. It is YOUR relationship. You cannot copy someone else's.

Kelly Muldoon

33 years old

Mother & Mentor

Gold Coast, Australia

346
The Real You

*W*e know all human beings are unique – but somewhere deep in our DNA we also know that we are connected. An invisible thread pulls us towards each other. We want to love and be loved. But all too often in our search for connection we lose ourselves.

As a five year old, I was quite the chatterbox. I was happy, confident, bright and courageous; quick to raise my hand in class to shout the answer. Until one day someone called me a "show off," I felt sad, scared, embarrassed. So I raised my hand less often. **I lost my voice.**

As a teenager, I felt uncool, unattractive, always on the edge of the in-crowd. One day I heard some girls mocking another girl. I felt uncomfortable; it wasn't right. But I so wanted to fit in. I didn't speak up. **I lost my courage.**

To be successful in my corporate career, I thought I had to be tough, hard-edged, no nonsense. But my heart wasn't in it. I was living a lie. The real 'me' was gentler – more compassionate. **I lost my heart.**

One day I realised I didn't like who I'd become. I had tainted my relationships with others by not being real with them. I had stopped being the very thing that makes me who I am. I felt like an imposter. I felt damaged. I felt ashamed. **I lost my integrity.**

So I started searching. The irony is that I had never lost any of those things – they were here all the time. They are part of my make-up. I just had to remember to be me – a compassionate, authentic, brave woman who has a voice and something important to say.

"Be yourself. Find your deep connection with others but don't lose yourself in the process. Be the unique person you were born to be."

Jo Stones
51 years old
Coach, Therapist & Writer
Plymouth, United Kingdom

347
Healing with Wild Dolphins

" *J*ust three seats left, perfect," the travel agent chirped. My heart lurched in recognition of our need for healing, especially after all that had happened.

"It's the worst possible outcome, she's been found," the teacher had whispered into the phone. My daughter's best friend had taken her own life. Never have I witnessed such utter gripping despair and disbelief as I gently told my daughter.

My inner critic laughed as we didn't have the money. Once, I'd have given up, but now I let go of the 'how' and trusted that it would happen. And it did. "Pay the deposit and we'll sort the rest out later," the organiser encouraged.

A month later, our journey from the UK ended as we touched down in Bimini. Our healing journey began as the beauty of the island distracted us from the pain. With heart-centred and loving people, we sailed six miles from shore to await the dolphins. And they came. In flippers and snorkel, we jumped into the magic. Diving playfully, 'chattering' and making eye contact, the dolphins embraced us in their energy. As a mother brought her baby to me, I felt an inexplicable internal shift. The privilege of swimming with these sentient beings touched my soul; we sensed they 'saw' us spiritually, and not just physically. My daughter (eighteen) and son (sixteen) were effervescent with excitement.

Later, as I sat on deck marvelling at the gift these wild creatures had chosen to share, my consciousness expanded and, with startling clarity, I was looking down at my life and the limitations I'd placed around myself while simultaneously being aware of the infinite possibilities before me that my blinkered vision had declined. We are each forever changed by the energy of these intelligent, spiritual beings, and I am truly grateful.

Janet Swift
58 years old
Author & Spiritual Traveller
Gloucester, United Kingdom

348
Me, Myself and I

By the time I was nineteen, there were three things that I feared more than anything: me, myself and I. I couldn't trust myself. I didn't love myself. Worst of all, I couldn't get away from myself. I consumed anything to flee from my feelings: drugs, alcohol, cigarettes. I hated myself for being so weak, for being powerless. I wanted to stop but couldn't. Sobriety meant reality, and that meant facing myself. That felt too vulgar, too annihilating, too utterly shameful.

And then, my world collapsed. I understood at some core level that I had to change or slowly die. I decided to try to learn to love myself. I chose to learn responsibility. I chose to create my life rather than let life happen to me. I literally had to relearn how to live.

The relearning was gruelling. There were days when I felt like I wanted to cut myself out of my skin, the inner turmoil was so agonising and pervasive. But I hung on with sheer determination and ultimately the desire to live. I found faith in both myself and a higher power. I worked consciously and vigilantly to alter my thinking. I was blessed to have people in my life who loved me in spite of myself and who truly believed in me when my faith in myself wavered. I absorbed myself in positivity and slowly, the changes arose.

As trite as it sounds, love for one's self is truly the only remedy for all our ails. My goal in life is to help others to know that they really do have value. Everyone has a purpose. Everyone is meant to be here. Everyone is important. If I could make it out, anyone can. We just need to believe that we deserve to.

Shawna Darch

45 years old

Graphic Artist, Writer & Mother

Lennox, Australia

349
Keep the Vision

J directed my first film at age twelve, completed a university degree in film production at twenty-five and by forty-one, a short film I had directed had won Best Film at a New York Film Festival. I felt my career was at least making some headway and I was enjoying the challenges. So why, at forty-three, was I sitting in a university lecture hall undertaking a teaching degree?

Any career in the arts is a gamble; will I succeed or should I do something else that offers a more reliable financial future? Perhaps I could do both, teach and make films? So back to university I went, unenthusiastic and unmotivated, and all the while fooling myself that I could make two careers work. But the reality was that if I continued with teaching, the safer path, my film career would invariably suffer. Teaching takes passion and commitment, but I had neither of those for it. I was only doing it out of fear of what my future might or might not be.

Then one day I had a rather nasty fall at university and it brought everything into focus; what was the point in putting in all this time, effort and money into a career I didn't want? Why not put all that effort into a career I did want? An absolutely simple revelation yes, but acknowledging it was liberating and exciting. Soon after, I cancelled my place in the teaching course.

All I ever wanted to be was a filmmaker, and while I cannot predict the future I can at least be absolutely sure of one thing, I am following my passion and living the life I want rather than doing something else simply out of fear.

Robert Braiden

43 years old

Film Director & Writer

Brisbane, Australia

350
You are Better Than This

So there I am, biking out to a cliff, wrists bleeding, tears cutting into my face, determined to end it all and what do you know - there is this voice in my head and its saying, "You are better than this. You can get through this, you will make it work, you always will." I figured I'd finally snapped.

Fate, God, the Universe – whatever you want to call it – had other plans. Due to leaving only a couple of minutes later then I had intended, circumstances lead to me not being able to jump off that cliff. Just as well really, I had a terrible fear of heights at the time.

Life has taken me on a roller-coaster ever since, and every time things have gotten bad something good has come of it. My experience with depression enables me to help others who are in that place. If it wasn't for my son's mother moving country, I wouldn't have met my wife, or have the amazing family I dreamed of when I was younger.

I've always had the belief since the day I tried to kill myself that I could get through this. Whatever 'this' is. If I can do it, anyone can, and once you have, you can start to change it from "I can get through this" to "I have everything I need for this" to simply "Everything I need is within me." What we say to ourselves matters more than many think. We have beliefs handed down to us that we don't even know are holding us back. So I ask you, how come you picked up this book? What are you searching for? What has life given you that others could benefit from? Everything you need is within you. You just need to trust.

Kaleb Ufton
27 years old
Hypnotherapist, Speaker & Trainer
Caboolture, Australia

351
You See Me

*N*ot long ago I was in a dark place, one where I was deciding whether to come out of or not. I had reached bottom, and it was a familiar place for me, not common but familiar. I didn't want to go on, not on my own, and not with the pain I was carrying. I thought of ways to end my suffering, to stop the mental torment. It was a burden I couldn't share with anyone, lest they be saddened and burdened as well. Mine was a pain owed to me, and I had reached the end of what I could bear.

And then I thought of how she would react to the news of me not being able to carry myself through one more day, and I saw her love for me. And when I turned my heart toward that love, I was lifted. It was as if a light shone from afar, from within, and they were one and the same. I saw her face, her smile, the gentle tilt of her head for my predicament, her caring. She understood. And it was as if she reached out a hand to me, a way forward. That hand held hope for another chance to speak with her, to hear the news about her day, about her struggles and triumphs, about how she walks through her life.

That woman is my dearest friend, my sister, my boss/enabler, my long-standing friend. That woman is Joni, is Sarah, is Fran, is Jenn, is Stephanie, is Deb, and that woman is me. I see myself in all of you, and I see the love from all of you. And today when I stumble and find myself down, I look up and see your face. I honour you, and I thank you.

Beth Nurnberger
50 years old
Executive Coach & Facilitator
Perth, Australia

352
From Lonely to Loved –
Stressed to Strong

*J*magine a world where we stopped looking to someone else to fill the void in our hearts, where we understand who we really are and why we are here, where we are free to be ourselves and speak our truth, where we embrace our differences with unconditional love and acceptance. We want to be loved for who we are, yet we get so tied up in trying to be somebody we are not.

I would often find myself in situations where I didn't feel loved, heard, or understood. I thought that if I just do more, be more, and give more love, then I will get more love and affection. But that was not the case. I blamed my husband for my problems. I didn't know what to do or who to turn to. I felt alone and powerless. I got sick with gallstones, which ate away at my gall bladder. I had lost my power.

One day my husband turned, looked at me and said. "I'm not the problem, you're the problem!" I felt shattered. Yet, it was the best thing he could have said to me. From that day forward everything began to change. I began studying relationships and learning self-development tools about how the mind works and how emotions affect the body. I learned numerology so I could understand my husband and me.

But what I got was so much more. I found myself. I found my purpose. I was no longer hiding underneath heartache trying to please others. I realized that other people can't make us feel anything – only we can. I reclaimed my power and self-worth, and discovered what it means to love deeply. I was free to be me. And so are you.

Sarah Batsanis

36 years old

Stress Specialist & Relationship Coach

Melbourne, Australia

353
Believe in Yourself

*Y*ou're loved. You may not feel it but somewhere inside you, you are. If you go deep down you will find it. You should know you are special because you are. One time at school, I saw my friend flip off a bar with a chain underneath. I wanted to try, but I remembered that once when I did I hurt myself. Then I never wanted to try again. Then, one day, I realised I should. I flipped off without hurting myself. I was proud of me! I overcame my fear. Another time was when I wanted to get into camp at school. I really wanted to get in. In my mind, I focused. As I kept on saying and believing that I got in, I finally did. I exploded with happiness! My friends got in too! I never knew I would get in. That's because I believed.

The past was then. All the bad worries and bad feelings about the past are gone. They're over now. You don't have to worry about them because you're starting a new life and a new year now. This is a short song to make you feel happy:

The moon is bright that the stars glow in the night

The river is so deep that you can hear the sound of a small creek

Please I know there's somewhere across the ocean

Footprints in the sand I can see

Everywhere I imagined the lights are shining on me

See...see the beautiful world above me

How magical it can be

See.... see the beautiful world above me....see.

When you grow up you can become whatever you want to be. No one can stop you. Follow your dreams. Even now if you want to accomplish something or do something, go for it.

Bethany Batsanis

10 years old

Student

Melbourne, Australia

354
Curiosity, Change and Creativity

A small, shy boy runs along a creek in country Victoria, eyes keen for lizards in the grass. He feels greater kinship with his pet goat, the galahs above, or the ants below, than his human classmates. Reaching a little precipice, he stops, and breathes in. Almost thirty years later, I reflect on the journey. Inspiration has been the delicate, trembling breath between inner and outer worlds. At eight, I moved to Melbourne. Land became concrete. My breath was forced inwards: across fantasy novels, encyclopaedia pages, and computer game screens. As a high school teenager, my imagination, shyness and studiousness drew beatings and continual verbal abuse from peers. I avoided mirrors as I hated looking at myself.

My curiosity for knowledge was finally nurtured at university, but it was through the accompanying years of environmental and social activism that shifted the tears formally shed for myself, to those for others. During a year volunteering in Bangladesh, I wept for the world's suffering. But tears of inspiration also flowed: for those whose faces glow in the continual process of renewing the world. Social change had a quietly missing piece however – it took art school to help me fully value my creativity, completing what are my three C's:

Curiosity: burning questions, sought after in
old books, late-night conversations

Change: continual struggle for a better world for all living beings

Creativity: unashamed ideation, seeing the possibilities, playfulness

Inspiration for me now is the spirit that dances within these three fires, born of all, but beholden to none. The dance now is ultimately for our planet Earth, ground of our being, currently threatened by our collective myopia. We all breathe, we all can join this larger dance through our own unique movements. I breathe out, and step forward.

Michael Chew

34 years old

Environmentalist & Community Artist

Melbourne, Australia

355
Overcoming Limitations

*R*unning into the Melbourne Cricket Ground my tears welled up. I knew in that moment I would complete my second half marathon in two months. Not bad for someone who was told they would be in a wheelchair at fifteen due to juvenile arthritis. As a six-year-old, I developed swollen knees. I was treated with splints, rest, needle aspirations and a permanent note from doctors saying I couldn't do anything physical. The last item was my greatest hurdle to overcome.

I was stuck with a belief that I couldn't do anything athletic. I would never know what it was like to run or walk a long distance. If I had not met my outdoorsy husband, I might never have found out. Watching him, I wanted to join in. We started with short bush walks, then longer ones. We set a goal to hike the 1000 km Bibbulmun Track. On many occasions my mind told me, "I can't do anything physical, stop now."

I decided to do a fun run. I would hear the same thing when I was out training, "I can't do anything physical, stop now." The next step up was a half marathon. My mind was shouting, "I CAN'T DO ANYTHING PHYSICAL! STOP NOW!" But I started training anyway, running, arguing, running, arguing. I crossed the finish line, arms in the air, 21.1km later. Michael and our friends were there cheering me on.

A month later we both did the Melbourne Half Marathon and ran triumphantly into one of the most iconic sporting grounds in the world. Overcoming physical limits can be tough. Battling with your internal limits is even harder. I still can hear than voice telling me to stop, but now I have proof that the little voice is actually wrong.

Jane Pelusey
48 years old
Author, Mentor, Speaker & Traveller
Scarborough, Australia

356
Cancer: My Catalyst to Live

*I*t's a funny place to be when you see an illness as a gift to fully embrace living instead of just existing. The irony is most people fear death, yet death wears many masks including the death of ego. Sometimes death represents an opportunity for new growth. You see, I'm a medium who connects to loved ones in spirit, and I know we are eternal beings who live beyond physical form.

I was recently diagnosed with thyroid cancer after having a five-centimetre tumour removed from my neck. It's the second time I've danced with this illness. Being told I have cancer has been a sobering reality check that begs me to question my core beliefs. Do I surrender to the fear this disease conjures up within our society, as I mentally hear nails being driven into the coffin when I share my story? Or do I delve deeper, on a soul level, for greater clarity in pursuing an alternative pathway? I've chosen the latter, as I believe it's the starting point for true self-healing. It comes down to a state of mind as opposed to a situation defining who you are. It's the age-old adage of the glass being half full or half empty.

For me, it's about becoming more self-empowered by speaking my truth with heartfelt conviction regardless of the fear others project. It's a conscious decision. I avoided expressing aspects of myself because I wanted to be accepted. The truth is, I didn't really like myself, let alone love myself. I didn't feel worthy. I denied my voice and its need to be heard. I created distractions so I didn't have to look in the mirror and recognize my own beautiful soul. Cancer has been the catalyst for me to become fully present within myself and life.

Franziska Boon

42 years old

Psychic Medium & Earth Mama

Romsey, Australia

357
Change Is In the 'Why'

The major life-changing chapter within my story came through awareness that overcoming addiction to alcohol and other legal drugs has its roots within the truth that we are wired for joy. But, before I arrived at this understanding, I disliked the person I had become. The previous chapters of my life were typical of families growing up in domestic violence and child sex abuse by a family 'friend.' Living with the complex issues of an alcoholic parent was an unconscious pattern I was set to follow.

My first drink was at age fifteen. I then became pregnant at sixteen. I signed adoption papers under pressure. However, I learned an undisclosed hidden secret – we had a thirty-day grace period. I collected my baby boy the day before the thirty days expired, and later I had four more children. Substance abuse, over many years, caused pain to both me and my beautiful children, and I was ashamed.

The strength to sobriety was born from my mind being fixed on the 'why' for change. It is our authentic design to feel joy and love to all living beings and ourselves. Addictions, suffering, and pain are the unconscious search for joy and who we really are. The why that keeps one on track was also what got me through my first fourteen day water fast, which healed my skin cancer eight years ago.

As my desire to be more grew, I replaced artificial means to 'feel good.' with high-energy vibration foods. I consciously seek things beneficial for my growth and authenticity. Addiction can be overcome one step at a time. The 'why' firmly in place steers one in the direction of the heart, which ignites every cell in your body to remember who you are, a being of brilliance and light and a treasure to the world.

Kathy Hughes
59 years old
Counsellor & Energy Therapist
Brisbane, Australia

358
The Birth of a Lion

J watched the words come out of my mouth, my voice trembling with fear. It was one of the most vulnerable moments I ever had with my mother before she passed. Although our relationship was always sound, it was only in her final year of her life that we began to uncover the depth of our emotional connection. We became the love we shared.

One day, we got into a heated conversation. As she grew frustrated, I realized how unimportant this conversation was; that there was something deeper yearning to be expressed. A sentiment emerged from the depths of my being, carrying with it the fear of vulnerability. As we sat in silence, these words coursed through my being, my body tensing at the thought of vocalizing them. Hesitating with the unknown, I hugged her. Surrendering to the fear and with gratitude beating in my heart I said: "Mum, thank you for giving birth to me."

Only in the last few days of her life did she share how much that simple line had meant to her, how she walked into the hospital glowing, her smile radiating, and how grateful she was for me. I see now that it fulfilled something deep within her. My mother gave her life for the family, and in that moment she experienced that love and gratitude reflected back at her. It became something real. Something she could touch. We both realized what our hearts yearned for.

It showed me the power in being real and allowing others to see me. Fear created an opportunity, a chance for growth. When we dance with fear it impacts not just our lives but also all those who come in contact with us. When fear is embraced, the dance is beautiful beyond words, masterful in all its craft.

Miroslav Petrovic
26 years old
The Lion – Coach/Speaker
Melbourne, Australia

359
The Entrepreneur's Revolution

*W*hat is the entrepreneurial revolution? It is a paradigm shift from the belief that after working forty hours a week for forty years, we will be rewarded with a comfortable pension to support our retirement. In reality however, we have never been more sick, tired and broke. We have become modern day slaves to an out-dated belief.

In a world of inflating prices and the rising cost of living, the set wage is a trap, and we are becoming more aware of a need for results-based compensation. In the midst of this current uncertainty, an opportunity for the entrepreneur presents itself.

What is an entrepreneur? An entrepreneur is an individual who thinks differently, who acts with initiative, provides solutions and contributes value to the world. To the entrepreneur there is no economic decline. As one industry crumbles, a new one emerges.

Change is the only constant, and this is recognised by the entrepreneur. It's time to wake up. Be grateful for the world that you live in, be grateful that you are alive and understand that you are not a victim of your circumstances. Look beyond your immediate problems and remind yourself that they're just not that scary.

Think possibilities, think potential, think different, think opportunity and take massive action. It is time to start living a life of your own design. It is time to live an inspired life. It is time to become an entrepreneur and become the architect of your own reality. Create the life that you were born to live. If you've been waiting for a sign, this is it! It is time to step up and master your health, wealth and self.

*"Become the CEO of your own life, a Spartan of
mind and an athlete of physicality."*

Marko Petrovic

22 years old

Entrepreneur & Speaker

Melbourne, Australia

360
Inspired to Ride

*T*he bullies hated my intellect. I was rubbish at sport. I was the last to learn to swim. My first bicycle was stolen before I learned to ride. I skipped playing rugby by feigning a knee injury. That lie worked until the master asked the doctor. I was the first kid to wear glasses. I had learned boxing. I used it... a lot. Every fight started with finding someone to look after my glasses. I loved squash. I played alone. I took my anger out on the ball and a few racquets.

At athletics I practised hard; so much so that I fractured my leg. I had high-jumped my own height and blew a chance of winning. I took to running. I could leave school and seek solace in the hills. The farmer shot trespassers. I took that risk to be free. I only ever came second. I rode my bike everywhere. At university, a friend and I rode a lot. We did a 1,000 km tour up the coast and over the mountains. We did not know what we could not do.

Many years later, I sold my business. I moved to Australia and started to ride again. I signed up to ride Perth to Melbourne. I trained a bit. "Ride 4,500 kms in five weeks," they said. I rode 100 miles for the first time. We did eight days like that. One hundred miles is just four training rides. I signed up again. I rode a day of 200kms. I joined a friend on a 360km ride. I became a randonneur, riding long distances in set times. The pinnacle of endurance riding is Paris Brest Paris – ride 1200km in 90 hours. I knew that I had found my place in sport. With seven trips across Australia, the open road is my oyster. I am inspired to ride.

Mark Carrington
58 years old
Business Consultant
Turramurra, Australia

361
A New Lease on Life

J lived most of my life assuming and believing that I had no mission or purpose. Back then, I didn't even know the real meaning of those words. I lived a life that I presumed needed to take a particular path, and essentially it was living the conventional, predictable and ordinary. I had no life-changing aspirations or goals, and sadly no empowering interests.

The Universe has a way of delivering certain messages to us, and I didn't notice them. Now I understand why, and I feel blessed to have had my life experiences. Without those, I would not be where or who I am today. The key here is that sometimes it takes time to recognise those blessings, and that is okay too. In the last few years, I learned to love myself and my newly acquired gifts. I overcame a health issue that directed me to my true mission and purpose. I had to reconcile my personal demons with what the spirit was trying to do, and that was to wake me up. I'm still a work-in-progress, but I feel that it will no longer be a battle. No more swimming upstream.

My long-term vision is to inspire people to know that nothing is set in stone. My other passion is being environmental and health conscious. It takes action to create action, just like it takes friction to create fire. Discover what your fire is! If things are not working out, take that as a sign that something needs to change. Start exploring and experimenting, most importantly, remove the box that you have created for yourself, and be true to yourself. Think in infinite terms. Life is not a rehearsal, so you might as well as enjoy it!

Batia Grinblat
44 years old
Life Journey Adviser
Melbourne, Australia

362
Travelling to Inspire Self Love

We all have dreams; we all believe deep within us that we were placed on this Earth for a reason. For many years I have sat with this notion, motivated to strive for something more than I've always had. In 2007, bored with a mundane job and feeling lost in life, I booked a one-way ticket to London, which led me to some of the most incredible adventures of my life: running with the bulls, watching the northern lights, summiting Mount Kilimanjaro, Machu Picchu, and visiting six out of seven continents in the world. After two years of traveling the world, I also fell in love. I had a fairy tale wedding in Sicily, relocated back to Australia and purchased our dream home near the mountains in New South Wales.

Everything from an outside point of view looked amazing; however deep within, I felt something was missing. I would often find myself crying without reason, feeling lonely and unloved. Through battling my inner demons, I began to externalise my pain and created destruction in relationships around me. I lost my marriage, and from that moment, I made a decision to go on a journey of self-discovery for inner peace.

I invested in life coaching, health courses, seminars, and I modelled some of the world's greatest leaders to understand the key to success, happiness and self-love. Through the hardships, I overcame my demons and now wish to inspire others to do the same. I believe happiness is a state, not a destination, and one which we must unite in together. My dream is to travel the world and inspire people to follow their dreams.

"Courage does not always roar, sometimes it's that quiet voice which says I will try again tomorrow."

Joseph Di Bennardo
31 years old
World Traveller
Sydney, Australia

363
My Mother

*T*owards the end of 2011, I had finally completed my university degree with great results. The next day, I went to hospital to visit my mum who had a bile duct blockage. When I arrived, something didn't feel right. She had terror in her eyes. My mum, scared? Impossible!

She slurred the words: "They found a tumour in my pancreas." I didn't want to hear it. I wanted to wake up from the nightmare. I felt hopeless and angry at the world. Why my mum? She was so healthy! But it didn't help... it wasn't going to change anything. I knew I had to find a solution. I was going to do everything to help her. As much as I tried, and as much as she fought, it wasn't enough. The inevitable was approaching.

That's when my whole life shifted. I began to understand it is not perfect. We must accept what comes to us and understand all challenges in life only exist to help us grow, to become better. My communication with my mother became very special, laughing and crying about our memories. It was open, flowing like never before.

I will never forget my final conversation with her. She told me to hold my head high and not listen to anyone who tries to bring me down, to help others reach their dreams, no matter how young or old. The final thing she said to me is: "No matter what you do, where you are or whoever you're with, smile and enjoy your life." She defined the life I have today. She gave me strength. She lives in my heart with every step I take. To my mother, Nadica Marinkovic, thank you for inspiring me to share my heart with the world. I love you, forever.

Milos Marinkovic

26 years old

Business Owner

Melbourne, Australia

364
Life

I live my life.

With passion and belief, with dreams and desires.

With challenge and support, with pain and pleasure.

I live my life in peace and harmony, in conflict and struggle.

In my own way, in every way.

I live my life.

It matters not what life has brought. It matters
not what you may have thought.

Your life is always a reflection of. All the things you're thinking of.

If life's not what you want it to be. The answer appears quite simple to me.

Change the way you see it now. Just think about the here and now.

Be present in this life of yours. Be true to you and all that's yours.

No matter what the past has been. The future is still yet unseen.

The gift you received is life itself. Go on and live it for yourself.

Share your joy and love and laughter. From here on in and ever after.

Worry not what others do. Do the things you want to do.

Don't let the past get in the way. Of enjoying every single day.

Dare to dream and dare to live. Dare to love and dare to give.

For when you give love to one and all. The gift of life makes sense after all.

If life's not what you want it to be. Then take this piece of advice from me.

The life you live is all your choice. You simply make a different choice.

For when you live the life you choose. No one else can ever lose.

The gift was given to you to enjoy.

So go ahead and live with joy!

David Nolan

59 years old

Property Investor

Brisbane, Australia

365
Grace Nouveau

*A*s a child I recall grace as people simply rattling off a list of things they saw as 'good' that day. Imagine taking the time to say grace where you recall something you perceive as 'bad' and look for the learning, character traits and skills you developed because of it. A grace where you express gratitude for both the support and challenge that encourages you to grow. A grace that insists you become present as you create meaning for yourself.

An eight-year-old boy was upset that some older boys threw sticks at him at school. I asked him what was good about them throwing sticks at him, and what he had learned from them doing it. At first he said there couldn't possibly be anything good. I asked him to look again. He took a few moments to think; then smiled and said it made him get really good at Dodgeball, as he was super-fast at getting out of the way of the balls thrown at him. He then added that it also helped him in soccer, as he could get around the other players. He kept looking; then added that it also made him good at diving onto the ground, and that he was now really fast at scanning the ground to choose the best place to land. He said that it helped him become really good at seeing where it was safe to walk when he was camping with his family, and that meant he could keep his little brother and sister safe!

I was inspired by this amazing eight-year-old. Imagine if we all took a few minutes every day to say Grace Nouveau and find enough 'good' lessons and benefits in a challenging experience until we feel a tear of gratitude in our eyes and remember how magnificent the world we live in really is.

Helene Kempe
54 years old
Self-Leadership Teacher
Brisbane, Australia

Share Your Inspiration

Inspiration exists within all of us. If you would love to share yours, I would love to hear from you!

Log on to www.inspirationbible.com/share to write your story or share a message of inspiration with the world!

I look forward to being moved by you soon,

With inspiration,
Emily Gowor
Creator of the *Inspiration Bible* project

Contact the Contributors!

I would love to encourage you to reach out and contact each of the contributors who moved you through their stories, poetry and messages.

All of their contact information can be found via their profile on:

www.inspirationbible.com/contributors

And, every person who has written a piece for the Inspiration Bible, has services that can benefit you in your life, and further inspiration to share with you.

They look forward to hearing from you!

Acknowledgments

I barely know where to begin in expressing my gratitude for all those people who have participated in bringing this book to life, as the depth and enormity of what has been created humbles me every single day.

Jamie Stenhouse, you hold the first page in the book, and rightly so. Without you, this book and project may have never come about. I clearly recall the conversation between us where we decided the *Inspiration Bible* was my next adventure – and the hundreds of long hours we put in behind the scenes to make it a reality. It was the most precious journey I could have shared with you; and to know that our hearts and minds were at the beginning of what is now a global movement brings tears to my eyes. Thank you; for everything that you are and so much more.

Rhi Butler, my love is extended to you for working an incredible number of long hours with me to collect the submissions and photos – and taking care of the 365 souls in the *Inspiration Bible*. Your heart, level-headedness and outstanding work ethic played a significant role in the production of the book; and I know that my "thank you" is spoken on behalf of every contributor. You have been and continue to be a formidable ally in manifesting this magnificent vision in the world. I couldn't have done this without you.

Thank you to all of the truly extraordinary 365 people who chose to step forward, share their stories, and contribute through this book. Because of your willingness to become part of our vision to inspire humanity, people's lives are being uplifted, saved and changed on a daily basis. I will love each and every one of you throughout my life; and walk with you as you continue to bring your heart and soul to the world.

I would love to thank the Gowor International Publishing team for the production of the book. I would also love to thank the other individuals, some contributors and some not, who have supported, loved and encouraged both my team and I along the way as we have brought this book to life. And finally, I would love to thank the grand intelligence that permeates human life, for bringing this vision to and through me and others so that I too, could share my own heart with the world. May millions of people find the inspiration they seek through the words that they read today.

About the Creator

Emily Gowor is an extraordinary author, speaker, book mentor and entrepreneur devoted to bringing books and inspiration to the world. As the Founder of Gowor International Publishing (GIP) — an Australian-based company delivering training and publishing services to entrepreneurs and writers — Emily is the author of several books and creator of the *Inspiration Bible* project. Harnessing her love of writing and human potential at an early age, Emily has built a profound, thriving career as an international icon for writing and human potential.

To date, Emily is the author of five books — *The Book Within You*, *The Inspirational Messenger*, *The Unlikely Entrepreneur*, *Transformational Leaders* and *The Lie* (co-authored) — with many more in the pipeline as well as a long line of content including a multiple award-winning blog, *Life Travels*. Driven to achieve extraordinary outcomes and produce her greatest creation on Earth, Emily founded GIP to blend her background in writing together with her love of coaching authors and publishing life-changing books.

As a winner of the 2012 and 2014 Anthill 30under30 Young Entrepreneur Award, Emily has been interviewed on several radio shows and, in 2012, was featured in the book *Young Entrepreneur World: How 25 Teen-trepreneurs Succeeded and Left World Leaders Scratching Their Heads*. Having already made a significant difference in the lives of thousands globally before age 30, Emily finds continual inspiration in the divine order of the Universe: her deepest reason for continuing to bring her brilliance in writing and love for humanity to the forefront into all she does.

GOWOR
INTERNATIONAL PUBLISHING

CPSIA information can be obtained
at www.ICGtesting.com
Printed in the USA
LVOW13s0322240617

539231LV00034B/1519/P